D. H. Lawrence, Artist & Rebel

D. H. LAWRENCE

ARTIST & REBEL

A Study of Lawrence's Fiction

E. W. Tedlock, Jr.

Albuquerque

THE UNIVERSITY OF NEW MEXICO PRESS

© The University of New Mexico Press, 1963
All rights reserved

THE PUBLICATION OF THIS BOOK IS MADE POSSIBLE
BY A GRANT FROM THE FORD FOUNDATION

Manufactured in the United States of America
Library of Congress Catalog Card No. 63-21085
Second printing, 1965

*To the Garnetts
and the endeavor at Hilton Hall*

Preface

THIS IS A STUDY of all of Lawrence's fiction except a few early, uncollected sketches. Its interest is in both the remarkable unity of his ethic and his imaginative means that can be seen in this way, and in their development as he responded to the major challenges of his life and times. The title is meant to indicate the essential inseparability of his art from his rebellion, using the latter term in the sense in which Albert Camus used it in his history and analysis of the perilous position of so many modern intellectuals—philosophers, political theorists, and artists—between the reformist side of their radical discontent and the disastrous nihilism that often resulted. Lawrence too was not satisfied to "push against something," as Elizabeth Bowen characterized the moral effort she felt possible after the Thirties had made writers wary of ideological and political commitment. He would, he once said in nihilistic bravado, shoot the masses of people who defaced and blasphemed against natural life with the "silent bullets" of his work. The ultimate interest of this study, then, is in his *vitalism*, which everywhere directs his imagination and provides his ethic. It is this that is responsible for the unusual involvement his work tends to produce, and that has made it difficult for critics to discuss him in detached, aesthetic terms. Like such other militant vitalists as Nietzsche, Butler, and Shaw, he was resourceful in altering familiar situations and genres to dramatize the struggles inherent in transvaluation by vitalist principles. Again and again he creates the tension between his religious, "pure" apprehension of the wonder and evolutionary purpose of natural life, and his revulsion against the modern civilization that he feels to be at cross-purposes with it. The nature, strengths, and weaknesses of the rebellion he made and the art which embodies it, are points on the life line of this tension.

The organization of the study is broadly chronological, developmental. The division of the career is by events and works which signal major changes in his drive toward a vitalist utopia. Each part begins with a biographical sketch, and this is followed by chapters on the relevant short stories, novelettes, and novels. In the interest of synthesis and space, discussion of the details of the life and the stories has been limited, and other readings extant in the voluminous criticism of Lawrence have been omitted. The synoptic passages and commentaries frequently incorporate bits of Lawrence's phrasing in an effort to maintain contact with the vitalistic implications of his diction; these phrasings are usually signaled by quotation marks, though the process is sometimes awkward.

E. W. T., Jr.

Contents

D. H. LAWRENCE, ARTIST & REBEL

A Study of Lawrence's Fiction

1. Early Patterns of Revolt

*L*AWRENCE'S SITUATION in childhood and youth contained certain factors that remain constant in his work and contribute to its remarkable unity. The outlines of his situation are by now familiar. His father had only enough schooling to read and write a little, and while still a child went to work in a colliery. He married a middle-class young woman whose father had been an engineer in the Sheerness dockyard, who had once been disappointed in a courtship closer to her normal expectations, and who for a time had taken one of the few ways to refined independence open to women by teaching school. She seems to have been unprepared by her nature as well as her background, to accept the social, economic, and personal realities of life as a miner's wife. She brought to her marriage rectitude and firmness that were reinforced by innate self-confidence. Apparently the reason for her choice of so different a person was the father's physical attractiveness and native charm. By ordinary standards of what works and what doesn't, within the *status quo*, the match was a mistake. The father did not care about getting on in the world and liked a good time with his friends at the pub. The mother's values were offended; the relative poverty humiliated her and her children; and the relationship turned into a series of violent quarrels and an ultimate estrangement in which the children were passionately involved on her side. The conflict involved a wide range of values allied to class as well as temperament. Even the father's speech, the dialect of the uneducated lower class, became offensive.

Ironically it was the mother who gave her children the opportunity to analyze the causes of failure and to make a fight against them by her encouragement of reading and discussion, and the company of young friends of similar interests. If she had sunk in the world, her children would rise. She scrimped and saved, indomitably battled her husband's contentment with the prospect of his sons becoming miners and his daughters servants, and got them considerable education. For David Herbert she opened a less conventional door than she dreamed of. Instead of accepting the values and ambitions of the middle class world of her origin, he adopted social, psychological, and religious views she could not have understood. What he retained was her seriousness about life, her stubbornness and tendency to dominate, and her probity.

The situations in Lawrence's fiction always resemble that of his mother and father. Her plight in its essential frustration, is like that of Constance Chatterley, and there are elements of the father in Mellors, and the means of fulfillment, in his last novel. This reversal of values that occurred as he explored and realigned relationships is suggested by the sympathies in his earliest work. He found in men who resemble his father an unconscious, vital power that might—if freed, purified, and above all directed—redeem the failure of his parents' relationship. This power, which vitalists call the life force, had its own laws. Immorality occurred when it was impaired, and all existing institutions tended to impair it. The full step to this position was not easy; he had his mother's strong sense of responsibility, and the profundity of his love for her can be, paradoxically, measured by the extremity of his means of salvation. The reversal of her values required by a vitalistic view meant personal as well as cultural alienation.

Other deep attachments contributed to the complication of Lawrence's problem and the forming of his imagination. Most important was the more natural world lying just outside the town and the miners' dwellings, a country world mingling the decaying lovely houses of the older aristocracy with the new houses of the industrial aristocracy of rich mine owners, the pit heads, slag heaps, and railroad lines with lake and wood and field and farm.

Years later, after long exile, Lawrence could recall this country in detail for a correspondent who inquired about the setting of *Lady Chatterley's Lover*. Historically and romantically it was what survived of a Sherwood Forest, medieval England, even further back of a Celtic, druidic England, and most remotely, though threatening because of possible reversion, of a primordial evolutionary origin. Despite its disfigurement in the modern era, the country had for Lawrence great beauty, as indeed, it still has, the disfigurement being comparatively slight by contrast to truly urban industrial areas. To Lawrence it was not so far in time from a heartier, more robust England. He never used Robin Hood as one of his outlaw-heroes, perhaps because the story was too romantic, but he missed few other historical analogies of his theme. In *Lady Chatterley's Lover*, for example, he remembered that not far off at Annesley, Byron had placed the heart above the head by courting Mary Chaworth.

Lawrence came to know intimately the natural beauty of the country and the life of the farm through his visits to Jessie Chambers and her family at The Haggs. His intense friendship with her is an extremely complicated story, in which her account of the reasons for their ultimate estrangement is at odds with his in *Sons and Lovers*. These aspects, bearing upon his development as a writer, may perhaps be noted justly. Lawrence and she passed through adolescence together in a relationship which was a mutual education in languages and reading, in appreciation of beauty, and in ideas and aspirations. As boy and girl and for a time as young intellectuals, they did not find it hard to maintain an easy, happy, and platonic relationship. According to her sensitively written account, *D. H. Lawrence, A Personal Record*, it was he who broke this rapport by introducing, apparently at his mother's suggestion, the difficulty of the implications of their intimacy, and the need of his showing responsibility by always having someone with them. Later, according to her, because of the conflict between his overpowering attachment to his mother and his consideration of marriage with her, he attributed to her hesitations and fears that did not exist. He made her a scapegoat for his own limitations. When she read *Sons and Lovers* in manuscript, and later again in print, she felt that he had betrayed her.

Waiving for the time being the question, raised by some critics, of whether *Sons and Lovers* itself is flawed by a failure to face up to the full truth, it can be said that Lawrence may have recoiled from attitudes in her of which she was not aware. His fairly frequent suggestions to her that there was a side to him she did not know indicate that he was well into a breakthrough to sexual fulfillment that would not take account of the spiritual, and perhaps found it impossible to do so. She was hurt by his suggestion that in marriage the sexual relationship was enough, the spiritual did not matter; she wanted both. As he eventually worked their situation out in the thematic unity of fiction in *Sons and Lovers,* he was split between the mother (soul) and the other woman (sex)—a tragic, death-tending conflict—and she as Miriam contended with the mother for his soul. Survival itself may have dictated something resembling the vitalistic ethic—whatever enhances life, in the sense of vitality, is good, whatever tends to lessen it is bad. When, at the very end of their relationship, he remarked to a friend that he liked "a gushing woman," he was surely speaking of Frieda Weekley, who, alone among the several women in his life at this time[1] apparently had the uninhibited, undamaged vitality that could match his need. This need, and the development of his central vision of the supreme value of intense life, took Lawrence out of Jessie Chambers' life. Yet like his mother, and the other women in his life, she retained a place in his affections and concern. The unfulfilled women who appear as characters in his fiction reflect them all. He explores their problems over and over in all possible situations and brings champions to fight for them against the culture which, through inculcated attitudes, causes their suffering.

In Jessie Chambers' world Lawrence found another kind of relationship crucial to his fiction in his friendship with her father and brothers. As a boy he had not led the ordinary village boys' life of gangs and sports. His health was delicate, and his sensibility and interests quickly grew beyond the ordinary. He was much in the company of girls, and a favorite of theirs. At the farm he made himself helpful and useful in the household chores, and was admitted into the company of the men in the farm work. These men were intensely physical, like his father, but not disintegrated by divided homes and aimless existence beyond their immediate work. They might be hurt and even destroyed by the opening of their consciousnesses to problems beyond their capacity to understand, but they could still be encountered working contentedly and joyously in

---

1. A letter by Alice Dax, the model for "Clara" in *Sons and Lovers,* in the *Memoirs and Correspondence* of Frieda Lawrence, makes clear Alice's feeling that she was not free enough of shame and antagonism to meet Lawrence's need. His sense of this is conveyed in the novel in Clara's ultimate torment over, and return to, Baxter Dawes.

the sun, feeling themselves a part of a great natural ritual and of an older English culture. Such men are the prototypes of Lawrence's male characters of true but limited potentiality, for whom eventually his "aristoi" would try to create an organically related, joyously vital way of life.

Perhaps most crucial was Lawrence's locating in the countryside's birds, beasts and flowers an ultimate wholeness of being to which he aspired and to which he could turn from divided, unhappy humanity. In these and their participation in the cycles of night and day, moon, stars and sun, and seasons, he found his basic imagery and symbolism, however varied later through accretion of the idiosyncratic life of other places, and alliance to myth. He must have felt quite strongly the contrast of this entire country world to the dark, underground life and nature of his father, and sensed night-world day-world, unconsciousness and consciousness, death and resurrection parallels for his father's daily emergence from the mine, and his own "psychological" experience of deathliness and rebirth.

Nature might contain a struggle for survival, but the trend was upward, and it erected no barriers in consciousness that made of life a living death. The old did not linger on in painful decadence, but cyclically perished and was resurrected fresh and vigorous. In this there were hints for a dynamic of constant change and renewal for the human being experiencing deathliness in life, a pattern of recurring cultural and psychic crisis in which the individual found salvation in the death and resurrection of an intrinsic self.

Contributing to this pattern was Lawrence's recurrent bad health. All of his life he alternated between illness, convalescence, and relatively short periods of physical well-being. One effect of this was to complement his exaltation of vitality with a constant, courageous and religious awareness of death. Never did he refer to tuberculosis—his trouble was colds, flu, or bronchial trouble. He tended to think of his illnesses as essentially psychosomatic. The disturbed inner man was what must be set right. In his work no character is ill in the ordinary sense. Even in the relatively early *Sons and Lovers* the family illnesses, even the mother's cancer, are closely related to if not caused by crises of relationship. In *The Rainbow* Ursula's terrible crisis of health toward the end is caused by the failure with Skrebensky. And in *Aaron's Rod* the doctor himself comes to see that what is apparently post-war flu is dangerous to Aaron only because he has given up inwardly.

Another probable effect of his bad health is to reinforce his frequent psychological preference for dark, southern peoples as more vital and less disintegrated than blond, Nordic peoples. In *Women in Love* Gerald's defeat and death take place on an icy slope in the Alps that corresponds to the mechanical, disintegrating nature of his psychic tendency, while Birkin and Ursula are capable of the Lawrencean resurrection of vital human relationship and turn away to the southern slopes leading to the warmth of Italy. It was in Mexico with its dark, primitive peoples, in some ways culturally akin to his father, that he sought to create his conception of an integrated people and culture in *The Plumed Serpent*.

Lawrence's consciously intellectual development of values counter to the traditional ones of his culture originated in the challenge of rationalism and science to his youthful religious feeling. His initial unorthodoxy seems to have developed as a distinction between religious experience and applied morality, between exaltation in a sense of cosmic significance and the meannesses and ugliness of the man-made world. A glimpse of his youthful seriousness is given by his sister Ada's account of his attitude when their group of young people, out walking at Easter, entered the church at Alfreton: " . . . When we saw the Easter decorations, masses of daffodils, narcissus and Lent lilies, he said we must sing a hymn or two, and threatened awful punishments if anyone laughed or treated the occasion lightly."[2] A very early poem, written while he was at Nottingham University College, contains a view of God dynamically revealed in nature that suggests the view of God as life force in the philosophy of vitalism:

> The grey phosphorescent, pellucid advance
> Of the luminous purpose of God shines out
> Where the lofty trees athwart stream perchance
> Shake flakes of its meaning about.

2. Ada Lawrence and G. Stuart Gelder, *Young Lorenzo* (Florence, 1931), p. 47.

> The subtle, steady rush of the whole
> Gray foam-fringe of advancing God
> As he silently sweeps to his somewhere, his goal,
> Is heard in the grass of the sod. . . .
>
> For what can all sharp-rimmed substance but catch
> In a backward ripple God's progress, reveal
> For a moment his great direction, scratch
> A spark beneath his wheel.[3]

In his early student days, before his reading of rationalistic authors, he hinted to Jessie Chambers that he might enter the ministry. During the University years he told her that the church was based too much on negation: "The chapel system of morality is all based upon 'Thou shalt not.' We want one based on 'Thou shalt'." He was troubled by the discrepancy between the old religious ideas and the new scientific discoveries. He thought of asking their minister to state his position on the questions raised by agnostic authors, particularly J. M. Robertson, T. H. Huxley, and E. H. Haeckel. But the indication is that he himself did not take an agnostic position for long.

His steps from doubt and question to a new religious faith are not entirely clear. By the time of his mother's death when he was twenty-seven, his counsel to his sister Ada, during the crisis of religious doubt she experienced, expresses much of the position that characterizes his mature personality and work.

> I am sorry more than I can tell you to find you going through the torments of religious unbelief: it is so hard to bear, especially now. However, it seems to me like this: Jehovah is the Jew's idea of God not ours. Christ was infinitely good, but mortal as we. There still remains a God, but not a personal God: a vast, shimmering impulse which waves onwards towards some end, I don't know what—taking no regard of the little individual, but taking regard for humanity. When we die, like rain-drops falling back again into the sea, we fall back into the big, shimmering sea of unorganised life which we call God. We are lost as individuals, yet we count in the whole. It requires a lot of pain and courage to come to discover one's own creed, and

---

3. *Ibid.*, p. 67.

quite as much to continue in lonely faith. . . . What does it matter the name we cry? It is a fine thing to establish one's own religion in one's heart, not to be dependent on tradition and second-hand ideals.

Here is the rebellion against tradition and at the same time the reconciliation of skepticism with faith. There seems to be cognizance of nineteenth-century science in the notion of the impersonality of God, the analogy of life and death with the cycle of sea and rain, and the belief in an evolving cycle. The later Lawrence inveighs against anthropomorphic readings of nature and seeks non-human gods and destinies. In this early statement he seems to appropriate scientific materialism to religious ends, rather than to reject it completely. The reconciliation of purpose and matter may be seen still functioning in a very late poem, "The Ship of Death," in which the cycle of the resurrection of being begins with an arduous, desperate venture in extinction. As a "wasteland" poem, it exhibits a faith in the natural cycle that Eliot's famous poem does not have.

Among the philosophers Lawrence and Jessie Chambers read was Schopenhauer. Lawrence persuaded her brother to give her the *Essays* for her birthday in 1908, read aloud to them "The Metaphysics of Love" chapter from *The World as Will and Idea,* and annotated the book. The remarks on mismating and discord might well have reminded Lawrence of his parents, and the preference for brown coloring has a parallel in Lawrence's vitalistic typology. Schopenhauer's concept of the will to live, of which the mind and knowledge are merely servants, rationalizing our instincts, suggests the most central possible influence. The pessimism inherent in this anti-ideal, anti-harmony view—the will through individuation being violently divided against itself—seems not to have affected Lawrence for very long. Individuality and conflict are conditions to be not only accepted but used and even preached as means of recovery of, rapprochement with, the life force, or God. Merging, dominance are evil; merely social relationships and adjustments, especially those counseled by ideals, distort and destroy the integrity of the religious way of life.

Another influence was Nietzsche, and here the resemblance between

Lawrence's values and the philosopher's ideas is much clearer. "The Birth of Tragedy" with its distinction between the Dionysian and the Apollonian, or, to use Nietzsche's descriptive terms, the Dionysian expression of the "whole outrageous gamut of nature—delight, grief, knowledge—even to the most piercing cry" and the Apollonian emphasis of self-knowledge and self-control; Nietzsche's view that Greek tragedy at its best exhibited a balance of these two from which, in western culture, there has been nothing but decline through Socratic logic's opposition to the Dionysian; his emphasis on the importance of myth as essential to Dionysian recognition; all this could have contributed to Lawrence's emphasis on what he called the knowledge of the blood or the "blood consciousness," non-rational experience and knowledge. Eventually Lawrence, like Nietzsche, denounced post-Socratic, Christian western culture as a disastrous development of mind at the expense of the vital nature of man. His concept of power as the means of retrieving the error of emphasis on love suggests Nietzsche's *will zur macht;* but Lawrence denied that he meant the same thing and tried to define a power of physical tenderness in relationship, and of vital restoration. He is closer to Nietzsche in expressing the notion of a slave morality engendered by exaltation of the lowly and disinherited in Judaic-Christian culture, broached by Nietzsche in *The Genealogy of Morals.* His late essays "Aristocracy" and "Blessed are the Powerful" are quite similar in attitude, the latter reversing the Christian beatitudes. The slave morality of spite against the superior man, and betrayal of him, can be seen in *The Plumed Serpent* and *The Man Who Died.* In "Him with His Tail in His Mouth" he expressed the vitalistic ethic—" . . . that which is good, and moral, is that which brings us into a stronger, deeper flow of life and life-energy: evil is that which impairs the life flow." This ethic, Lawrence's willingness to rely on "the life force" as God evolving manifold forms of life in different planes of evolution, and his belief in the necessity of control and direction of the lower by the higher, resemble also the views of Samuel Butler and George Bernard Shaw.

A much earlier statement of his view that is often used to get at the nature of his vision of life is the one made to Ernest Collings in a letter of 1913:

> My great religion is a belief in the blood, the flesh as being wiser than the
> intellect. We can go wrong in our minds. But what our blood feels and
> believes and says, is always true. The intellect is only a bit and a bridle.
> What do I care about knowledge. All I want is to answer my blood, direct,
> without fribbling intervention of mind, or moral, or what-not. I conceive a
> man's body as a kind of flame, like a candle flame, forever upright and yet
> flowing: and the intellect is just the light that is shed onto the things around.
> And I am not so much concerned with the things around—which is really
> mind—but with the mystery of the flame forever flowing. . . .

Elsewhere he elaborates on this belief, taking cognizance of psycho-
analytic theory as supporting the notion of an "unconscious." But this
simple statement, containing a sense of his dedication to the mystery
of life itself as a lovely, proud central phenomenon, will serve as an ade-
quate touchstone by which to judge the poetic nature of the vitalism in
the early fiction.

Lawrence's statements of a philosophy, it should be remembered,
came, or so he thought, at intervals after his experience had been explored
first in the fiction. He was careful, in talking of the novel, to distinguish
between such "philosophy" and the art, which had an internal development of its own that might contradict the didacticism.

The "social" aspect of Lawrence's early situation is important to an
understanding of his alienation. As a gifted young man from the lower
class and the provinces he was in the position of the present "angry
young men" in England who challenge, with much of his contrast of
values, the establishment. "Room at the top" could involve considerable
humiliation through condescension, if not the active persecution Richard
Aldington and F. R. Leavis think were accorded him—"a genius, but
. . . ," a writer of pornographic books, a primitivistic, anti-intellectual
obscurantist. A moving indication of Lawrence's sensitivity to his early
situation is his account of the appearance of his first novel.

> The very first copy of *The White Peacock* that was ever sent out, I put
> into my mother's hands when she was dying. She looked at the outside, and
> then at the title-page, and then at me, with darkening eyes. And though
> she loved me so much, I think she doubted whether it could be much of a
> book, since no-one more important than I had written it. Somewhere, in

the helpless privacies of her being, she had wistful respect for me. But for me in the face of the world, not much. This David would never get a stone across at Goliath. And why try? Let Goliath alone!

His first venture into an intellectual career was through extended training as a teacher, at the British School in Eastwood, at the Ilkeston Pupil-Teacher Centre, and in the Teachers' Training Department of Nottingham University College, where he qualified for the Board of Education Teacher's Certificate. He then took a teaching post at David-son Road School in Croydon. During these years he was writing poetry and fiction with the advice and criticism of Jessie Chambers, who sent his first published work to Ford Madox Hueffer of the *English Review*. The editor who had most to do with the shaping of his work, through the writing of *Sons and Lovers* and into the crucial break and experimentalism of *The Rainbow*, was Edward Garnett, encourager and friend of so many beginning talents. Illness precipitated Lawrence's resignation at Davidson Road School in March, 1912. Then, with his climactic meeting with Mrs. Frieda Weekley in April, and their leaving for Germany in May, Lawrence was fully committed to writing and to the complex relationship that permeates all his fiction after *Sons and Lovers*, and marks the beginning of a new, more mature period.

This first part, then, views Lawrence's fiction through *Sons and Lovers* as constituting the development of the young, immature writer. Frieda Weekley had a strong influence on *Sons and Lovers*, and the early short stories revised for book publication as *The Prussian Officer and Other Stories*. She brought to bear on the psychology of relationship and the hierarchy of values involved in sexual fulfillment, an extraordinary faith and capacity, a strong, intransigent championship of the underdog, a sympathy for the fighting and suffering of the male as a leader and teacher, and truly exceptional vitality. Her encounter with Freudian theory during an earlier affair had brought her to a crisis of self-understanding, a belief in the rightness of fulfilling one's nature, and the necessity of a revolutionary effort to change the conditions of life. But *Sons and Lovers* had been in progress for some years and was essentially a backward look for Lawrence at the malaise of his youth at home in Eastwood, and through all the analysis of the causes of his failure in the relationships with Miriam and Clara runs the death-drift brought by the mother's suffering, ending in almost fortuitous, and rather blind choice of life.

The time span, then, is from a point in Lawrence's late teens, when he began *The White Peacock*, through revision of *Sons and Lovers* in his twenty-seventh year—c. 1905-12.

I 🐚

Lawrence's earliest notions of the art of fiction are reported by Jessie Chambers in *D. H. Lawrence: A Personal Record*. When he began to talk definitely of writing, he decided to do a novel, and said of planning one:

> The usual plan is to take two couples and develop their relationships. . . . Most of George Eliot's are on that plan. Anyhow, I don't want a plot, I should be bored with it. I shall try two couples for a start.

Such a way of beginning, with a situation, and creating the story through development of relationships, continues into all of Lawrence's work. It suggests why his method of revision was to rewrite completely; external action may be tinkered, but inward, "psychological" action develops through every detail.

He also felt that it was Eliot who had begun the placing of the action inside the characters, where with Fielding and others it had been outside; he wondered which was right, and said he thought there should be some of both. The origin of the strongly subjective and personal nature of his fiction, much less conventionally masked later on, may also be indicated by his remark that *The White Peacock* would have to be a mosaic of moods because interruption of his writing by teaching meant that he returned to it a different man, and by his pleased approval of Borrow's having so subtly mingled autobiography and fiction in *Lavengro* that critics could not clearly distinguish between the two. He also thought of fiction as a deep personal commitment. When he had finished the first revision of *The White Peacock,* he said: "Everything that I am now, all of me, so far, is in that. I think a man puts everything he is into a book —a real book." Earlier, when his first sheer delight in reading was changing into a seriousness that Jessie Chambers found almost frightening in intensity, he said: "I feel I have something to say. . . . I think it will be didactic."

The relevance of these remarks to the early short stories is not so apparent as it is to *The White Peacock.* Many of these stories were written while the novel was in progress, and by comparison with its slow pace and elaboration are no more than sketches, hardly accommodating to the intricacies of the two-couple situation. They are perhaps by-products of the major effort. But all of them show the interest in situation rather than plot, and a tendency for the "action inside the characters" to predominate.

One group employs a young man narrator who resembles Cyril Beardsall of *The White Peacock,* but is frequently much less masked off from Lawrence's situation and experience. He appears most frequently in sketches that, if they were submitted for publication, were passed over by editors, and perhaps by Lawrence himself, in the making of the first collection, and were collected posthumously in *A Modern Lover.* This young man reflects to some extent the feeling of the statement "I think a man puts everything he is into a book," but more often than not the "stories" represent a stage of development in which personal experience is somehow not transmuted into the greater objectification and unity of art. They occasionally contain striking bits of surprisingly mature Lawrence.

The narrator is a sensitive, brooding young man who regards the history of his region and the contretemps of his provincial society with self-conscious, rather literary, and impotent irony. He has a highly developed taste for painting and music, savors bits of beauty and moments of intense experience in a Paterish fashion, and has read with increasing personal rebellion most of the iconoclastic literature of the day. Sometimes he explores without satisfaction the possibility of sexual fulfillment to relieve a painful spiritual and psychic intimacy. Culturally, emotionally, and morally he stands between two worlds—one appealing to the stable, "everyday," responsible side of his nature; the other appealing to sides of his nature that drive him toward intense, even fierce and dangerous experience that has nothing to do with scruple and sentiment.

In the very early "A Fragment of Stained Glass" (collected in *The Prussian Officer* volume), this young man participates in a bit of sardonic iconoclasm containing many elements of the mature Lawrencean fable. He is the friend of a bachelor, slightly paralyzed vicar who is disliked by serious, puritanical people because of a tendency to be ironic that is actually one side of his tolerance and generosity, and because of his fondness for pagan and Italian Renaissance statuary. As an amateur archeologist, the vicar is no mere antiquarian. He is compiling a Bible of the hearts of the English people, and has found a paragraph for it in the record of the breaking of a stained glass window in Beauvale Abbey. The record interprets the breaking as the work of the Devil, the blood on the snow outside as the miraculous blood of Christ. The vicar's interpretation of the event is surprisingly mature Lawrencean reversal of piety.

A fugitive serf and a passionate girl who is his only ally, are attracted by the light and warmth of the stained glass. But the spiritually dedicated window excludes their need. When she longs for "such a little light like a red flower—only a little, like a roseberry scarlet on one's breast," and he climbs the window to gather it, the glass figure of Christ, the "cold man," breaks, and he falls, cut and bleeding. They flee to the wood that is so often a refuge later for Lawrencean outlaws. Here the fragment of glass becomes a means of vital communion when, echoing the Christian ritual, he gives it to her as his blood and his life-stone. She is fearless in their sexual consummation; but they awake next day to the threat of death. Here the unconventional vicar breaks off his story with "Nay, they lived happily ever after." His young auditor's "No" tacitly recognizes the ironic untruth of this romantic cliché.

In spite of a degree of preciousness in the frame story, and an awkward quality of *tour de force* in the vicar's archaic language, the story has a feeling over and above the paraphrasable content, that is uniquely Lawrencean, having to do with the intensely created rejection and isolation, the accompanying peril of the blood relationship, and, perhaps above all, a certain kinesis in objects and environment as well as action.[4]

"The Shades of Spring," though essentially a rather weak, self-conscious sketch, contains the basic story of Lawrence's last novel, *Lady Chatterley's Lover*. An educated young married man is drawn back to the natural world of the countryside by his desire for life and his inability to forget the sweetheart with whom he had failed. He had thought that her nature and need were entirely spiritual and ideal. Now she reveals to him his misunderstanding by showing him, in orchard, garden, and bird nests, a series of natural matings. At the hut of the gamekeeper who is her lover, her final revelation of the way she has chosen is to put on a cloak of animal skins. As the young man leaves, he sees her sucking the poison from a bee-sting on the keeper's arm while he embraces her, "one rough rope of dark brown hair . . . across his bare arm."[5] In an existential touch that anticipates *Lady Chatterley's Lover*, the keeper's voice, as he asks her to marry him, is troubled by fear as well as passion. Such trouble in the midst of the Lawrencean reversal of values is developed in the later work as an acknowledgment of the world's hostility to, and the intrinsic difficulty of, a vital relationship that crosses class and moral boundaries. It becomes part of the complex awareness that saves Lawrence's fiction from unrealistic, oversimplified solutions and from merely primitivistic and sexual apotheoses.

"A Modern Lover"[6] also treats a young man's return—after two years in the city—and his rejection. He, too, is a young esthete and intellectual, but his crisis is that of a virginal young man who, unable to marry because he is in debt, has decided to persuade his sweetheart to become his

---

4. Kingsley Widmer says ("Our Demonic Heritage: D. H. Lawrence" in *A D. H. Lawrence Miscellany*, 1959) of the relevance of the story to the later work: ". . . The scene of violence and extremity, the rebellious devil-hero rending both the social order and Christian forms, the totemic animals of passion (horse and fox), the imagery of fire, blood, and darkness, and the concluding deathly sexual consummation become substantial and recurrent elements in Lawrence's art."

5. There is a possibility that this climactic scene was suggested by a painting Lawrence copied in his youth. Among the copies reproduced in *Young Lorenzo* by Ada Lawrence and G. Stuart Gelder, is one of the painting by M. Greiffenhagen titled "An Idyll" which shows such a primitivistic embrace. It would be surprising if the very early work did not contain "literary" influences of this sort.

6. Posthumously published in *A Modern Lover* (London, Secker, 1934).

mistress. The style is at times unbelievably precious; the statements of need and the good life suggest Walter Pater's esthetic hedonism and hard, clean flame. Yet the attack on decadence and the belief in the value of its destruction by unchecked, "fierce" vitality, is recognizably Lawrencean.

> What was it he wanted, sought in the slowly-lapsing tide of days? . . . Of many people, his friends, he had asked that they would kindle again the smouldering embers of their experience; he had blown the low fires gently with his breath, and had leaned his face towards their glow, and had breathed in the words that rose like fumes from the revived embers, till he was sick with the strong drug of sufferings and ecstasies and sensations, and the dreams that ensued. But most folk had choked out the fires of their fiercer experience with rubble of sentimentality and stupid fear, and rarely could he feel the hot destruction of life fighting out its way.
>
> Surely, surely somebody could give him enough of the philtre of life to stop the craving which tortured him hither and thither, enough to satisfy for a while, to intoxicate him till he could laugh the crystalline laughter of the star, and bathe in the retreating flood of twilight like a naked boy in the surf, clasping the waves and beating them, and answering their wild clawings with laughter sometimes, and sometimes gasps of pain.

At times the psychological pattern is like that of *Sons and Lovers*. The girl's submissiveness makes the young man shrink from her, a reaction that he thinks may come from the throwing of full responsibility upon him. He proposes a flint-steel relationship in order to overcome the paralysis of their speculating and poetizing together. Ironically, it is this mutual move towards knowledge that has brought him to his decision. When he graphs their reading—from *Jane Eyre* and George Eliot through Carlyle, Ruskin, Schopenhauer, Darwin, Huxley, Omar Khayyam, the Russians, Ibsen, Balzac, de Maupassant, *Madame Bovary*, Nietzsche, and William James— the iconoclastic line runs from moral and esthetic criticism of the Victorian milieu through natural science and skepticism, a hedonistic view of the sensual, the irony of the relativity of morality in action, the romantic schizophrenia of Madame Bovary, to vitalism and a pragmatic skepticism of the ideal and absolute.

This argumentative young intellectual is hardly the Lawrencean hero of the later fiction. But he foreshadows him when he advocates against himself the nonintellectual man, a mine electrician, who is the girl's fiancé. His mixed judgment of this man betrays a rather self-conscious sophistication. The fiancé is "among the men of handsome, healthy animalism, and good intelligence," but also deserves the sophisticated judgment of George Moore as one whom "his wife would hate after a few years for the very way he walked across the floor." Yet when the young intellectual helps him ready his bicycle by the light of a match, in a darkness that is not yet the full Lawrencean darkness of touch, he feels that he must take him into his protection. Here, so early, is a suggestion of Lawrence's mature championship of the nonintellectual but vital man through a more knowledgeable leader, as in *Aaron's Rod*. The importance of the man and man relationship is extended when the young intellectual, completely frustrated by the girl's remaining within his spell of esthetic and intellectual intimacy while refusing him sexual fulfillment, expresses love of the physical beauty of the farm men he encounters. Thus very early in Lawrence the problem of relationship is also that of love between men, as it is more critically in *Women in Love*, *Aaron's Rod*, and *The Plumed Serpent*.

In these short stories, the protagonists oscillate queasily between their Midland origin and tokens of the world of Lawrence's college and teaching days. Other stories focus more closely on the latter world, of Croydon, but explore essentially the same problems.

"The Old Adam"[7] sketches a brief break-through to passion that lapses into the ludicrous and a victory for the *status quo*. Again the young man is chaste at a critically advanced age, twenty-seven. The story turns on his relations with the family with whom he boards—a lawyer husband of forty, a wife of about thirty-five, a girl-child of three, and an attractive nineteen-year-old maid. The immediate catalyst of the possibility of sexual fulfillment between the young man and the wife is a storm which, by its intensity, as in *The Virgin and the Gipsy*, sweeps them out of ordinary consciousness into rapport. The analysis of the young man's block to such fulfillment, in its distinction between the subconsciously

---

7. Posthumously published in *A Modern Lover*, 1934.

passional and the resistance of the "conscious soul," and its running inter-mixture of abstraction and sensation, is surprisingly mature Lawrence.

> Being highly civilized, he prized women for their intuition, and because of the delicacy with which he could transfer to them his thoughts and feelings, without cumbrous argument. . . . There was a pain in his chest that made him pant, and an involuntary tension in his arms, as if he must press someone to his breast. But the idea that this someone was Mrs. Thomas would have shocked him too much had he formed it. His passion had run on subconsciously, till now it had come to such a pitch it must drag his conscious soul into allegiance. This, however, would probably never happen; he would not yield allegiance, and blind emotion, in this direction, could not carry him alone.

The anticlimax when the husband arrives is rather good Lawrencean intellectual-psychological comedy. There is an argument over a point of politics involving the Women's Bill, and consequently the wife's emancipation from such a boorish male as her husband. The wife takes her husband's side against herself and enjoys inciting a battle of words. The fight that follows turns upon Lawrence's use of another female character in counterpoint to the antagonism.

The maid has the "insolent pride" and the challenge of handsome young womanhood. The most significant thing about her, in terms of Lawrence's mature art, is that she is a semi-outcast because of her lower class position and because she has just enough Jewish blood to enrich her beauty. She is attracted to the young man and offended by his indifference to her. The vital potentiality she suggests is also developed through the young man's love of the girl-child, a love that figures strongly in Lawrence's early poems and fiction.

> She was a beautiful girl, a bacchanal with her wild, dull-gold hair tossing about like a loose chaplet, her hazel eyes shining daringly, her small, spaced teeth glistening in little passions of laughter within her red, small mouth. The young man loved her. She was such a little bright wave of willfulness, so abandoned to her impulses, so white and smooth as she lay at rest, so startling as she flashed her naked limbs about.

The maid is leaving on the day of the argument over women's rights.

As the antagonistic husband and young man carry her trunk downstairs, they are unaware of her as a woman. A contest develops; they fight, and the wife's sympathy goes to the husband. As passional loser, the young man retreats into remorse and apology, and relations become formal and distant.

"The Fly in the Ointment" or "A Blot,"[8] perhaps based on an experience in this same Croydon household, sketches the conflict for the young man between his sense of beauty at home in the Midlands, revived when his girl sends him a box of flowers, the consequent interruption of his attention to the work of school, and, as the central experience of the story, his encounter late at night, after finishing a letter to his girl, with a degenerate young burglar. The reaction to the rat-like nature of the burglar expressed in his sardonic, baffled questioning, contains Lawrence's characteristic nausea at what he later called the "social beast" aspect of man.

> He could affect and alter me, I could not affect nor alter him. . . . It was like a nightmare. I thought he was a blot, like a blot fallen on my soul, something black and heavy which I could not decipher.

Recalling his girl and the life her gift had recalled to disturb him, he feels sudden anger against her "perfect serene beauty," and prepares for bed, alone and wretched.

In "The Witch *à la Mode*"[9] Lawrence's young protagonist has made a move toward stability by becoming engaged, but he is restlessly driven by needs his fiancée cannot satisfy. He seeks out another woman, Winifred, with whom these needs are connected. As he approaches this encounter, his troubled division of feeling is linked with the night-moon-star imagery that expresses the nonhuman, otherworld drift of the early mother poems, the love poems, and *The Trespasser*.

The central question of the story is put by the young man to the older generation as "Why do we do things?" The older generation's discussions of Free Will are passé. Lawrence's protagonist is caught in a situation that is unbearably painful yet impossible to break out of. When Winifred

---

8. Published posthumously in *Young Lorenzo,* by Ada Lawrence and G. Stuart Gelder.
9. Published posthumously in *A Modern Lover,* 1934.

talks of resolving their love-hate duality, he objects to what he calls the "misleading symbols" of her speech and says that he is going to wander blind, go by instinct. When he tries to explain the reasons for his engagement, he defines his conflict as one between love of change, which he equates with love of life, and his desire to be nailed to something, if only to a cross.

The situation suggests Lawrence's complicated position between the traditional values and sense of responsibility he inherited from his mother, and his need to escape them as part of the process of freeing himself from arresting love and grief for her and achieving fulfillment. His betrothed, says the protagonist, possesses that side of himself that idealizes her and loves her pityingly and tenderly. But this leaves out the greater part of his nature, fascinated by playing with fire with Winifred, and expressed by his eyes, which are sometimes "hard and insolent," sometimes full of "warmth and tenderness," and sometimes "flaring like an animal's." Winifred is cruel to the "common, everyday" part of himself that requires stability and marriage. Her case is worse than his. As she puts it, he is jetsam, while she is flotsam that will be stranded. He cries out against her acceptance of wreck and loss, as the young Lawrence cried out against the fatalistic resignation to suffering of Helen Corke, who may be the model for Winifred. His final response is a violent act of revulsion and flight, when she gives him her first genuine kiss, but wants no more than the kiss, and so places on him the unbearable strain that characterizes relationship this side of fulfillment in the early fiction. The creation of his sense of strain with its stages of consciousness, and his violence toward a symbol of what resists and arrests him, through combined analysis and sensation building to a climax, is rather mature Lawrence.

> Dazed, he was conscious of the throb of one great pulse, as if his whole body were a heart that contracted in throbs. He felt, with an intolerable ache, as if he, the heart, were setting the pulse in her. . . .
>
> The hurt became so great it brought him out of the reeling stage to distinct consciousness. She clipped her lips, drew them away, leaving him her throat. . . . He opened his eyes as he bent with his mouth on her neck, and was startled; there stood the objects of the room, stark; there, close

below his eyes, were the half-sunk lashes of the woman, swooning on her unnatural ebb of passion. . . . His whole body ached like a swollen vein, with heavy intensity, while his heart grew dead with misery and despair. This woman gave him anguish and a cutting-short like death; to the other woman he was false. As he shivered with suffering, he opened his eyes again, and caught sight of the pure ivory of the lamp.

In a scene resembling the crisis in Dickens' *Great Expectations,* he kicks over this image suggesting his conscious misery and a bloodless purity; the flames catch her dress, he crushes them out, and flees with his burning-red hands held out blindly. The power of the ending is lessened by the self-consciously witty remark that this demonstrates the danger of playing with fire.

I have grouped Lawrence's other stories broadly by the "worlds" with which they may be said to deal, reserving two of the longest and best, approaching the novelette in complexity, for the last. By "worlds" I mean those segments of his environment that come, through his organization of them into the imagined worlds of his fiction, to have special characteristics and significance. In an expanding order, these are the worlds of the miner's home and life; the town of trade and manufacture, fairs, churches and vicars; and the countryside of wood, lake, farm and field. The relations in and between these worlds are complex, often involving rude differences of education, language, attitude, and behavior. The values offered to Lawrence's imagination were, of course, correspondingly complex. Always, as later, he concentrates on the difficulties of the love-sex relationship.

"The White Stocking," one of Lawrence's earliest stories, seems to have grown from an incident in his mother's life before her marriage.[10] The milieu is town and middle class. The husband is a traveler for a small firm; his rival owns a lace factory in which the wife was employed before her marriage. The mood of the story is light almost to the point

---

10. In *D. H. Lawrence: A Personal Record* Jessie Chambers says rather strangely that this is "an idealised picture of his mother as a young girl going to a ball at the Castle and drawing out a long, white stocking in mistake for a pocket handkerchief." She seems to mean "idealised" in the sense of social idealization. She may also have been thinking of an earlier version.

of bedroom farce before the tension reaches the point of violence. It is a mood Lawrence was to refine into the laconic satire of "The Captain's Doll" and other mature stories.

The lively, impulsive wife receives a white stocking as a valentine, one of a pair given her before her marriage by the factory owner. At that time, mistaking it for a handkerchief, she had taken it to a dance where he, allegorically named Adams, had nearly claimed her sensually from her fiancé, who was negligently playing whist at the time, and is not very subtly named Whiston. Adams' Adamic power while they dance is quite Lawrencean.

> Every moment, and every moment, she felt she would give way utterly, and sink molten: the fusion point was coming when she would fuse down into perfect unconsciousness at his feet and knees.

Adams had reclaimed the stocking. Now, she puts the stockings on and boasts of them to her husband, not only refusing to let him burn them but letting him know she really would like the other man to see her pretty legs. What starts out as no more than her pleasure in harmless freedom within the security of her husband's power turns into a battle. Her jeers move him enough to want to kill her. He reacts from the violence of striking her, into shame and nausea, and she is accusatory; but at the end there is a reconciliation in her submission and his anguish in the touch of an embrace. It is interesting that the violence that makes Paul Morel in *Sons and Lovers* hate his father here has a very different resolution, as if Lawrence the artist, here freer to invent, was already in advance of Lawrence the son. A touch that is later to have an almost ritualistic use is the wife's awareness of her husband's male power in the nakedness of washing.

The attitude toward the town's middle class sometimes resembles the burlesque that marks the opening chapters of *The Lost Girl*. "Goose Fair" explores the grotesque nature and consequences of the holiday, during a strike, taken by the young son of a factory owner—a holiday not only from his business duties but a more Jamesian moral holiday from his conscience-keeping fiancée. Contrasted to her, and in a sense victorious over her, is an unkempt, rather sullen country girl who drives her geese to market through the "morose atmosphere of bad trade" that pervades the town.

He excuses himself from dinner with his fiancée on the ground that he must guard the works from arson by the unemployed hands. When the mill burns and he cannot be found, the fiancée's father suspects him of setting the fire for the insurance money. The girl herself is characterized by the kind of idealism that is a characteristic Lawrencean target. She is preoccupied with Ruskin's *Sesame and Lilies* and oblivious to the human reality of the economic situation, and the lack of the fun that should be going on at the fair. She imagines herself defending her lover from the accusation of arson, and is certain her life is ruined. Her romantic longing is comically contrasted to reality through high-flown diction.

> She felt an intense longing at this uncanny hour to slough the body's trammeled weariness and to issue at once into the new bright warmth of the far Dawn where a lover waited transfigured. . . .
> Then she went downstairs and found her father eating a mutton chop.

The truth about her fiancé is excellent Lawrencean realistic, psychological comedy. He has spent the night teasing, and fighting with, the country girl at the fair. When he is faced with the fact of the ruined factory and the anger of his betrothed, and must submit to her as his conscience-keeper, there is contempt in the curl of his lip.

The impingement of town and country worlds is more serious and poignant in "Second Best." The marriage of Lawrence's own mother had been, apparently, a second best choice, "downward" not only in class and status but in sensibility, as in the story.

The young woman's first choice, an educated young man who is nothing less than a Doctor of Chemistry, has become engaged to another. The second best is a young farmer resembling George in *The White Peacock*. She moves toward him reluctantly in the setting of wood and field that constitutes the vitalistic side of Lawrence's cultural, psychic contretemps. Here, as she talks about her problem with her more robust younger sister, she finds the natural strange and unfriendly. The appearance of a mole establishes for her a correlative of her feeling. He is like a "very ghost of *joie de vivre*." She pities him in his blind delight in sun and touch. But when her unsqueamish, untroubled sister captures the mole and, when he bites her, kills him in sudden anger, she admits that such creatures have to be killed, and moves from her grief to dreary indifference.

Rapport with the young farmer requires of her a parallel inward death. To the young farmer, the killing of moles is a matter of simple necessity about which he does not think. She must respond to this, and, inseparably, to his passional feeling, that, as Lawrence puts it, "had never become conscious, purposive." Still offended by his use of the dialect and other uncouthness, she makes a submission by killing a mole and bringing it to him. Though she feels that this act involves a death in herself, she takes a thrill of pleasure in it, and is passionally aroused. His response to her suggests the prelude to Lawrencean fulfillment that reaches all the way to *Lady Chatterley's Lover*—passion and tenderness, aroused by a specific physical feature, overcoming the barriers to fulfillment.

> The blood came up in him, strong, overmastering. He resisted it. But it drove him down, and he was carried away. Seeing the winsome, frail nape of her neck fierce love came upon him for her, and tenderness.

Here again, so early, are all the elements of the Lawrencean parable of the modern sensibility—a culturally bred, class allied, highly conscious, self-dramatizing fastidiousness and consequent severance from the natural and the passional common denominator, capable of being overcome only by an experience of the fierceness and mastery in nature, and an inward death. The fight in nature is a catalyst of the passional self of even the vitally strong male, whose fierceness is tempered by tenderness for the vulnerable woman.

In six early stories Lawrence explored the nature of relationship among the miners and their families. His most intimate beginnings lay in this world of divided allegiances and anarchic emotions unpalliated by genteel manners. The five years of his concentration on the major effort of *The White Peacock*, 1905-10, represent a relative avoidance of this subject in favor of the country world and the young intellectuals of his reading, dreaming, and thinking, and struggle for fulfillment. His second novel, *The Trespasser,* continued this preoccupation with their world, into which he had grown, or risen, from his origins. Not until the third, *Sons and Lovers,* did he engage in a concentrated and sustained look at his most intimate experience, in his family's life. Inevitably one guesses that the reasons lay in the painfulness, the preoccupation with the evolving means of escape to life, and perhaps the beginner's tendency to avoid realism in favor of something more romantic and artistic. Yet, on the whole, these six stories are sharp, acutely perceptive vignettes, reflecting an analysis of the causes of anarchy in relationship that is surprisingly close to Lawrence's mature reflections.

"The Shadow in the Rose Garden" contains the effects of crossing class and cultural lines. Perhaps like his mother, this miner's wife keeps emotional allegiance to a lost love higher in class and superior in sensibility. She has secretly chosen for her honeymoon the neighborhood of her affair with a man she thinks is dead. Her mood is one of abstraction and distance from her husband.

When she revisits the rose garden in which her love was experienced, the place itself is an emblem of the delicacy of sensibility and class that separates her from the miner. That it belongs to a rector assigns it to the religious emphasis on resigned suffering that Lawrence could not abide. The use of natural objects as correlatives of psychic states is characteristic Lawrence. As she wanders abstractly, the pink roses arouse in her the former softness of intimacy; the white roses, greenish like ice at the center, suggest her frustration. Surprised by a shadow over the color and sunlight, she encounters her old lover, reported dead in the Boer War. Now, in the living death of insanity, his hands, "her symbols of passionate love," fill her with horror, and instead of recognition she feels the threat of violence. (The psychic effect of war haunts Lawrence's fiction after World War I and produces the concept of another kind of soldier, the vitally resurrected man fighting for a new life.)

When she returns to her husband, he is at a climax of fury over her distance and forces her to tell the story of her love. His blunt miner's suspicion of such an affair is that it is "going the whole-hogger" before marriage. When he drives her to admitting a sexual relationship, she does so with her own brutality. The cost to her of adding that her lover is now a lunatic, reveals to the husband "the width of the break between them. . . . They were both shocked so much, they were impersonal, and no longer hated each other." The story leaves them in this traumatic suspension of relationship of which Lawrence was always so acutely aware.

"Odour of Chrysanthemums" is at first glance a sort of English miners' "Riders to the Sea" with its stark treatment of the effects of a miner's death in an accident on his family. But through it runs the extreme failure in relationship which is the Lawrencean tragedy. A mother and her children await the late homecoming of a father who, to her, is surely wasting money drinking at the pub. The children must bear the mother's irritation, which deepens into anxiety and dread. She is forced to move completely from her moral and economic value judgment when she receives his corpse, emblematic of her inability to realize the basic living man. After superficially reassuring the children, she must, in laying out her husband's ironically unmarked, handsome body, and listening to his mother's querulous, but passionate grief, face up to the death in life meaning of her situation.

> In her womb was ice of fear, because of this separate stranger. . . . Was this what it all meant—utter, intact separateness, obscured by heat of living . . . ? There had been nothing between them, they had come together, exchanging their nakedness repeatedly. Each time he had taken her, they had been two isolated beings, far apart as now. He was no more responsible than she. The child was like ice in her womb.

She experiences full force, in sensation, the passional and psychic horror against which Lawrence labored all his life. By the time of Constance Chatterley and Mellors the means of violation of relationship have been enormously multiplied by exploration of attitudes and practices in the whole of modern culture.

Much more should be said of this story than that it is characteristically Lawrencean in perception and theme. It is an example of his art at its organic best. Tone, setting, dialogue, and action, a pervasively suggestive imagery of deathliness through ragged garden, autumn, and odor of chrysanthemums, all create a felt meaning of cumulative fatality now being climactically realized. A temptation to conceptual analysis was overcome in revision between the *English Review* version and that in

The Prussian Officer collection, the earlier one ending with a rather sociological account of the causes of the frustration and misdirection of the miner's vitality.

"A Sick Collier" also suggests that the basic cause of conflict in marriage is a difference of sensibilities stemming from different values and expectations from life. The miner teaches his bride to use a newspaper instead of a cloth on the table, and she, in her beautiful cleanliness, discovers the reason when he comes home from the pit and does not trouble to wash up before dinner. Like Mrs. Morel in *Sons and Lovers*, she is attracted to her husband physically—this "tight little fellow; short, dark, with a warm colour, and that upright set of the head and chest, that flaunting way in movement recalling a mating bird, which denotes a body taut and compact with life." But she is repelled by his physicality when it is revealed in the daily ritual of nakedness while washing, the ritual Constance responds to passionally in *Lady Chatterley's Lover*.

Her revulsion is not so complete as to destroy their relationship; but the shocks she must endure because of her husband's occupation suggest those of Mrs. Morel. She must worry about money and contrive during a fifteen weeks' strike. When he is hurt in an accident, he deliriously threatens to kill her. Her final, ironic fear is that if his ravings are overheard in the privacy-lacking miners' community, gossip that he is insane will stop their compensation. Lawrence's hatred of possessions and any sort of fixed dependency, and his ultimate advocacy of vitalistic cultural revolution rather than tinkering with the socio-economic *status quo*, develop from this sort of basic indignity.

In "Strike-Pay"[11] the miners take a moral holiday from which they gain a desultory, temporary sense of adventure and mastery, and one of them, less robust than the others, wins a small, inconclusive victory over his mother-in-law and his wife.

The men gather at the Primitive Methodist Chapel, a "bulwark of the women's conscience-keeping role," to receive their meager strike-pay, while up and down the streets the women are busy with the family washing. A gang of them, starting in high spirits on a lark to Nottingham, tease the pale young married man who is the central character of the

---

11. Published posthumously in *A Modern Lover*.

story into joining them. Their spirit is one of battle and triumph that is "beyond all consciousness." When they encounter a troop of idle pit-ponies, there is a suggestion of Lawrence's ubiquitous use of horses as symbols of thwarted vitality. The men try to have fun by riding and running the ponies, but find them inert because they are so unused to freedom. Lawrence says of the ponies as he was later to say of the miners: "They missed the warmth and the life of the pit." During the horse play, the young married man loses his money. The others share with him, so that he can continue, through more visits to pubs, gambling on skittles, and a soccer game; but then he gives in and goes home. The unaccustomed freedom, the loss of his strike-pay, his anticipation of trouble at home, and his seeing a man killed in a cart accident give him a sense of death and strife. At home he is taunted by his mother-in-law, and his remaining money is expropriated. He asserts himself enough to demand his tea, and even sends the mother-in-law sailing indignantly off to her other daughter's house when he swears a bit; but his wife serves his tea, not because she is really meek, but because he is her man rather than her mother's. The story portrays a world in which male strength and pride sometimes take the relatively inconsequential freedom of the brief moral holiday. The problem of how such men's joy in life could be made integral with all the other aspects of their lives was to be an important theme in Lawrence's later work.

The contest between these men and the "conscience keepers" who thwart them is treated more comically in "Her Turn."[12] The husband is "one for the women," even being liked by the prudish neighbor women because of his bigness, naiveté, and courtesy. He earns good money, and gives his wife what he considers a generous allowance before applying the rest to his pleasure. The story turns on his wife's dissatisfaction when, during a strike, she cannot get his strike-pay from him, and the stratagem she uses during the next strike.

He is inconspicuously visiting the wife of a pub-keeper, an easy-going woman with whom he enjoys talking in the bar-parlour, to which men she likes are invited. She provides a rudimentary Bohemian-intellectual escape that foreshadows the more elaborate one in *Aaron's Rod*. This mildly

---

12. Published posthumously in *A Modern Lover*.

Byronic man loves conundrums, and sometimes writes down his thoughts in a series of simple sentences that he calls his "poetry." His wife interferes with these visits by getting his strike-pay. She has a real passion for him, localized in Lawrencean fashion in his strong neck, so that she is not a puritanical shrew, but a clever combiner of the main chance with passional claim.

By using up her savings in buying things for the house that he cannot prove she does not need, she robs him of his excuse that she does not need his strike-pay. One by one, as her purchases are brought into the house, they pile up on his freedom. He must even help carry them, while the neighbors watch, and tip the carter. Angry at her smug sense of satisfaction, he lifts his fist to strike her, but turns away to the garden to pet the tortoise which earlier, putting out its head in awakening to the warm spring day, was a correlative of his limited freedom—" 'He's like th' men, wakened up for a holiday,' said the wife." The next week he brings home his strike-pay and receives the allowance of a shilling.

Though the young Lawrence hated his father, there is in these early stories remarkable empathy for and understanding of one side of his father's situation and nature. This was to grow, in the full Lawrencean rebellion, into the creation of men who insist on the mastery that will permit them activity beyond the woman's sphere, and a more complete and fulfilling life. A late analysis of the miners' predicament that is consistent with this early story occurs in "Nottingham and the Mining Countryside": "The colliers were deeply alive, instinctively. But they had no daytime ambition, and no daytime intellect. . . . The collier fled out of the house as soon as he could, away from the nagging materialism of the woman. With the women it was always: This is broken, now you've got to mend it! or else! We want this, that and the other, and where is the money coming from? The collier didn't know and didn't care very deeply —his life was otherwise. So he escaped."

In these early vignettes of the miners' world, disorganized life rather than immorality is the subject. "The Christening" is a story of the miners' unconventional, mixed response to illegitimacy that Lawrence remarked in early letters to Edward Garnett. The complex contradictions of the passional, social, and moral aspects of the situation—the clandestine christening of an illegitimate baby—are created through an old, retired miner who dominates his children. One daughter, educated as a schoolmistress and suffering from a weakened heart, is pathetically vulnerable to the social stigma imposed by the town. Another, decisive and effective, tries cheerfully to make the best of a bad situation. The daughter who is the baby's mother is ashamed and sullen, but when she touches the baby, feels only love for it. The son of the family has no respect for the old father's inchoate religious feeling for life, and brutally mocks his sister.

Propriety and ideality are contrasted to this chaos of feelings in the response of the clergyman. Women are "unliving, Biblical things" to him. Holding the baby, he "shines with an unreal," abstract love. His remoteness contrasts with the bold, emotional prayer of the old father, whose talk with the Lord is an intimately personal confession of failure to yield his self-will to a higher power. The vitality of the old miner has been crippled by locomotor ataxia. Gossip has it that his mind is weakening. The children are opposed to him. Yet he dominates them. The focus is on the disintegrative nature of his power. "They had never lived; his life, his will had always been upon them and contained them. They were only half-individuals."

I have reserved two rather long, very good stories with which to end this discussion of the early short fiction. One, "Daughters of the Vicar," the longest and most complex of the stories collected in *The Prussian Officer* volume, is the richest and most revolutionary exploration of the clash between the miners' natures and lives and the spiritual and moral expectations of their cultural supervisors, near in time to the relative dead ends of *Sons and Lovers* and *The Trespasser*. Clearly the Lawrencean move to salvation had been plotted while the defeat was still dominant in other stories. One aspect of the technique is particularly interesting, the skillful and more mature use of the strategy of exploring the situations and destinies of two couples, involving sisters, with which Lawrence began, in *The White Peacock*, and which he continued through his last novel.

The sisters, Mary and Louisa, are the daughters of an Episcopal vicar who is isolated among the unsympathetic, chapel-going miners. The mother become an invalid broken by the suppression of her anger and misery. The girls are, in Lawrence's terms, repressed into gentility, urged to ambition, and weighted with duty.

The opposite tendency of the socially anarchic, emotionally and indi-
vidually oriented miners can be seen in the wonderfully alive and humorous dialogue between the vicar and the mother of the man who is to
save Louisa from disintegration.

> "I don't feel like eating," she sighed.
>
> "Why—aren't you well?" asked the clergyman, patronizing.
>
> "It isn't that," she sighed. She sat with shut, straight mouth. "I don't
> know what's going to become of us."
>
> But the clergyman had ground himself down so long, that he could not
> easily sympathize.
>
> "Have you any trouble?" he asked.
>
> "Ay, have I any trouble!" cried the elderly woman. "I shall end my days
> in the work-house."
>
> The minister waited unmoved. What could she know of poverty, in her
> little house of plenty!
>
> "I hope not," he said.
>
> "And the one lad as I wanted to keep by me——" she lamented.
>
> The minister listened without sympathy, quite neutral.
>
> "And the lad as would have been a support to my old age! What is going
> to become of us?" she said.
>
> The clergyman, justly, did not believe in the cry of poverty, but wondered
> what had become of the son.
>
> "Has anything happened to Alfred?" he asked.
>
> "We've got word he's gone for a Queen's sailor," she said sharply.
>
> "He has joined the Navy!" exclaimed Mr. Lindley. "I think he could
> scarcely have done better—to serve his Queen and country on the sea . . ."
>
> "He is wanted to serve me," she cried. "And I wanted my lad at home."
>
> Alfred was her baby, her last, whom she had allowed herself the luxury
> of spoiling.
>
> "You will miss him," said Mr. Lindley, "that is certain. But this is no
> regrettable step for him to have taken—on the contrary."
>
> "That's easy for you to say, Mr. Lindley," she replied tartly. "Do you
> think I want my lad climbing ropes at another man's bidding, like a
> monkey——?" . . .
>
> "I shall respect all men who serve God and their country on the sea, Mrs.
> Durant," said the clergyman stubbornly.
>
> "That is all very well, when they're not your sons who are doing the dirty
> work.—It makes a difference," she replied tartly.

The assistant clergyman who becomes Mary's husband has little range of feeling and acts from a strong, philosophical mind. In marrying him, she rejects her body, as a "lower thing," for the "higher freedom of pure will towards right." The consequence is a split between body and mind that troubles her relationship with her child, which she alternately loves and hates because it makes her live again in the flesh when she wishes to live in the mind.

Louisa, who feels indignant distaste for her sister's marriage, re-encounters the miner's son, Alfred, home from navy service. Her recognition of him is Lawrencean in its connection of the physical with the reality of love—"his small teeth showed in a glimpse of the greeting she used to love." In contrast, the clergyman looks "queer and obliterated," and his praying is "like a foretaste of inexorable, cold death, a taste of pure justice."

Louisa unconsciously gravitates to Alfred's mother's home, just as later Constance Chatterley is drawn to the gamekeeper's hut. The portrait of the mother and her meaning to her son contains anticipations of *Sons and Lovers*. She is suffering from a tumor as did Lawrence's mother and Mrs. Morel. Alfred has matured during his navy service, but for him as for Paul Morel, his mother is "the fact and hope of belief." Connected with this is a split between his "idea of women, with which he sometimes debauches himself," and real women, with whom he feels a "deep uneasiness and need to draw away."

Louisa achieves her vitalistic Lawrencean salvation from ideal love in the physical intimacy of washing the coal-grime from Alfred's naked back. In creating the qualitative differences in her feeling, which combines the force of sex with a comical human response, Lawrence anticipates his later semantic method, emphasizing and repeating key words.

> He ducked his face round, looking up at her in what was a very comical way. She had to harden herself.
> "How funny he looks with his face upside down," she thought. After all, there was a difference between her and the common people. The water in which his arms were plunged was quite black, the soap-froth was darkish. She could scarcely conceive him as human. Mechanically, under the influence of habit, he groped in the black water, fished out soap and flannel, and handed them backward to Louisa. Then he remained rigid and submissive, his two arms thrust straight in the panchion, supporting the weight

of his shoulders. His skin was beautifully white and unblemished, of an opaque, solid whiteness. Gradually Louisa saw it: this also was what he was. It fascinated her. Her feeling of separateness passed away: she ceased to draw back from contact with him and his mother. There was this living centre. Her heart ran hot. She had reached some goal in this beautiful, clear, male body. She loved him in a white, impersonal heat. But the sun-burnt, reddish neck and ears: they were more personal, more curious. A tenderness rose in her, she loved even his queer ears. A person—an intimate being he was to her.

Through Alfred is passionally aroused by such Lawrencean stimuli as her heavy, bright hair and the pointed wisps at the nape of her neck, he regards her as a vision, "everything that is beyond him of the exquisite and ideal." And like Paul Morel he is drawn from life by his mother's illness and death, felt through a communion with night and stars—night enclosing him as his mother carries him into an "unformed, unknown chaos." During this death drift, Alfred makes no response to Louisa until she forces a choice by offering herself. Then he is restored through the touch of an embrace and what can be described as an experience of death and rebirth. This healing of the split between ideality and passional fulfillment is such advanced Lawrence as to seem anachronistic. Suggestive also of later work is the tentativeness of the victory because of the consequent intensification of class and moral antagonism. When Alfred asks for her in marriage, the father cannot understand why Louisa should not behave in the normal way, and thinks that she ought to spare him the loss of prestige. His being mollified by their plan to make a new start in Canada suggests the ultimate exiles of the later work.

"Love Among the Haystacks" is one of Lawrence's best handlings of the farm world he so loved, especially of the natures of the farm men he was so sympathetic to. Somehow it was passed over, for publication, until after his death. Like "Daughters of the Vicar" it uses the strategy of exploring the situations of two couples without the subjective intermediacy of the observer-narrator of *The White Peacock*. Stylistically and formally it is quite mature Lawrence, creating the drama of fulfillment through ordinary work, manners, and speech, and the latent metaphorical and symbolic suggestions of the setting.

The counterpointing of needs and potentialities involves two brothers, and the women who match them. Maurice is handsome, careless, and debonair, and is assigned the swarthy skin that often marks the passionally powerful Lawrencean character. Geoffrey, heavy and hulking, is distinguished by a painful self-consciousness—"The idea of going through life thus coiled up within himself in morbid self-consciousness, always lonely, surly, and a misery was enough to make him cry out." Both brothers are fiercely shy of women until the hay-harvest of the story, because the whole female sex has been represented by their mother, proud, strange to the country world, quiet, and speaking pure English. The common girls of the region, loud-mouthed and broad-tongued, are beneath them. They have grown up virgin and tormented.

As they work at the hay-harvest, the scene suggests Lawrence's later sun symbolism of life-giving power, as in "Sun."

> The stack they rode was high, lifting them up above the hedge-tops, and very broad, a great slightly-hollowed vessel into which the sunlight poured, in which the hot, sweet scent of hay was suffocating. Small and inefficacious the brothers looked, half-submerged in the loose, great trough, lifted high up as if on an altar reared to the sun.

The brothers become involved in a furious male contest in building the stack because of their attraction to the governess of the family of the local vicar. Lawrence makes characteristic use of sympathy, tenderness, and touch in the development of this situation. Geoffrey has first been drawn to her by seeing her fall, and sympathetically picking her up and rubbing her nettle-stung arms with dock-leaf. When he causes Maurice's fall from the stack, she is drawn to Maurice through her concern and tenderness. Another means of arousal is the passionate wildness and foreignness of the voice of this German-speaking Polish girl, whose strongly passional nature is in ironic service to a vicar. Her being an outlander not only in nationality and language but in freedom of feeling, is a combination that runs all through Lawrence's mature work. A Polish woman of a more complex kind appears in *The Rainbow* both to fulfill and trouble the farmer Tom Brangwen.

A further Lawrencean stroke is this vital outlander's being judged harshly by the representatives of morality. The vicar has given her notice because to him she is a completely wild, disobedient, insolent animal.

Lawrence's descriptions of her exemplify his tendency to substitute for the familiar anthropocentric and moral conception of character, a purely vital, unconscious force, later so associated with animals, as in "The Fox."

> Her hair was blonde and full of life, all crisped into many tendrils with vitality, shaking round her face. Her fine blue eyes were peculiarly lidded, and she seemed to look piercingly, then languorously, like a wildcat.

Her fierce concern for Maurice after his fall from the stack gives him the sense of male power so often denied their men by the women in these early stories.

The fulfillment of Maurice and the governess takes place in the Lawrencean activity and darkness that accomplish the death of consciousness and antagonism. After their running and their daring riding of a horse, that ubiquitous Lawrencean correlative of vital power, they work together to protect the stack from rain, their unison in such work linking them to the natural fulfillment of harvest. When the ladder falls the stack is their sanctuary as well as comic trap.

Geoffrey's achievement of a parallel fulfillment is an interesting variation of the traditional underdog's-coming-even plot. His woman is a native lower-class outcast, the wife of a tramp. Trapped and debased by her husband, the totally irresponsible man Lawrence never makes a hero, she is characterized by a sullen antagonism that obscures her potential comeliness.

Geoffrey, jealous when he overhears the happy intimacy of his brother and the governess, finds shelter in a hut that suggests the gamekeeper's hut in *Lady Chatterley's Lover*. When the tramp's wife seeks shelter there, their rapport follows the mature Lawrencean pattern of hesitant, gradual development of tenderness through touch and nakedness—the overcoming of self-consciousness, hurt, and withdrawal by entry into the vital unconsciousness. The wetness and coldness outside the hut are correlative to inward defeat and misery, as is the weather in *The Virgin and the Gipsy*.

> He warmed her feet as best he could, putting them close against him. . . . Leaning forward, she touched his hair delicately with her fingers. He thrilled. She fell to gently stroking his hair, with timid, pleading finger-tips.

"Do they feel any better?" he asked, in a low voice, suddenly lifting his face to her. This sent her hand sliding softly over his face, and her finger-tips caught on his mouth. She drew quickly away. He put his hand out to find hers, in his other palm holding her feet. His wandering hand met her face. He touched it curiously. It was wet. He put his big fingers cautiously on her eyes, into two little pools of tears.

"What's a matter?" he asked, in a low, choked voice.

She leaned down to him, and gripped him tightly round the neck, pressing him to her bosom in a little frenzy of pain. Her bitter disillusionment with life, her unalleviated shame and degradation during the last four years, had driven her into loneliness and hardened her till a large part of her nature was caked and sterile. Now she softened again, and her spring might be beautiful. . . .

Both couples must face the exigencies of what might be called the nonvital, outside life in society. The governess avoids discovery of her night's escapade, becomes engaged to Maurice, and when her notice is up, joins him at the farm. But the problem of Geoffrey and the tramp's wife is more difficult, suggesting the wider range of social difficulty that troubles the ending of *Lady Chatterley's Lover*. The possibility of mar-riage is ruled out by the existence of the inferior but legally protected and sanctioned man. When Geoffrey proposes flight to Canada, she hesitates to injure his fortune. Their final wistful agreement sounds very like that of Constance Chatterley and Mellors. She will take farm service until spring. With a lack of faith that he knows she has reason for, she can only say that she will go with him to Canada when the time comes. He is angrily afraid that he will never see her again. They will write each other.

Study of the sequence and nature of Lawrence's development must take into account an apparent relationship between technique and the "world" a given story dealt with, and certain facts of revision. The stories posthumously published in *A Modern Lover* indicate that when he was dealing with his young intellectual's position at home, or between home and his teaching at Croydon, he was apt to use the young narrator strategy that results not only in an effect of preciousness but of queasy paralysis of sensibility. This strategy occupied his attention during the years of work on *The White Peacock*, 1905-11, and lingered on in the frame story of *The Trespasser*. After that it very seldom reappears in the fiction, though it may be said to continue in the point of view of some of the poetry. The more successful early stories apparently depend on the greater objectivity of the omniscient point of view, and its use seems especially connected with the miners' world, to which he may well have felt himself a sharply observant outsider. It must be remembered, too, that these stories, collected in *The Prussian Officer* volume, December, 1914, gained from revision at a time when he was under the discipline of Edward Garnett, who urged him toward the formal unity of art as distinctly different from life. (This is particularly evident in their exchanges over *The Trespasser, Sons and Lovers* and *The Rainbow*.)

Yet Lawrence resisted formal perfection, as an end, and relied on the dynamic of his experience as the shaper of an exploratory art having clarification and growth, if not, more didactically, a better life in view. The early stories show a maturing of, and increased confidence in, the original insights afforded by his basically "vitalistic" way of seeing and the reversal of values it called for—at twenty, faith in the blood as being wiser than the intellect; at twenty-seven, after long struggle and search, fulfillment and commitment in his relationship with Frieda Weekley.

There is a barrier between men and women, and sometimes between men, and a consequent frustration of relationship that ranges from the comic to the intensely tragic. The barrier originates in attitudes of "mind" connected with culture and class—broadly gentility, idealism, and Christian religious emphases—which cause people to shrink from physical life and intimate contact. The split is usually strongest in, and is carried by, the woman, who is nearly always drawn as superior in education and class. The split in the man usually originates in his attachment to his mother. Lawrence does not handle this split psychoanalytically as a completely unconscious force, or complex, but understands it as a product of culturally transmitted attitudes reinforced by love. This attribution of the origin of the split to the woman suggests why her plight is so central to all of Lawrence's work, and why she can only be saved by the mastery of a vital man from the lower class, or of an alien culture, who is opposed to the values of her culture.

The theme of the split naturally sought a series of contrasts, a contrapuntal handling of character and incident, and Lawrence's decision to begin his first novel with the situation of two couples, was perfectly suited to developing such contrasts. Characters, especially sets of lovers, tend to pair themselves on either side of the conflict, to succeed in vital rapport or to fail, and so to be, in a sense, pro-life or anti-life characters. Among his women Lawrence's favorite pairing is of two sisters; among men, two friends, usually of different classes. As their dual destinies are worked out, incidents tend to structure themselves in thesis-antithesis cycles of crisis moving to an ending that is often a last anti-social choice in the series, like the exile of Louisa and Alfred in "Daughters of the Vicar," rather than a complete victory.

Perhaps Lawrence's greatest problem was semantic—the development of a language that would adequately express an adventure that on the physical side challenged the taboos of the culture. His words and images tend to cluster around the two poles of the split, dividing broadly between abstract words made detrimental to life within a single phrase or in a larger context, and concrete words enhanced by the vitalistic struggle and even given mystic significance. Thus the importance attached to blood— warm, pulsating, somewhat like the older value term "heart"—and touch linked with sex, the most intimate physical and emotional contact, and the most difficult in a *natural* way for the highly developed consciousness. Not until late in his career did Lawrence really venture into the forbidden dictionary of four-letter words. But even *blood* was a loaded word to the attitude he opposed.

The barrier between the sexes, anti-contact and anti-life, is expressed in such terms as "stranger," "utter, intact separateness," "dread," "deadly," and its effects on the mother's attitude towards her child, born or unborn, as "almost hatred," "anguish of love," and "in her womb . . . ice of fear."

Around the forces of gentility, ideality, and religion cluster the ab- stract terms of their values: "good and purely just," "free of mundane care," "pure will towards right," "a higher thing, her freedom from material things" with its counterpart "a lower thing, her body." The culture urges the child toward "gentility," "ambition," "duty." Its methods are anti-life: "repressing," "pruning," "weighting," and its ef- fects are natures "unwarmed and rather rigid." The attempt to live "in the mind" is accompanied by a lack of "the full range of human feelings," "unreal love," "no sense of any person," a "mathematical working out" of charity, a "calculated well-doing," and if the split functions very violently personalities are "broken by the suppressing of violent anger and misery and disgust," or their purpose is "broken in two." The encounter with this creates in the vitalistic "rebels" a sense of inhuman judgment and domination and death: "something that dominated," "something dispassionate that governed," "a foretaste of inexorable, cold death," a repulsive "taste of pure justice."

Around the vitalistic counter-force of feeling and touch in the world of the miner and the country, represented chiefly by the lower class man, cluster concrete, "physical" terms. He is "a tight little fellow," "a laughing, warm lad" with "something kindly and something rich about him." He is "short, dark, with a warm colour" and an "upright set of head and chest," a "flaunting way in movement recalling a mating bird," "a body taut and compact with life," "a straight, fine jet of life." The woman apprehends him physically, through "his small white teeth," his "naked breast" or "the fine outline of his breast," his "sunburned skin" or, revealed as he washes, skin "beautifully white and unblemished," of "an opaque, solid whiteness," the latter terms as if in qualification of whiteness as potentially sickly and anti-life. Not conscious in an intellectual sense, he is "intensely himself, like a vigorous animal."

When the woman of the dominant cultural attributes is saved by this man and his physical world, her "feeling of separateness" passes away, and she ceases "to draw back from contact." His body becomes "a living centre." Her physical response is in terms of warmth, countering the terms of coldness: "made her feel warm," "her heart ran hot," "like a flame through her." While her love may have as one quality a "white, impersonal heat," it gains realization of "a person—an intimate being," through the quality of "tenderness." This key Lawrencean term and feeling is concerned with specific, comic and humanly limited qualities, such as reddened neck and ears, and counters both the abstractness of ideal love and that side of physical love that is fierce and nonhuman.

Sexual contact, if only through an embrace, becomes a ritual which accomplishes psychic death and rebirth for either the man or the woman: "she nearly lost consciousness," "she yielded up, swooned to a kind of death of herself," "his brain reeled round, and he felt himself falling from himself," "a moment of utter darkness came over him," "they began to wake up again as if from a long sleep," "he was himself."

When the man is split by his idealization of the mother and consequently of a sexual and marriage partner—"all that was beyond him, of revelation and exquisiteness," "all that was ideal and beyond him"—he is characterized by a "deep uneasiness" and "need to draw away." Beyond this, his very will to live is based on his attachment of "the fact and hope of belief" to his mother, and a death-drift is caused in him by her illness and death. Her passing is "a new night ringing about him" and a being carried "into an unformed, unknown chaos." He is afraid to think of her but cannot help himself—"his chest was conscious of her." His predicament is given extraordinary dimensions by the story's devaluing of ideal conscious attitudes, which in a sense attacks the mother as representative and carrier, and by the claim from death. That Lawrence was aware of painfully paradoxical championing of his dead mother, as if he maintained a contact with her, is clear in the late, New Mexico poem "Spirits Summoned West." All of his work is touched by this; in some it is a major theme.

The miner's son become artist was beginning, in his early fictions, a revolutionary war with the *status quo,* not an economic war of strikes, but a war of sensibility. His insight into the cause of failure in relationship and his desire for and vision of intense, unthinking, integrated life was potentially in conflict with the whole weight of the injunction and law, manners and attitudes, of society. His fiction was increasingly not the old fiction of character and moral conflict, but of the psychology of the vitalistic struggle. The struggle was not only outward but within him, and it would require a lifetime of exploration.

2

To turn to *The White Peacock* at this point is to re-encounter the dominant mood and the technique of those short stories that explore Lawrence's position as a young intellectual. Here he stands queasily and unhappily between the young people's world, centered in the farm, that had provided the essential means of his first development, and a drive toward fulfillment and an evolving conception of means that demanded a break. The novel too is narrated by a young man who views defeat in love with a rather precious sophistication and sadness very unlike Lawrence's mature attacks on the problem. There are few signs of the realism and less studied style he seems to have been developing during the late stages of the book. The diction of his young provincial intellectuals has the stiltedness of the self-consciously bookish, poetic, and romantic. The fate they yield to, without the active fight that goes on in the later fiction, may be indebted to the nineteenth-century novel tradition with which Lawrence began, and to Schopenhauer's view that the individuation of will results in hopeless conflict; but it must also be an aspect of the highly indirect, essentially complete rendering of self Lawrence said good novels achieved. This may be what Jessie Chambers meant when she called the novel "a subtle study in self-portraiture" in which Cyril and Lettie contain aspects of Lawrence to which Emily is a foil.

The novel's narrator, Cyril Beardsall, comes from a vague as to class but highly cultivated home from which the dissipated father is exiled. Early in the novel the father returns to the neighborhood for a last furtive sight of his children, and dies in a lower-class cottage much closer to Lawrence's experience than the Beardsall home. Cyril describes his father as frivolous and rather vulgar, but plausible and possessor of a good deal of charm. His lies to the mother have caused her soul to revolt. Cyril and his sister Lettie are thankful that the mother has saved them from contact with such a father, but recognize profound trouble for themselves in the failure of relationship. To Lettie this brings a fatalistic, deathly feeling that causes her to behave perversely towards the men she must choose between, and to destroy the one by choosing the other against her deepest tendency. To Cyril it brings a sense of decadence and a moody yearning connected with the family in his saying of his father's death: "It was not that we suffered a great grief; the chief trouble was the unanswered crying of failure." The story Cyril has to tell extends that failure to the lives of nearly all of his generation and suggests a radical flaw in their milieu.

Cyril and Lettie have rather natural and easy ties of friendship to Leslie Temple, the cultivated son of a mine-owning family, and to George Saxton, the earthy son of a farm family. Potentially the situation is the old love triangle involving a choice between high and lowborn, cultivated

and uncultivated, rich and poor. Lawrence's originality consists of trans-
forming this convention into a complex story of psychological-cultural
conflict. Physically and emotionally Lettie is attracted to George, but she
regards him as an animal whose mind and sensibility need awakening.
She awakens him by arousing his passion, and then marries the graceful,
charming Leslie because of a defeatist sense of the necessity of conformity
and duty. George, now divided between the conscious and the passional,
reacts to one extreme by marrying the common, physically attractive Meg.
Lettie, thwarting also the passionate male in Leslie, carries on a non-vital
marriage in which she eventually lives for her children, as had Mrs.
Beardsall. George ends up a drunkard, both psychically and physically
disintegrated by his rejection. Cyril watches this development with complex sympathy for both the kinds of sensibility involved, eventually
affirms his affinity and preference for George, but, unlike the Lawrencean
protagonists of the vital, passional side of man, is primarily the sad, departing observer of the breakup of a cherished, but irretrievably disintegrated way of life.

The first half of the novel creates the stages in Lettie's awakening and
rejection of George, the second half the consequences. At the very center, affording the title and illuminating the essential Lawrencean conflict at this critical point, is the savage symbol of the white peacock. It
rises like a monstrous perversion of nature from the thematically contrapuntal story of the gamekeeper, Annable.

The intricate class-related antagonisms of Lawrence's early environment are nowhere more clearly drawn than in the keeper's position. His
employer, a decayed squire, has fallen back on grazing rabbits as a means
of income. This threatens the farm crops. Both the farmers and the striking miners poach and are the enemies of the gamekeeper. His job is to
him chiefly an answer to the distintegration around him. It provides him
with a life close to and preservative of nature from which he may sardonically look out and strike back at the antinatural, and in which he may
rear his children as good animals.

His significance is led up to through a series of incidents that suggest his antisocial philosophy. He catches Cyril and George trespassing, and beats both the aesthete and the cultivator of the land. He enters
the conflict between the sexes when he catches Leslie and Lettie, and

Cyril and George's sister, Emily, enjoying the beauty of masses of snow-drops in the wood, which suggest to them a romantic past. For Cyril the girls bending and touching them symbolize his yearning. "Folded in the twilight, these conquered flowers are sad like forlorn little friends of dryads." To Emily they are the symbol of tears, perhaps of some strange-hearted Druid folk. To Lettie they belong to some knowledge she has lost and needs. The keeper rudely interrupts this musing like a malicious Pan. Recognizing the upper-class Leslie, he apologizes ironically by say-ing that you can't tell a lady from a woman at that distance at dusk. He shocks all but Cyril with his philosophy:

> "Do as th' animals do. I watch my brats—I let 'em grow. . . . They shan't learn to dirty themselves wi' smirking deviltry—not if I can help it. They can be like birds, or weasels, or vipers, or squirrels, so long as they ain't human rot. . . ."

Leslie and Emily make the judgment that he has no soul. Lettie, as fits her struggle between two worlds, is made thoughtful.

The challenge of the keeper's philosophy is extended by two encoun-ters with the untamed children who illustrate it. Lettie and Emily con-demn the keeper's neglect of amenities for his distracted wife, and try to bring some order into the comically created overrunning of her and the house. A remote counterpoint is the revisit of the young people to his house after his death to find an unfriendly, prim good housekeeper and her *Christian Herald* reading husband.

The full meaning of the keeper explodes in the symbol of the white peacock. The brooding Cyril, attracted and curious, seeks him in the wood. Not finding him at once, he explores the ruined old church near the abandoned hall and finds its prayer books dragged from their ledges, scattered on the floor in the dust and rubble, and torn by mice and birds. This destruction of Christian forms by the natural becomes a recurrent symbolic action in much later Lawrence, for example, "The Last Laugh" and *The Plumed Serpent*. But here decadence rather than nihilistic ren-ovation, *Weltschmerz* rather than revolutionary anger, are suggested. When Cyril does meet the keeper it is in the graveyard just as a scream-ing white peacock flaps up onto the neck of an "old, bowed" angel which has "long ceased sorrowing for the dead and died also." From that vantage point, and soiling it, the bird bends, peers, lifts its head and yells. The effect is violation of the natural. The sound tears the sanctuary of twilight. The dead grass seems to stir, and Cyril fancies that the smothered primroses and violets beneath it "wake and gasp for fear." The keeper reads the symbolism for Cyril: "Perched on an angel, too, as if it were a pedestal for vanity. That's the soul of a woman—or—it's the devil."

Lawrence accounts for the keeper's attitude in one of those caricatures of the culturally disintegrated he could strike off so deftly even in very early work. As a young curate, the keeper had been led into sexual relations by "a Lady Christabel, a lady in her own right," who seemed very fine, frank, and unconventional. But one of their amorous adventures had originated in her reading a sloppy French novel, the *Romance of a Poor Young Man,* and he became her poor young man. After marriage, though they were infatuated, she appreciated his fine physique as she might Greek sculpture. And after three years she tired. A related cause of their difference was that she would not have children. Later and more Lawrencean was her rejection and humiliation of the "pride of his body." She became souly, like one of Waterhouse's women, or the romantic Lady of Shalott, and he became her "animal—*son animal —son boeuf.*" After leaving her and being reported dead, he had seen her obituary notice of him, a warning to other young ladies not to be seduced by plausible "Poor Young Men."

An echo of the terms "son animal—son boeuf" involves Lettie Beardsall in the white peacock symbolism. Her teasing names for the young farmer, George, as she awakens him early in the novel are "Taurus" and "bos-bovis." When she finds he lacks appreciation of the pictures of Clausen, a "true Realist" who makes common things beautiful, she judges him as "gross with good living and heavy sleeping." Never developing intellectually and aesthetically, he is "like bulbs which spend all summer getting fat and fleshy, but never awakening the germ of a flower." But she is hardly such a caricature as the keeper's lady. The direct connection of her with the peacock symbol comes late, when, as the mature woman married to Leslie but keeping up the troubled friendship with George, she triumphs over both of them. She "let her cloak slide over her white shoulders and fall with silk splendour of a peacock's gorgeous blue. . . . There she stood, with her white hand upon the peacock of her cloak. . . . She knew her own splendour, and she drew up her throat laughing and brilliant with triumph."

Lettie's vacillation between Leslie and George is created complexly. In her attraction to George, she does not have to contend with the deceit and dishonesty that repelled her mother, though the probability of moral failure in the physical side of life assumed by her mother's culture, is an indirect factor in his being rejected. The integrity of his fine body and his psyche is the source of the Lawrencean ritual of attraction of the superior woman. When, in the world of the farm, she sees him drying himself after washing—"the swelling of his arms as he moved them, and the rise and fall of his breasts, wonderfully solid and white"—her mind is attacked; he "scatters her words like startled birds." This develops into the ritual of touch when she sees him mowing, "the muscles of his back playing like lights upon the white sand of a brook." She touches his arms, "such a fine brown color and so hard," and withdraws blushing. When he praises his work as "a pleasure to one's self, one's own physique," she sees him as if he were "some great, firm bud of life."

Of course among the cultivated young townspeople gathered around Leslie and Lettie, George is awkward, uncouth. When they appreciate him and his world, it is through the literary filter of the Greek pastoral. When she is pressed for her reason for not choosing him, Lettie pleads the fatality of the social system, its cultural expectations linked with its moral suasion. "I have been brought up to expect it—everybody expected it—and you're bound to do what people expect you to do—you can't help it. We can't help ourselves, we're all chessmen. . . ." (The chess-fatality motif is repeated when, after the snowdrops episode in the wood, she brings those metaphors of a lost natural rapport to George just as he is checkmated in a game.) One of the means of moral suasion Lettie yields to is duty toward the sick, so crucial later in the question of Constance Chatterley's responsibility to the maimed Clifford. Leslie, hurrying home to attempt a reconciliation after Lettie's revulsion from premarital intercourse with him, is hurt in a car accident. While she is nursing him during his convalescence, she asks to be released from their engagement; but at the moment of trying to make him understand her need, she sees his fear and perplexity, "like that of a child that cannot understand," and capitulates in pity and despair.

George's failure to capture Lettie during her indecision is attributed by Cyril to a failure of courage and action against an "inhuman fatality." After Leslie's accident Cyril has rebelled against the sense of fatality that has invaded the natural world. The night sky is "a great, hollow vastness in which the stars are only sparks." The voice of a corn crake, pleasantly romantic on past summer evenings, is now the "intolerable voice of fate." "Here on earth," he thinks, "is sympathy and hope, the heavens have nothing but distances." To George he says, "You should have insisted and made your own destiny." The importance of a fight against any sort of social fate is to become a major theme in Lawrence's later work.

It is characteristic of Lawrence that, as he explores here the destinies of his two couples after marriage, lack of vitalistic integrity proliferates almost uncontrollably. Eventually he even locates it in the animal-like Meg. George's decline is linked to his removal from the world of the farm to proprietorship of a pub and to its harsh, vulgar life. Such a rise in the world involves him in land speculation and horse-dealing. He gains some higher purpose when, after a visit to Cyril in London, the poverty and suffering in the city stimulate him to an interest in socialism. But this ranges him against Lettie and Leslie during a strike, and Lettie, impelled almost against her will to interfere in his life, is mainly responsible for his loss of interest. Another and perhaps more Lawrencean cause is George's perception of the human inadequacy of the socialists, which resembles the judgment Lawrence made of them. His final isolation occurs in the family, where, without the dishonesty and deceit of Cyril's and Lettie's father but in the dissipation of drinking, he repeats the other man's psychic and moral rejection. In a vividly created scene characteristic of the novel, Emily, with Cyril looking on, helps Meg bathe the baby, tasting with her lips and her cheeks all the softness, warmth, and life of the baby's body. Cyril feels shut out by this intimacy, which suggests to him the readiness with which women disclaim "the body of a man's love," fondling him for the soul's meaning while shrinking from his "passionate limbs." George says to him bitterly, "Meg never found any pleasure in me as she does in the kids." In the marital duel between Meg and George, the children coalesce about the mother and apply to George the moral judgments they have learned at Sunday school. When Meg complains of George's drinking and irresponsibility in front of the youngest boy, the child is full of "wild pity" for his mother, and "furious hate" of his father, who seems to him the source of all their trouble.

Running through Cyril's relationship with George is the important Lawrencean theme of love between men. Cyril feels that their friendship is at its "mystical best" while they work together on the farm. A foreshadowing of ritual nakedness and physical touch develops when, after bathing in the pond, the two men dry themselves. Cyril, watching George's fine body, is reminded of the story of the gamekeeper, and forgets to continue drying himself. George begins to rub him as if he were a child, or "a woman he loved and did not fear." The touch of their bodies satisfies in part the vague yearning of Cyril's soul, and when they look at each other with "eyes of still laughter," their love is perfect for a moment, "more perfect," says Cyril, "than any love I have known since, either for man or woman." Rituals of male love appear in *Women in Love, Aaron's Rod,* and *The Plumed Serpent.* Though never overtly sexual, and always connected with the problem of overcoming the barrier between the sexes, they suggest to some Lawrence critics the possibility of latent homosexuality in Lawrence and his heroes. If he and his heroes betray what seems an excessive need for intimate male relationship in the nonsexual sense, this need appears not as a real alternative but as an extension of Lawrence's basic vision of more vitally and humanly based relationships of all kinds.

George's body is a key image-metaphor throughout the novel. Its degradation parallels his psychic disintegration. At the end, during Cyril's last visit to him, he can only watch with shame and despair the strength of the men at harvest in the fields near Emily's home. Emily's marriage is the one success, significantly achieved only by her leaving the old life at home, and by choosing a manly, physically warm husband. Cyril finds in her house a kinship, now rare, between a room and the one who inhabits it, a bond of blood-relation. Emily has escaped what Cyril calls "the torture of strange, complex modern life."

The dominant mood of the novel is a brooding over failure. The world of wood and farm, nature and natural man, is too strongly assailed by disruptive cultural and psychic forces. One hope is a new start somewhere else, and there is, though not as strongly as later, the feeling that it must be sought not merely outside the Midlands but outside England. Economically beaten, the elder Saxtons emigrate to Canada. If George had made that choice, it would have been to escape an England in which "you've no freedom for thinking . . . and everything round you keeps the same, and so you can't change yourself—because everything you look at brings up the same old feeling, and stops you from feeling fresh things." His and Meg's holiday with Cyril in London suggests that the way may lie in a freer, southern culture. He and Meg are fascinated by the opera *Carmen*. Its "gaudy, careless Southern life," and Carmen's bold way of playing with life "startle them with hints of freedom." But George is powerless to develop these hints into action, and Cyril, unlike the later heroes, cannot make an effort to lead him. Hearing the unanswered crying of failure and seeing the horror of life in George's destiny he is sad and haunted as he leaves his country world.

Of course as a first, apprentice novel *The White Peacock* comes off badly in comparison with the mature work, yet it should not be dismissed from the critical canon. Archaic and precious though it may be, there is much in it that is powerfully realized. Relationships are developed so intensely, with such a sense of felt experience, that the aura of a sentimental idyll is overcome. Essentially Lawrence's imagination worked organically here, too; that is, everything is significant to, even alive with, the struggle for and against free and whole vitality. An example of this simultaneous awareness of the life in nature and the barriers to a correspondence in man is the parting between Lettie and George.

> He stood looking at her; his face was coloured only by the grey-brown tan; his eyes, the dark, self-mistrustful eyes of the family, were darker than ever, dilated with misery of helplessness; and she was infinitely pitiful. She wanted to cry in her yearning.
> "Shall we go into the wood for a few minutes?" she said, in a low, tremulous voice, as they turned aside.
> The wood was high and warm. Along the ridings the forget-me-nots were knee deep, stretching, glimmering into the distance like the Milky Way through the night. They left the tall, flower-tangled paths to go in

among the bluebells, breaking through the close-pressed flowers and ferns till they came to an oak which had fallen across the hazels, where they sat half screened. The hyacinths drooped magnificently with an overweight of purple, or they stood pale and erect, like unripe ears of purple corn. Heavy bees swung down in a blunder of extravagance among the purple flowers. They were intoxicated even with the sight of so much blue. The sound of their hearty, wanton humming came clear. . . . The sight of their cling-ing, clambering riot gave satisfaction to the soul. . . .

"If there were fauns and hamadryads!" she said softly. . . . "If you were a faun, I would put guelder roses round your hair, and make you look Bacchanalian." She left her hand lying on his knee, and looked up at the sky. . . . The clouds rose up like towers, and something had touched them into beauty, and poised them up among the winds. The clouds passed on, and the pool of sky was clear.

"Look," she said, "how we are netted down—boughs with knots of green buds. If we were free on the winds!—But I'm glad we're not." She turned suddenly to him, and with the same movement, she gave him her hand, and he clasped it in both his. "I'm glad we're netted down here; if we were free in the winds—Ah!"

3

Lawrence's second novel, *The Trespasser,* originated in his interest in an autobiographical narrative by Helen Corke, a member of the Croydon teachers, young intellectuals circle to which he removed from Eastwood. Her story of the holiday of a middle-aged music teacher with his young woman pupil, ending with his suicide, moved Lawrence deeply, touching as it did his own search for fulfillment. There is no question that much of his interest lay in helping her recover from the paralyzing effects of such an experience of love. The frame story he uses in the first and last chapters presents as a mask for himself a young man, Cecil Byrne, who is trying to arouse Helena from the living death of her trauma. At the end, they sit in the shelter of a yew tree in the touch of an embrace, as do the characters of the death-haunted early love poem "The Yew-Tree on the Downs." Clearly Lawrence was personally involved in the central story as well as the frame. He wrote to Edward Garnett, who as editor wanted less personal subjectivity and more verisimilitude and form (in an argument between them that was to reach a crisis over revision of *The Rainbow*):

. . . this is a work one can't regard easily—I mean, at one's ease. It is so much oneself, one's naked self. I give myself away so much, and write what is my most palpitant, sensitive self, that I loathe the book, because it will betray me to a parcel of fools. Which is what any deeply personal or lyrical writer feels, I guess.

The rather affected manner, the overwriting, and the hectic oscillations of sensibility suggest not so much *The White Peacock* as the short story "The Witch *à la Mode*," which is filled with a similar *Sturm und Drang*, and his early poetic manner in the mother and love poems. The result is neither very good poetry nor fiction. The psychology, and the ethic suggested through it, are characteristic Lawrence. The protagonist of the central love story, Siegmund, is victimized by the conflict between vital fulfillment and the blocks to it that are propagated in the mind and sensibility by the culture, and by the kind of woman it produces.

In age Siegmund is at the far end of the familiar Lawrencean crisis in life situation. For this man of thirty-eight, the holiday with Helena is a breaking free from years of "suppressing his soul" (in the sense of his deepest self) and, in despair, doing his duty. He is to have at least a few days for "his own joy." But this means to a man of his integrity a "painful breaking of bonds and severing of blood-ties," the accompaniment of vitalistic rebirth that is characteristic of much later Lawrence.

At moments during the five days of his escape, Siegmund fully achieves what may be called his vital resurrection, expressed ritualistically in the natural setting of sea, sand, and cliff, and in the sexual relation with Helena. Bathing alone, he scrubs the sand from his body as if he were washing away "years of soilure." After this purification, he becomes a "happy priest of the sun." For both him and Helena "the marionette procession of days is broken; the labels are gone off everything." The freshening of Siegmund's perception makes it preconscious and pre-moral. He feels as if he were the first man to discover things, like "Adam opening the first eyes in the world." The stone by which he undresses to bathe becomes his altar-stone, and he senses in nature the nonhuman religious significance that characterizes Lawrence's later displacement of the forms of Christianity.

The serpent of moral guilt makes itself felt in this Eden at the nadirs of cyclic attraction and repulsion, vitality and deathliness. By turns

Siegmund and Helena suffer the sickening detachment which follows their "moment of intense living." At one such purely existential moment, she is assailed by the moral sense. Being a moralist rather than an artist, and coming of Wesleyan stock, she punishes herself and is haunted by "lives that cry out against her." All the radiance leaves her vision of the natural world and of Siegmund, whom she now sees as past the buoyancy of youth, stooped, and walking and whistling rather stupidly.

A less actively moral barrier between them is the limitation of passion apt to exist in the Lawrencean woman. Helena belongs to "that class of 'dreaming women' with whom passion exhausts itself at the mouth . . . in a real kiss." The cause of this is explained in terms like those of *The White Peacock*:

> For centuries a certain type of woman has been rejecting the "animal" in humanity, till now her dreams are abstract, and full of fantasy, and her blood runs in bondage, and her kindness is full of cruelty.

To her the sunlight on the sea is "the Rhine maidens spreading their bright hair to the sun." She does not really care for people, who usually seem vulgar, ugly, and stupid.

Physical intimacy with Siegmund frightens her with suggestions of an unknown power, beyond the confines of her fancy and her religious training. When she hears Siegmund's heart, she is fascinated by its "expulsions of life" and wonders if there is in the cosmos a "great God thudding out waves of life." Frightened, she listens for Siegmund's soul, but only hears his heart. The heart imagery is extended to a scene of identification with the life force through touch and sex. To Helena the water beating the rock is like a great heart with something brutal about it that she cannot bear. Siegmund's enjoyment of the power of the water makes her hate the brute in him. But in his embrace she is reduced to identity with this nonmoral, essential force. His body, lifting and sinking away, seems to force "a new rhythm" into her.

The oscillations of this vitalistic struggle between deathliness and life are often imbedded in the imagery, as in the early poetry. Helena's blocks to sexual fulfillment are relatively plain. But Siegmund is troubled by more than the genteel, ideal, and fanciful in Helena. Constantly, in their five days' struggle, he plays the child to her. In most love scenes she rests above or upon him, and he, sometimes oppressed by her weight, looks up. He resents her mother aspect, which would draw him to her, hide him from fate, and save him from searching the unknown. His crying in the night is a "crying that a woman cannot still."

When Helena senses this direction, associated with acute suffering, she responds with the mother aspect he wants to reject. " . . . Delicately, she fondled and soothed him, till he was child to her Madonna . . . till at last he raised himself to lay his lips on hers in a long kiss of healing and renewal—long, pale kisses of after-suffering." Sequentially, a star seems to him "a lantern hung at the gate to light someone home," and he imagines himself following the star-track. This desire for transcendence is plainly linked to a death direction. After he suffers shame from her admission of moral revulsion, she, full of passionate pity, moves her mouth on his face "as a woman does on her child that has hurt itself." Her compassion goads him deeper into life, while he feels despair and prefers death.

Contrasted to this imagery of night and release from life, is another of day, active life, and passion. Here the woman plays a subservient fructifying role. After passion, in which he is "burning and volcanic" as if he would destroy her, he becomes like the sea, musing by itself. She is merely the "earth in which his strange flowers grow." He loses his customary yearning, an "ache outwards towards something," which is like that of Cyril in *The White Peacock,* and is as whole and perfect as the day. She serves to connect him with the beauty of things as if she is "the nerve through which he receives intelligence of the sun, wind, and sea, and of the moon and the darkness."

This pairing of images of psychic alternatives of death and life directions suggests a long range of such pairings throughout Lawrence's work. It seems to originate in the early poetry, where it expresses his conflict between love of his mother and the temptation to death through her death, involving faith in the ultimate meaningfulness of that death, and his drive towards fulfillment and life with the woman who is not-mother. When Siegmund, half-conscious, sees Helena as "Hawwa-Eve-Mother," he seems to place all these meanings together:—woman as a star in the mystic universe entered through death; the life and euphoria giving mate; and the mother role that soothes the hurt man but renders him powerless either for life or death.

The novel is filled with a sense of fatality by other, more conscious means than the night imagery. Out of Siegmund's and Helena's musical backgrounds come motifs from Wagner's *Tristan and Isolde,* which run through their minds as they enact their own love tragedy. A foghorn suggests to them the horn call to Tristan, Wotan's wrath, and Siegfried's dragon. On the way back to London and moral judgment, Siegmund thinks of the movement from the Valkyrie Ride. In spite of its grandeur, its "insistence of catastrophe" hurts him. Helena often quotes passages from German romantic poetry that link love and magic. Siegmund's response is to recall this poetry's concern also with fatality and death. In Helena's vision of tragedy as endued with grandeur he sees a kinship with Ibsen's destructive Hedda Gabler

Helena's having a volume of Nietzsche with her, their thoughts of Wagnerian tragedy, and the sense of doom that builds up toward the end of the novel, suggest that Lawrence is contrasting the Nietzschean concept of tragedy to romantic and domestic tragedy. Nietzsche's concept of slave morality, and his anti-Christian vitalism generally, are suggested by Siegmund's and Helena's responses to Christian symbols earlier. When they come across a chapel whose carved Christ looks down on the dead in the graveyard, she is filled with the "yearning and pathos" of Christianity. There is a vitalistic choice for her in having on the one hand the dead and on the other Siegmund, strong and vigorous though walking dejectedly. Although her embrace is motivated by the Christian sentiment of pity, it arouses him, his passion burns away his heaviness, and he seems "tipped with life." Once, roaming at night and using the church cross as a landmark, they feel free only after they lose sight of it. When they return to the chapel, Siegmund makes their plight and the Christ symbolism fatalistically analogous.

> Thirty years of earnest love; three years' life like a passionate ecstasy—and it was finished. He was very great and very wonderful. I am very insignificant and shall go out ignobly. But we are the same; love, the brief ecstasy, and the end. But mine is one rose, and His all the white beauty in the world.

Lawrence returned again and again to this antithesis yet parallel through love and death, and in *The Man Who Died* resurrected Christ as a man seeking healing in the love of a priestess of Isis.

A related Lawrencean value is touched on when, during the return to the mainland, Helena and Siegmund see a launch nearly run down by the ship. He admires the poise of the people threatened with sudden death, and muses that he shall at least "enrich death with a potent shadow" if he does not enrich life. In this there is a suggestion of Nietzsche's antislave-morality pride, and of later Lawrencean resolution in a threatening world.

Siegmund's defeat in life receives its final Lawrencean location in the family. The older children consolidate with the mother in cold, sneering condemnation. His beloved baby daughter's turning away is the culminating blow. The most cherished child of George Saxton in *The White Peacock* is his daughter. Girl-children seem to have been Lawrence's favorites. It is as if in his imagination they become mother-surrogates, their disapproval touching a raw nerve of conscience and rejection.

The future of the wife and the older daughter is as sardonic social satire as much later Lawrence. The mother evades any personal, emotional responsibility for Siegmund's suicide, and is last seen as proprietor of a boarding house enticing, with Vera as bait, young male boarders into the marriage trap in a way that suggests Joyce's boarding house story in *Dubliners*.

The framework story, of course, ends the novel on something of a vitalistic, anti-surrender note in Cecil Byrne's effort to restore Helena to life through the touch of an embrace. But here, as in *The White Peacock*, the dominant note is that of failure and decadence, with little sense of hope or direction. The rebellion and the fight for a new life are latent rather than active.

4 🐌

In *The White Peacock* Lawrence had omitted or elaborately masked a large part of his most intimate experience, especially the turbulence of life in the miner's family kind of home, the children's constant awareness of battle, their defensive love of the mother, and their profound revulsion from the father. In *The Trespasser* he had moved even further from his root experience, casting into the young intellectual's tone and "poetic" language another person's experience, though, to be sure, this masking was a means to a highly subjective exploration of his own problems in love. In the early version of his next novel, *Sons and Lovers, he did not deal very directly and realistically with his background.* Jessie Chambers (Miriam in the novel) has said that she urged him to greater boldness and frankness, because, as the woman who felt she had been defeated by the son's blind, overpowering allegiance to his mother, she thought this might lead him to understanding of his situation, and to mature freedom.

Another force was pushing Lawrence toward writing a more objective, formally realized kind of novel, though with a different analysis than Jessie Chambers thought should be made. As editorial taskmaster he had the sympathetic but exacting Edward Garnett, to whom he wrote when he posted the finished manuscript:

> . . . I want to defend it, quickly. I wrote it again, pruning it and shaping it and filling it in. I tell you it has got form—*form:* haven't I made it patiently, out of sweat as well as blood. . . . Now tell me if I haven't worked out my theme, like life, but always my theme. . . . If *you* can't see the development—which is slow, like growth—I can.

He wanted to dedicate the book to Garnett, if Garnett thought it really good, and part of his gratitude may have come from his sense of being saved by Garnett from the potentially disastrous dead end in the subjective quasi-tragic poetizing of *The Trespasser*.

The force that perhaps pressed him hardest toward understanding the causes of his suffering in such a way as to be certain of a theme was the personality of Frieda von Richtofen Weekley, with whom he went to Germany in 1912. It may well have been she who made him so sure of the devastating effects of profound attachment to a certain kind of woman as mother and sweetheart. When Lawrence encountered her she was the wife of Ernest Weekley, professor at Nottingham University College, and the mother of three children. Her memoirs and correspondence make clear that she was a remarkably vital, unconventional woman who felt from childhood a strong attraction to and sympathy for men and the burden of responsibility they carry, and was indignant at whatever defeated life in the vital sense. Essentially she had married the older man of such different background because he represented a strength, solidity and responsibility unknown in her German world of Metz and its army garrison life. But he was unable to understand the very free, relatively anarchic side of her nature, and a serious conflict with his restraint and respectability developed. She tried self-education through reading, having as an example of the emancipated woman her sister Else, doctor of philosophy and wife of a professor at Heidelberg. Among her affairs was one with a young student of Freud. In Lawrence's combination of genius with intense commitment, she found an irresistible attraction. To him she was, in the discreet description he gave Edward Garnett, "the woman of a lifetime," "perfectly unconventional, but really good—in the best sense." With her he found sexual fulfillment, the lack of which had so troubled his writing and given it at times the limitation of immaturity. He also found a redoubtable antagonist in that side of vitalistic faith that sees in nature a precedent for the battle of the sexes. Altogether, both vitalistically and through Freud and her understanding of the dangers of repression, she opened as no one else all the sides of his nature.

During the revision of *Sons and Lovers,* Lawrence sometimes consulted her about how a woman would feel in certain situations. It is likely that then, as later, she exclaimed against what to her would be the crippling influence of his mother and of Jessie Chambers. How Freudian an analysis she made of the son's situation is not clear, but it is not likely that, despite her association with the student of Freud, she gave Lawrence a very full or accurate account of the Oedipus Complex. Probably she was not much more satisfied with the finished novel than was Jessie Chambers, since Lawrence's deep, empathic involvement with his past, that gives the novel such a rich texture, may well have interfered with present happiness. As for Jessie Chambers, she felt that Lawrence evaded full understanding, indeed was dishonest, in not placing the full blame for the failure of their relationship on the mother and his blind allegiance to her.

When Lawrence himself formulated, for Garnett, the theme he had developed, he did so in terms that are not a radical departure from the implications of much of his earlier work.

It follows this idea: a woman of character and refinement goes into the lower class, and has no satisfaction in her own life. She has had a passion for her husband, so the children are born of passion, and have heaps of vitality. But as her sons grow up she selects them as lovers—first the eldest, then the second. . . . As soon as the young men come into contact with women, there's a split. William gives his sex to a fribble, and his mother holds his soul. But the split kills him, because he doesn't know where he is. The next son gets a woman who fights for his soul—fights his mother. The son loves the mother—all the sons hate and are jealous of the father. The battle goes on between the mother and the girl, with the son as object. The mother gradually proves stronger, because of the tie of blood. The son decides to leave his soul in his mother's hands, and like his elder brother, go for passion. He gets passion. Then the split begins to tell again. But, almost unconsciously, the mother realizes what is the matter, and begins to die. The son casts off his mistress, attends to his mother dying. He is left in the end, naked of everything, with the drift towards death.

It is a great tragedy, and I tell you I have written a great book. It's the tragedy of thousands of young men in England. . . .

This carefully reasoned synopsis is a helpful guide to the reader exploring the destiny of the eldest son, William, through childhood and youth to marriage to Lily Western and a psychosomatic death, and the entrapment of the younger son, Paul, between the mother and Miriam Leivers, and passion with Clara Dawes. But no synopsis could show the subtle, perhaps partly unconscious, weighting of values. The novel is so rich in empathy, despite Lawrence's later feeling that he had been unfair to his father, the characters so complexly created, that the reader must eventually ponder just where the tragedy centers. Is it in the tormented sons, whose fate Lawrence's synopsis stresses, the beloved but doomed mother, the hated and destroyed father, or the painfully rejected women who rival the mother? In a sense, of course, it is in them all as victims. But what lies behind their tragic failure? What fate victimizes them? Out of the novel's own complex emphasis there rises as fundamental cause the deadly cultural-psychological conflict between the mother's sensitive, cultivated, idealistic and moral world; the father's lower-class, irrespon-

sible, enslaved but physically vital and carefree world; and, allied with
him, the beautiful, vitally natural world of farm and countryside.

Lawrence gives his characters cultural and psychic genealogies, as if his
search for the exact nature of their failure forced such an extension
to root causes. The mother descends from an old burgher family through
a grandfather who went bankrupt in the lace market to an engineer
father who was particularly proud of his integrity, and from whom she
inherits her pride and unyielding temper. But even she contains the
father-mother split, having favored her gentle mother, and hated the
father's overbearing manner. As the novel begins, she is taking one more
step down in the world by moving into a house in the Bottoms, a company housing project much nicer than its predecessor, Hell Row, but still
a place where conditions are unpleasant because people must live in a
kitchen opening onto an alley of ash-pits. From generations of Puritans
she has inherited a high moral sense which causes her to scourge her
husband for his carelessness, and his drinking though it is not detrimental
to his health. Lawrence makes a vitalistic judgment of her attitude in the
first pages. "She could not be content with the little he might be. . . .
In seeking to make him nobler than he could be, she destroyed him."
She and her values already stand indicted for harmful good intentions toward a people to whom moral improvement and self-conscious effort are
fatal. Such a cultural impasse is responsible for Lawrence's later anti-
democratic pronouncements and belief in the need of a new aristocracy
who could integrate the concept of a higher life with the potential of the
vital unconscious, and lead to full self-realization those who could not
find a way unaided because of their limited though vital natures, whether
English miner, Italian peasant, or Mexican Indian. The plan is evolutionary; the aristocracy resembles Nietzsche's and Shaw's superman.

The father's genealogy is traced from a French refugee who married
an English barmaid—if there had been a marriage. He is ruddy, with a
vigorous black beard, a red moist mouth, and a rich, ringing laugh. His
humor is not satiric or ironic like Gertrude's father's, but soft, nonintellectual, warm, and playful. Her father had been like the Apostle Paul,
"harsh in government, in familiarity ironic," and ignorant of sensuous
pleasure. His daughter, though like him, had found something comple-
mentarily enriching in the miner—"the dusky, golden softness of this

man's sensuous flame of life, that flowed off his flesh like the flame from a candle, not baffled and gripped into incandescence by thought and spirit as her life was." But soon after their marriage, his inability to take part in the serious discussions she liked had killed her efforts at a "finer intimacy." Her discovery that, despite his protestations of affluence, the furniture was not paid for, the bills were neglected in his coat pocket, and their house was rented from his mother for more than it was worth, had hardened her proud and honorable soul against him.

Part I, about a third of the novel, creates the stages of her total rejection of Morel and the development of a "soul" relationship with William, ending with William's death, which is *felt* to be an inevitable outcome of the split. But Paul's involvement in this begins when, as a baby, he receives what might be called a baptism with the mother's blood. While Morel is drunkenly fumbling with a kitchen drawer, and is being scolded by Mrs. Morel as she sits holding the baby Paul, it jerks out and falls on his shin, and on the reflex he flings it at her. Irresistibly metaphorical of the split between their natures is its hitting her on the brow. She is sick to "the very soul," and Morel, his natural anger turned into remorse and anxiety, watches a drop of blood fall into the baby's hair. A series of such scenes as Paul grows up confirms his allegiance to his mother.

The occurence of these crises at night calls up Lawrence's characteristic imagery of deathliness and the vitalistic nonhuman source lying beyond what is familiar and reassuring. When, after a quarrel, Morel locks the mother out of the house, she first shivers in the moonlight, whose coldness shocks her inflamed soul. After a loss of full consciousness, she becomes aware of the night again, and stands panting and weeping in the "immense gulf" of light. Her return to her usual self is through flowers that suggest both her frustration and the preferences of her sensibility. She is first relieved by awareness of the scent of lilies, whose flowers are pallid and whose pollen hardly shows. After achieving self-forgetfulness in what Lawrence calls the mixing-pot of moonlight and then coming to herself, she is invigorated by the strong scent of phlox. But the more delicate roses in her garden smell "sweet and simple" and remind her of "morning time and sunshine." She prefers the less violent flowers and "conscious, purposive" life, and feels forlorn in the mysterious out-of-doors. This fear of the death-source mystery of night carries over to Morel, who, finally awakening from his drunken stupor to let her in, is afraid of the dark outside the door, though he is a man without physical fear.

Part II, nearly two-thirds of the novel, creates Paul's struggle between his mother and any other woman, whether the other woman vies for his soul, like Miriam Leivers, or his passion, like Clara Dawes.

It is chiefly through Miriam's reactions to the natural that both her rivalry of and resemblance to the mother are created. In Part I, when Paul and she first meet when they are about fourteen, she blushes at his use of the common flower-name, "maiden-blush." She is afraid to let a hen peck corn from her hand, and follows Paul's reassuring teaching in pathetic fear of pain. She is romantic in the Victorian literary tradition, wanting to be a grand person like the Lady of the Lake.

In Part II, when they are older and Paul has fully assumed the son-lover role, he feels that there is no looseness or abandon in her movements while she dries the dishes, or while she walks with him. She is "gripped stiff with intensity." Running with him in the fields, she is capable of a kind of ecstasy that frightens him. But she is physically afraid, even of climbing over a stile. She is identified with the anti-vital, tragic side of Christianity, as is the mother. "She might have been one of the women who went with Mary when Jesus was dead." When she shows him a wild-rose bush, her response to his look is as if her soul quivers. It is "soul-communion" she wants, and he turns away in pain to the flowers, which to him are alive like butterflies, but associated with her have a virgin scent that makes him feel anxious and imprisoned.

At Easter when they visit a church, Paul is afraid of the things he must not do. On the more positive, Lawrencean side, he feels the fascination of shadowy religious places; his latent mysticism is aroused. She loves him for his respect, and he is "a prayer" along with her. But later when she thinks about love with him, she feels as if her soul were coiled into knots of shame. In a touch that suggests Hardy's Sue Bridehead, she prays, "O Lord, let me not love Paul Morel. Keep me from loving him, if I ought not to love him." She develops out of this religious scruple the attitude of resignation and sacrifice that opposes the passional and vital by essential negation. She reasons that if it is God's will that she love Paul, it is her duty to be a willing sacrifice. She falls into a "rapture of self-sacrifice, identifying herself with a God who was sacrificed, which gives to so many human souls their deepest bliss." It is this that repels Paul in the ultimate test of their relationship by intercourse. At first he sees only the beauty of her body. But the look at the back of her eyes, like that of "a creature awaiting immolation," arrests him, and makes his "blood fall back."

The failure in the most purely vital side of relationship produces in Paul a death-direction. He wonders why the thought of the after-life seems so consoling to him. Night, death, stillness, and inaction seem to him like *being*. Day seems only a white shadow, and urgency and insistence *not-being*. The highest thing was to "melt out into the darkness and sway there, identified with the great Being." The mysticism involved in his reaction is related to later creations of dark, unconscious states, as in "The Blind Man," and the peace and relief they bring; and to the longing expressed in the midst of great human disappointment, for nonhuman gods and destinies. It is, in a sense, the obverse side of Lawrence's vitalism, recession to the source for peace and renewal. In Lawrence's later fiction, the male may recoil from life, as Paul sometimes does, but more frequently, in an effort that amounts to cultural and psychic seduction, he draws the woman's conscious, spiritual, day self into the night, unconscious state of being, or, even, the underworld of death for reassurance, if her trauma is great.

Paul Morel turns to a more mature and passionate woman, Clara Dawes, separated from her husband and so troubled also by a failure in relationship. His passion is aroused by "the nape of her white neck and the fine hair lifted from it" (this stimulus suggesting vulnerability and arousing a protective tenderness is frequent in the early fiction), her breasts swelling inside her blouse, the curve of her shoulder, the "beautiful, strong" curve of her back. Her response to the natural vitality of the country world is very different from Miriam's romantic, soul response. Walking together, the three encounter that fundamental Lawrencean symbol of vital power, a stallion. He is linked, as is St. Mawr in the novelette of that title, with a Celtic past:

The big red beast seemed to dance romantically through the dimness of green hazel drift, away there where the air was shadowy, as if it were in the past, among the fading bluebells that might have bloomed for Deirdre or Iseult.

Clara, in her own trouble, is half-fascinated and half-contemptuous. Miriam is shy and embarassed by the frankly earthy speech of the farmer who leads the horse. At the farmhouse, the spinster of thirty-five who is the stallion's owner, holds his head against her breast and, when Miriam remarks that the horse is splendid, connects Paul with the horse's power by looking straight at him.

Paul's sexual consummation with Clara is not without a touch of the mother, Miriam limitation.[13] The "tightness in his chest" because of Miriam, which in "Daughters of the Vicar" is how Alfred was aware of his mother's death, relaxes and the "hot blood bathes" him. But when Clara senses the hurt and need in him, she soothes him into forgetfulness as a mother might a child. Not until he forgets the struggle in his soul is she only a woman. Even this stronger woman is frightened by something "blind and ruthless" in his love that is almost terrible to her. But through intercourse they do succeed in entering Lawrence's marvelous, nonhuman, natural world. When they return to consciousness, they feel small, half-afraid, childish, and wondering, "like Adam and Eve when they lost their innocence and realized the magnificence of the power which drove them out of Paradise and across the great night and the great day of humanity." The simile may suggest Lawrence's Nietzschean conception of the origin of the split in the logical, Socratic Greeks, and in Christianity. The reapproach to Paradise is towards vital integration, and consequent innocence, from the moral-vital, mind-body dichotomies of Western history.

Any such integration is, of course, threatened by Paul's attachment to his mother. She pleads that Miriam will not leave any part of his soul to her, and this is the reason, consistent with her portrait and Lawrence's synopsis, that he begins a serious break with Miriam. Against Clara the

---

13. A remarkable letter by Alice Dax, the model for Clara, in Frieda Lawrence's *Memoirs and Correspondence,* make it painfully clear that she was hurt by the severest kind of female distaste for sex, and resentment towards men.

mother pleads that he will tire of the merely passional relationship with her. Paul is finally absorbed in attending his mother in her illness and death, which is felt as psychosomatic through fear of the loss of the son. His giving her an overdose of morphine makes him, in a sense, active against her suffering and fate. (The possibility of euthanasia, real as well as fictional, has startling bearings on the later death of women in his fiction, and the theme of the man powerful in death.) Earlier, when Paul goes with his mother to Lincoln to see the "great cathedral lying above the plain," he feels it as a symbol of her—her nobleness, her submission to fatality, and her defeat in life: " . . . there was on her the same eternal look, as if she knew fate at last." In the next sentence, the deepest motive of all Lawrence's rebellions is expressed: "He beat against it with all the strength of his soul."

Who escapes the cultural-psychic split in this novel of tragic failure? Most of all the middle Morel son, Arthur, who is so like his father that Mrs. Morel is anxious about his behavior. Though he gets into scrapes, they are "manly scrapes" easily condoned. He and his girl play freely and unselfconsciously in the physical touch of courtship. She is moved by his strong chest and his thighs in close-fitting trousers. In a passionate kiss, she acts of "her own free will." "What she would do she did, and made nobody responsible." Essentially undivided, they escape the fatality in love; yet when he is at home with the mother, even Arthur is disturbed and restless.

The great sufferer, of course, is Paul, lost as was Lawrence, after the mother's death, or perhaps more accurately, wanting to lose himself. Again, as after his failure with Miriam, the darkness of night becomes the most real thing, "whole, comprehensible, and restful." This resource, foreshadowed by the earlier imagery and experience of night, is ultimately a drift towards death. The need it reflects is satisfied this side of death by entry into the unconscious. Extinction of consciousness and physical death are dealt with so synonymously, as in the very late poem "The Ship of Death," as to be nearly indistinguishable. Both close with essential being, or God, and in this represent faith in the intrinsic meaning of the universe and human life. Paul Morel's final turn from the death direction toward the lights of the city is an acceptance as well as a reaction.

The first furor over the "Freudian" perceptiveness of the novel has long since subsided. The book still ranks high, but for other reasons than being that sort of intuitive, genius-produced illustration of a theory. The tragedy remains, and may well have been as widespread as Lawrence thought, though now, after so much emancipation, one wonders about the lasting quality of that sort of novelistic relevance to life. The question is finally one of art. The novel's power lies in the intensely felt objectification of the experience. This is probably marred by the rather frequent long passages of exposition, in which Lawrence analyzes and explains the nature of relationships already created, although this tradition of the novel, as opposed to Flaubertian exclusion of the author, is defensible and far from dead. Such passages are relatively distanced and undidactic; in later Lawrence they sometimes lose this impression of integral relevance and suggest the nervously tormented and occasionally quite unbalanced predicament of the man.

As for the challenge of the integrity of the novel on the ground that at some point in it Lawrence abandoned courage and honesty and made Jessie Chambers a scapegoat for his mother and himself, it ought to be said that Jessie may have been blind to her own nature and the ultimate necessity behind Lawrence's response. It ought also to be remembered that what may be called Lawrence's "depth psychology" really spares no one; aspects of himself appear in other characters than the primary mask. Anti-life manifestations were everywhere.

His interest was now to center more and more in the cultural-psychological forces that propagated the anti-life, in the hope of successfully combating them. He would eventually evolve a program of cultural leadership and revolution.

2. Alienation & Exile

*A*FTER he had established his relationship with Frieda Weekley in 1912, and completed *Sons and Lovers,* Lawrence could deal more freely and hopefully with life in England. The novel had been an act of self-confrontation and understanding, and the relationship brought the fulfillment that had been so painfully delayed, to the age of twenty-six. He inherited new personal problems, but the effect on his writing was catalytic and his best work lay just ahead, before censorship, the war, and a series of related defeats, inflicted a shock from which he never fully recovered. During the war he made several efforts to leave England and the European violence. In 1919 he resumed residence in Italy, and reformulated his plans for self-imposed exile and a search for a new kind of world and life, his crucial move coming in early 1922.

In retrospect it seems inevitable that Lawrence found his fulfillment with a woman who in cultural heritage and class was not English and was an aristocrat. This in itself was not enough to insure that she would be free from the traumatizing limitations of his mother's world, but when in the next few years he read *The Golden Bough* on totemism and exogamy, and connected this with his belief in the blood consciousness, he encountered an explanation that might well have confirmed the validity of his intuitive direction. Frieda's very youthful marriage to Ernest Weekley, professor of languages and literature at Nottingham University College, had been in large part a matter of sympathy for the responsible, intellectual man, and a reaction against the aimlessness and narrowness of German army garrison life in Metz. But her nature was also what her mother had called atavistic, a combination of vitality, sympathy, and passion whose relationship with society was anarchically uneasy. By the time Lawrence met her, the marriage had turned into a situation very like that in much of Lawrence's fiction—a powerful and intelligent, but essentially unintellectual nature struggling between self-assertion and accommodation to the restrictiveness of an opposite nature of strong mind, and formal and moralistic conceptions of life. She had experimented unhappily with affairs, and had been most deeply disturbed by her encounter with a pupil of Freud who preached a completely new kind of relationship and world cleansed of the traumatic past. Lawrence's taking her from this situation is irresistibly like the raids made by the lower class, foxlike men of his later fiction, who have the power, and in a sense the program, of the blood consciousness. He told her that she was unfulfilled, and, refusing the irresponsibility of an affair, claimed her in the name of the rightness of their passional attraction, and by the right of his genius.

Their liaison reversed the situation of his second novel, *The Trespasser*. It was the woman who, in the rebellion against a dead life, must bear directly the judgments of the social, moral world and the pain of alienation from children. Lawrence was far from insensitive to her troubles, and far from unscathed by them, but he fought stubbornly to keep her in his orbit, as if he would triumph over the fatality of the system that had defeated his father, and many of the characters of his early fiction. The fight was to continue throughout his life, particularly when she worried about her children, and always when she was drawn away from him by any tendency to compromise. He put her into his work, and created champions, both comic and heroic, to do battle for and against her. She troubled and enriched his fiction by providing his strong personality and stubborn intransigeance with a powerful counterfoil that he must acknowledge. Most significantly she remained satisfied with fulfillment in love and with his creativity, and opposed his involvement in a prophet-leader role.

The first phase of their relationship is recorded in the poems of *Look! We Have Come Through!* with its suggestion of somewhat surprised survival. The problems that arise in the poems extend far beyond notions of easy rapport, and continue past problems. His mother haunts them like an unexorcised ghost as well as a beloved person who should not be forgotten. The relationship with Frieda becomes at times an unbearably Oedipal imprisonment.[1] The solution is that the relationship be made to transcend the personal and find its place in a metaphysic. The woman must yield precedence to larger relationships and purposes, granting the man the higher activity of cultural and religious pioneer. For Lawrence this included a lifelong desire for vital male friends with whom he could wage war against decadence and found a colony of kindred spirits in some new environment. Love for a woman as a supreme value isolated that side of him that cared so much about the destinies of underdogs, and was so strongly didactic.

No single poem in *Look! We Have Come Through!* can adequately illustrate the intense dedication with which Lawrence conceived his relationship. His longing for a paradisal state of being through purification is suggested by such lines as

> Beautiful, candid lovers,
> Burnt out of our earthly covers,
> We might have nestled like plovers
> In the fields of eternity.

His faith in the connection between personal vital integrity and a force in the universe that creates order in chaos is expressed by

> If only I am sensitive, subtle, oh, delicate,
>   a winged gift!
> If only, most lovely of all, I yield myself
>   and am borrowed
> By the fine, fine wind that takes its course
>   through the chaos of the world
> Like a fine, an exquisite chisel, a wedge-blade
>   inserted . . . .

---

1. As late as 1918 Lawrence sent Katherine Mansfield a volume of Jung that he said had prompted him to confession and warning. Though the idea of mother-incest could become an obsession, there was much truth in it. " . . . At certain periods the man has a desire and a tendency to return unto the woman, make her his goal and end, finds his justification in her. In this way he casts himself as it were into her womb, and she, the Magna Mater, receives him with gratification. This is a kind of incest." He confessed that he had been involved in such a situation with his wife, and was struggling to get out of it.

But for the purpose of illustrating how he came to see his past, and conceive the solution to the problem of relationship, "Manifesto" probably serves best. Here he carefully summed up all his debts to his culture. He had never feared the want of food. He felt that despite his illnesses he had never had to hunger for health. He had barely escaped the "hunger of the mind for the knowledge that the great dead opened up." He had suffered the phallic hunger, and a woman had fed it so that he had lost the fierceness of fear of starvation. One hunger remained in him—"the ache of being." He admitted difficulty in expressing the nature of this. In the relationship he had had the experience of dropping to "sheer, hard extinction, a death, a ceasing from knowing, a surpassing of self." The woman was then all that was beyond him, in an inviolable limitation of identification. This having surpassed oneself, this not being self, is the major fact of being. But the woman did not recognize this and still regarded him as part of herself. He wants her to perish as he has, so that they will be separate beings having pure existence and real liberty. When she does this, they will be glad not to be confused with each other, and will live in the paradox of "unutterable distinction and unutterable conjunction." There will be no laws but the laws of the individual being, for all men and women. Relationships will be like music—sheer utterance, "pure being in the mystic now."

Here Lawrence had conceived the ultimate goal of social anarchy inherent in his vitalistic religious view. His desire is for an existence untroubled by time and consciousness, governed only by the laws of being, or the life force revealing itself in nature. This is a lovely but terrible vision, putting an impossible strain on mere mortality, subject to practical exigencies and more familiar, human emotions. Lawrence's passionately felt need for it in a deathly, materialistic world informs *The Rainbow*. Birkin preaches it to Ursula and Gerald in *Women in Love*. Lilly expounds it to Aaron in *Aaron's Rod*, with the ironic concession to realistic limitation of the necessity of submission by less developed natures to higher ones (in a vitalistic frame of reference suggesting evolutionary hierarchies; in a political frame of reference, Lawrence's opposition to democracy). Its realization later on in *The Plumed Serpent* was a program for gods and supermen.

When Frieda Weekley at last received her divorce in 1914, Lawrence and she returned to England and were married. What may be called his first exile, from English respectability and its animosities, was over. But any promise of social equipoise for Lawrence was destroyed by the immediate advent of the war. It was the climactic crisis of his life, driving him into total rebellion and exile.

During the war, everything he attempted went wrong. *The Rainbow* was suppressed on charges of indecency shortly after publication in 1915, so that several years' work went for nothing. Other literary ventures failed. The Lawrences were desperately poor, and he was often ill. Because of Frieda's German origin and, probably, indiscreet honesty, they were suspected of spying and expelled by the police from Cornwall, where Lawrence had taken refuge in a remote region containing relics of the pagan Celtic past that attracted him. They were shadowed by detectives in London, and felt afraid even in his native Midlands. He deeply resented the violation of physical privacy by the physical examinations for conscription he underwent. His repeated efforts to go to South America or the United States were thwarted. The cumulative effect was to embitter him beyond recall. It can be measured by his saying in 1916: "I wish one could be a pirate or a highwayman in these days. But my way of shooting them with noiseless bullets that explode in their souls, these social people of today, perhaps it is more satisfying. But I feel like an outlaw. All my work is a shot at their very innermost strength, these banded people of today. . . . Let them make way for another, fewer, stronger, less cowardly people."

His sense of insane dislocation of values drove Lawrence to nightmare and illness. The war sanctioned mutilation and murder, the triumph of perversity over physical, natural integrity. It was the inevitable outburst of the psychic disintegration he had so long been describing. He assessed the effects of the war in terms of the vital damage that would plague the survivors, rendering many of them incapable of vigorous life. For others there must be a vital resurrection.

> After the War, the soul of the people will be so maimed and so injured that it is horrible to think of. And this shall be the new hope: that there shall be a life wherein the struggle shall not be for money or for power, but for individual freedom and common effort towards good. . . . It is no good

plastering and tinkering with this community. Every strong soul must put off its connection with this society, its vanity and chiefly its fear, and go naked with its fellows. . . .

The change of emphasis in his fiction can be measured by comparing two statements about his intention in *The Rainbow*, one made in 1913, the other in 1916 in the midst of the war. In the first he said that what he felt strongly about as the major problem of his day was the establishment of a new relation, or the readjustment of the old one, between men and women. In the latter, he said that as far as he could express the message of the novel it was that "the older world is done for and that it is no use for the men to look to the women for salvation, or the women looking to sensuous satisfaction for their fulfillment." There must be a new world.

When Lawrence tried to formulate a plan of action with Lady Ottoline Morrell, Bertrand Russell, John Maynard Keynes, and other intellectuals associated with Cambridge, a disagreement with Russell developed that illustrates how religious Lawrence's direction was, as opposed to the pragmatic, rational, materialistic views that were so prevalent.

> Bertie Russell is here. I feel rather glad at the bottom, because we are rallying to a point. I do want him to work in the knowledge of the Absolute, in the knowledge of eternity. He *will*—apart from philosophical mathematics—be so temporal, so immediate. He won't let go, he won't act in the eternal things, when it comes to men and life. He is coming to have a real, actual, logical belief in Eternity, and upon this he can work: a belief in the absolute, an existence in the Infinite. It is very good and I am very glad.
>
> We think to have a lecture hall in London . . . and give lectures: he on Ethics, I on Immortality: also to have meetings to establish a little society or body around *a religious belief, which leads to action*. We must centre in the knowledge of the Infinite, of God.

Russell has delivered a sweepingly condemnatory final opinion of Lawrence. His thinking was dreamlike. Pressed for specific action—books, speechmaking in Hyde Park—he was evasive. "He had no real wish to make the world better, but only to engage in eloquent soliloquy about how bad it was." His soliloquies "were designed at most to produce a little faithful band of disciples who could sit in the deserts of New

Mexico and feel holy." His theory of a blood consciousness as distinguished from a mental and nerve consciousness was mystical rubbish. Worst of all, he "had developed the whole philosophy of fascism before the politicians had thought of it." At the time, he, Russell, was accustomed to being accused of undue emphasis on reason, and thought that Lawrence might give him "a vivifying dose of unreason." Lawrence's challenge of the good intentions of his pacifism, which Lawrence said masked an unconscious lust to destroy, was so unsettling that he contemplated suicide. But he recovered his confidence, and the ultimate result was a stimulation to his work that did not come from anything good in Lawrence's ideas. Lawrence's central characteristic was domination. His excessive emphasis on sex was "due to the fact that in sex alone he was compelled to admit that he was not the only human being in the universe. But it was because this admission was so painful that he conceived of sex relations as a perpetual fight in which each is attempting to destroy the other." Finally Lawrence must be seen as part of the world's attraction to madness between the wars.

This is an extreme example of the attack that can be made on Lawrence from the position of skeptical humanism. As Russell once put this position, in "A Free Man's Worship," the world was formed by the fortuitous collision of terrible physical forces, and will probably end in the same way. God was invented by man out of fear. The conception of God must be made as high as man's own moral capability, giving up primitive notions of a God of force and fear whose demands on men are unjust by the highest human standards. Freedom lies in this, and in a giving up of all earthly desire. Such a credo is of course diametrically opposed to Lawrence's vitalism with its faith in the divinely centered purpose of life, in a vital force that takes regard for mankind, and in the importance of relationship of the individual being with ultimate being, or God. Russell's denial of profound efficacy in the physical is the opposite of Lawrence's religiously based trust in the sacredness and goodness of sensuous experience.

John Maynard Keynes, in one of the memoirs published as *Two Memoirs*, took a more sympathetic view of the Lawrence of this period. There were two causes of emotional disturbance. One was the movement of Lady Ottoline Morrell and David Garnett away from his group to

Russell's group, which made him jealous. The other was his distaste for "Cambridge rationalism and cynicism, then at their height." There was some truth in what Lawrence felt. "His reactions were incomplete and unfair, but they were not usually baseless." The Cambridge group had imperfect understanding of the outside world and their relation to it. They "recognised no moral obligation . . . , no inner sanction, to conform or to obey." More important than this shocking aspect of their code was "the fact that it was flimsily based . . . on an *a priori* view of what human nature is like . . . which was disastrously mistaken." They were "among the last of the Utopians, or meliorists . . . , who believe in a continuing moral progress by virtue of which the world consists of reliable, rational, decent people" who can be left to their own devices. Keynes concluded with a considerable admission of Lawrence's rightness. " . . . If I imagine us as coming under the observation of Lawrence's ignorant, jealous, irritable, hostile eyes, what a combination of qualities we offered to arouse his passionate distaste; this thin rationalism skipping on the crust of the lava, ignoring both the reality and the value of the vulgar passions, joined to libertinism and comprehensive irreverence. . . . That is why I say that there may have been just a grain of truth when Lawrence said in 1914 that we were 'done for'."

Lawrence's uncompromising stand that the disintegration of civilization threatened by the war could only be prevented by a reorienting of life to a religious absolute, is worked out in *The Rainbow* and, somewhat less plainly, in *Women in Love*. The theme is harmony, or the disastrous lack of it, between the relative and the absolute, the lesser world of man and the greater world of God, or the life force.

This effort, resulting in his best work, was, seemingly paradoxically, carried on at a time when he was often very ill, and sometimes driven and distracted to a pitch that his intimates regarded as insane. If his achievement of such organic imaginative vision seems to be rendered impossible by this, it ought to be remembered that he had great powers of recovery, and that during these difficult times, complicated by their personal battles, Frieda and he often led a rather peaceful, even gay life together in the cottages that were their refuge. The vitalistic view involved acceptance not only of fight in nature through the evolutionary struggle, but a similar fight in relationship, whatever ludicrous or repulsive sides it might exhibit to the sensibilities of such friends as Middleton Murry and Katherine Mansfield. Without fight, followed by rapport, one could suspect that "love" was not the active, living reality.

Behind Lawrence's bitter quarrels, stubborn didactic excursions, and anti-institutional, vitalistic art, moved a dedicated man. To lose sight of his sense of personal responsibility is to lose the essential Lawrence. At the time of his 1913 blood consciousness credo, he said:

> . . . I do so break my heart over England. . . . And I am so sure that only through a . . . making free and healthy of this sex, will she get out of her present atrophy. Oh, Lord, and if I don't "subdue my art to a metaphysic," as somebody very beautifully said of Hardy, I do write because I want folk —English folk—to alter, and have more sense.

His letters from the war years illustrate his sense of crisis vividly. Immediately after the declaration of war, he felt as if his soul were in the tomb—"not dead, but with a flat stone over it." In January, 1915, walking on the downs, he had become aware of the natural life about him, and had risen from his state of living death, though he was still feeble and only half alive. Upset by meeting a young, handsome, one-legged soldier, he could see him under the chloroform having his leg amputated, and he feared the ghosts of the dead "marching home in legions over the white, silent sea." He relapsed into one of "those horrible sleeps when one is struggling to wake up, and can't," a feeling which persisted much later in the New Mexico poems of *Birds, Beasts and Flowers*. Once he dreamed that all the stars were moving out of the sky, and he was more terrified than ever before. Hatred of the enemy was a madness. He felt in himself a struggle with the Powers of Darkness and a desire to kill. He would even enjoy killing if he could select his victims, and those who cant so much about the goodness of man ought to recognize the existence of such malignant will. He had many periods of revulsion when he did not care about the things he had formerly cared for. One had to "get one's soul ready" for the new life, and an important part of the process was submission to being "helpless and obliterated." One must become dark "like winter which mows away all the leaves and flowers, and lets only the dark underground roots remain," where the plants "sleep in the profound darkness where being takes place again."

His experience of psychic death was accompanied by the conviction that the English culture of his past was dying, and with it the Christian era that contained it. In the autumn of 1915, when he thought Frieda and he would be able to go to America, he viewed the countryside as the past of two thousand years crumbling with the leaves. At the country house of Lady Morrell, he saw the Tudor house and the farm harvest going on around it as "the vision of a drowning man, the vision of all that I am, all I have become, and ceased to be. It is me, generations and generations of me, every complex, gleaming fibre of me, every lucid pang of my coming into being." And he exclaimed, "Oh, my God, I cannot bear it." He felt that his heart was so quartered that it could never be gathered together again as had that of the mutilated Osiris (later the mythic basis of *The Man Who Died*). The "Gethsemane, Calvary, and Sepulchre" stages of his suffering must come to an end. He must begin again in a resurrection with "sound hands and feet and a whole new body and a new soul." His friends who were parents should not let their children be drawn into this slow flux of destruction and nihilism. If the children became contaminated by it, they should be taken away into a new life, no matter what the cost.

The means to a new life became for Lawrence the founding of a new kind of community. Part of his conception suggests the wistful, naive spirit of his remark to Jessie Chambers, when they were very young, that he wished they and their friends could live in a house together. He wrote of it to Lady Ottoline Morrell:

> I want you to form the nucleus of a new community which shall start a new life among us—a life in which the only riches is integrity of character. So that each one may fulfill his own nature and deep desires to the utmost, but wherein tho', the ultimate satisfaction and joy is in the completeness of us all as one. Let us be good all together, instead of just in the privacy of our chambers, let us know that the intrinsic part of all of us is the best part, the believing part, the passionate, generous part. . . . We can laugh at each other, and dislike each other, but the good remains and we know it. . . . I hold this the most sacred duty—the gathering together of a number of people who shall so agree to live by the *best* they know, that they shall be *free* to live by the best they know. The ideal, the religion, must now be *lived*, *practised*.

In the same letter he warned against "the will to Power: the desire for one man to have some dominion over his fellow men." But the aristocratic and theocratic implications of his conception, ultimately "realized" in *The Plumed Serpent*, were also revealed:

> We will be the Sons of God who walk here on earth, not bent on getting and having, because we know we inherit all things. We will be aristocrats, and as wise as the serpent in dealing with the mob. For the mob shall not crush us nor starve us nor cry us to death. We will deal cunningly with the mob, the greedy soul, we will gradually bring it to subjection.

Actually it was impossible for Lawrence to cooperate with anyone for very long. Though this may have been due largely to an extraordinarily stubborn and dominant nature, a subtler and more creditable cause is the purity and beauty of his religious vision, apocalyptic in its intensity. Its gravest limitation and danger was the sweeping misanthropy that resulted from his hurt and anger when others did not understand it, and accept it. Thus when prospects of the lectures with Russell were bad, he wrote:

> I am so sick of people: they preserve an evil, bad, separating spirit under the warm cloak of good words. . . . Bertie Russell talks about democratic control and the educating of the artisan, and all this, all this goodness, is just a warm and cosy cloak for a bad spirit. They all want the same thing: a continuing in this state of disintegration wherein each separate little ego is an independent little principality by itself. . . . That is what they all want, ultimately—that is what is at the back of all international peace-forever and democratic control talk: they want an outward system of nullity, which they call peace and goodwill, so that in their own souls they can be independent little gods, referred nowhere and to nothing, little mortal Absolutes, secure from question. That is at the back of all Liberalism, Fabianism and democracy.

When, instead of formulating his idea of a new world, Lawrence imagined it, a nonsocial and even nonhuman naturalness was revealed. At the English seashore as he contemplated his departure for America, the original world he longed for was nature without human beings in it— "perfectly clean and pure, many white advancing foams, and only the gulls swinging between the sky and the shore; and in the wind the yellow sea poppies fluttering very hard, like yellow gleams in the wind, and the

windy flourish of the seed-horns." What he could not bear was the un-
clean world that civilization had imposed on the natural world. What he
really wanted to do was go to a land where there were "only birds and
beasts, and no humanity, nor inhumanity masks." When he felt so poignantly the death of the English past, and saw a flock of turkeys ruffling
themselves like flowers, he thought of Florida as a place where they would
go in droves "like metallic clouds, like flowers with red pistils drooping in
the shade." In his passion and imagination he desired something essentially like the early world of the country around Eastwood with the
human failure expunged. Late in his career he wrote rather wistfully to
Dr. Trigant Burrow that what ailed him was the absolute frustration of
his primeval societal instinct, an instinct "much deeper than sex instinct
—and societal repression much more devastating."

Toward the end of this nine-year exploration of the ways and means
to a new life, Lawrence formulated his psychology in *Psychoanalysis and
the Unconscious* (1921). This work should be read with its sequel,
Fantasia of the Unconscious (1922), which develops an "anthropological," geographical-historical analogue of his theory of the unconscious
that he followed with surprising consistency when he left Europe in
1922. The latter book is reserved for the next part, on his "exile" and
search. The former is discussed here for the light it throws on situation
and "psychology" of character in the fiction. Lawrence's plots are basically the development of the psychological, ethical consequences of succumbing to, or breaking with, a culturally distorted view of relationship.
It ought to be remembered that his theoretical views were, to him, a
periodically imperative stocktaking, through conceptualization, of what
he had already explored intuitively in his fiction.

He begins with the crucial point that psychoanalysis, whether it wants
to or not, challenges religious faith and morality when it reduces the
psyche to an automatic incest motive. This automatism is an additional
weapon against individuality already enslaved by a machinelike culture.
He likes Dr. Trigant Burrow's view that sin begins when the mind turns
to consider and know the affective-passional functions and emotions.
Adam and Eve fell because they made the sexual act a mental object. The
Freudian assignment of the origin of incest-craving to the unconscious is

a reading into an area of being whose pristine nature has not been determined, and Lawrence argues that the incest impulse is propagated by the ideas and ideals of the conscious mind. Applying an ideal to the affective soul as a fixed motive converts it into a supreme machine-principle; the result is the death of all spontaneous life.

The nature of the infant is not just a new permutation and combination of elements contained in the natures of the parents, but something entirely new and individual. Religion is right about this, science wrong; the child exhibits the old mystery of the divine nature of the soul, and, Lawrence says, he would use the word *soul* had it not been vitiated by idealistic usage. In a touch that both suggests and, through psychoanalysis, brings up to date transcendentalism's organic view of life, he asserts that the great laws of the universe are no more than the habits of the unconscious. This view establishes the ground of his self-reliant anti-institutionalism. The paradox of his own intellectuality co-existing with his fierce anti-intellectualism is explained when he says that we must trace still further the habits of the unconscious (or, the great laws of the universe) and by mental recognition of these habits break the limits we have imposed on its movement.

It is characteristic of his attempt to bend science to his purpose that he sketches a physiology of the unconscious. The navel is its first center (as, obviously, the original vital connection between mother and child). In the adult the same region, the solar plexus, is the primal affective center. His phrasing of his conception of the interchange of knowledge between mother and child resembles the metaphors of relationship in the novels of this period. There is "a lovely, suave, fluid creative electricity that flows in a circuit between the great nerve-centers in mother and child." The goal is the "perfecting of each single individuality, unique in itself— which cannot take place without a perfected harmony between the beloved, a harmony which depends on the at-last-clarified singleness of each being, a singleness equilibrized, polarized in one by the counterposing singleness of the other." As the individuality of the child separates from that of the mother, there are violent reactions. "Sweet commingling" is complemented by the "sharp clash of opposition." "Clumsy old adhesions" must be ruthlessly destroyed. There can be no creative development without this duality of "direct, spontaneous, honest interchange, the primal unconscious pulsing in its circuits between two beings in love and wrath, cleaving and repulsion." Such a duality is both characteristic of Lawrence's own experience and behavior, and the central aspect of relationship in his fiction, giving it that alternation between attraction and repulsion, love and hate, that is disturbingly inconsistent and even immoral to readers accustomed to an either-or logic of behavior. Here he defends it in vitalistic terms. "The essence of morality is the basic desire to preserve the perfect correspondence between the self and the object, to have no trespass and no breach of integrity nor yet any defaulture in the vitalistic interchange."

Lawrence's physiological structuring of the psyche develops an elaborate eight-fold polarity. For the purpose of understanding the relationship of this to his fiction it is perhaps enough to note a few emphases. One direction of love is outward from the center of the breast. When the infant's hands seek the mother's breast, its eyes wake to perception. Northern culture emphasizes a sympathetic mode of communion, making the breast and heart the only "source of sun, light," and way of seeing. In the south, in Italy, for example, and in Renaissance Italian religious painting, one can see in the eyes of the child looking at the mother the "dark look of the pristine mode of consciousness established in the lower body," the so-called sensual mode. An example of this southern way of looking in the fiction is Ciccio in *The Lost Girl*, whose dark eyes disturb Alvina by their lack of familiar sympathy, yet offer her salvation from the living death of a culture which has denied the sensual mode. In "The Rocking Horse Winner" both modes have been lost, and the boy's eyes become frenzied, glazed, and at last dead.

Through the pedagogic jargon of this treatise, which may owe something to the former schoolmaster, there runs Lawrence's deeply felt, revolutionary sense of crisis. The two modes, the sympathetic and the sensual, the merging and the separatist, should be complementary to one another. "It is the absolute failure to see this, that has torn the modern world into two halves, the one half warring for the voluntary, objective, separatist control, the other for the pure sympathetic."

I 🐚

Several of the short stories collected in *The Prussian Officer* volume came out of Lawrence's experience in Germany during the first months of his relationship with Frieda Weekley. In the milieu of her father's army connections and her youthful experience, he encountered a new kind of external discipline and authority, caste and corruption, bad marriages and affairs. He explored this experience with essentially the same insights and values as those of the earlier short stories, complicated by a new psychological awareness.

While the antagonism between the captain and the orderly in "The Prussian Officer" is essentially psychological, the awareness of cultural causes in Lawrence's characteristic opening exposition of the situation is quite strong. The captain is a haughty, overbearing aristocrat who in his youth ruined his prospects of advancement with gambling debts. He has remained unmarried not only because his low rank and pay prevent it, but because no woman has ever really moved him. He takes a mistress now and then, but this only intensifies his hostility and irritability. He is just on the point of breaking through a self-discipline that merely reflects the mechanical military discipline.

The orderly is young, vigorous, unconscious. His movements seem clumsy in comparison to the captain's skill with horses—a skill that also suggests control of the natural and vital through sheer will—but he has the "instinctive sureness of movement of an unhampered young animal." The sense of his person is like a "flame" upon the captain's body, so tense and rigid as to seem almost unliving. It is this vitalistic challenge that causes the captain to insult and degrade the orderly because, says Lawrence, he does not choose to be touched into life by his servant.

The history of their relationship to climactic present time is one of increasing strain from the captain's first awareness. The break in the captain's self-discipline involves the orderly's relations with his girl. She eases him after the strain of the antagonism; when the captain seeks release with a woman, he finds the relationship "a mockery of pleasure." Since the orderly must not be permitted to have what the captain lacks, he is forbidden to go out in the evenings. A bit of pencil stuck behind his ear, with which he has been writing poetry for his girl, becomes the excuse for a disciplining. When he is forced to acknowledge its use for an intimate, natural purpose, the completely abstract, socially sanctioned authority of the captain punishes his vital integrity by the perverse kicks at his thighs, and brings on his painful delirium during the heat of the march.

The remainder of the story focuses intensely on the vitalistic derangement of the orderly. His perception of the scene about him is mirage-and-dreamlike. The fever that blazes through him is not merely the effect of sun and heat, but the rebellion of his manhood. His killing of the captain is a "passion of relief in which his blood exults."

From what remains of his natural feeling he pities the broken body, that is, the vital side, of the man he has killed, and conceals it under boughs and leaves. In the forest, he can momentarily appreciate the prettiness of a bird, and be pleased by a squirrel, but his trauma places him in a condition between life and death that resembles the beginning of *The Man Who Died.* A woman he sees is now an unreality, and he has no language with which to speak to her. In the morning when he awakes, the distant mountains image the integration he has lost.

> He was divided among all kinds of separate beings. There was some strange, agonized connection between them, but they were drawing further apart. Then they would split. . . . Then again, his consciousness reasserted itself. He roused on to his elbow and stared at the gleaming mountains. There they ranked, all still and wonderful between earth and heaven. He stared till his eyes went black, and the mountains, as they stood in their beauty, so clean and cool, seemed to have it, that which was lost in him.

The use of fever and delirium as correlatives of an inward sickness, and the cool mountains as a counterimage, suggests Hemingway's similar effect in "The Snows of Kilimanjaro," with the difference that Lawrence's visionary man is the integrated man needlessly destroyed, Hemingway's the hopeless victim of a long, inevitable decay. The difference is perhaps significant in that Lawrence's feeling for decadence and defeat is ultimately less fatalistic than Hemingway's, as if he expressed the religious experience and faith Hemingway's heroes can only long for. The story deserves its very high ranking among his short stories because of the intensity and completeness with which the conventional aspects of the situation are transmuted into the vitalistic, psychological-ethical conflict.

"The Thorn in the Flesh" takes a young man through an instinctive act of rebellion against military discipline to fulfillment with his girl and a plan of escape to a new world and life in a more episodic, less powerful way.

As in "The Prussian Officer" the beauty of the country side contrasts with the vitalistic deformity revealed in the barrenness of barracks, decorated compensatorily by the soldiers with brilliant nasturtiums, the hard surface of the drillground, and the disfigurement of Bachmann's body by his uniform. Self-conscious, and almost girlish in his good looks and grace, he cannot complete a postcard to his mother because of the "knot of consciousness" that anticipates shame during that day's military exercise.

Climbing a rampart, located above a moat where the completely free and natural is expressed in the beauty of flowers, he is betrayed by his kidneys, hauled up, and subjected to a verbal disciplining that is, in Lawrence's lexicon, also a laceration of his body. In instinctive reaction to this violation, he knocks the sergeant over the ramparts, and flees.

His sense of vindication and peace is reflected in his appreciation of the beauty and freedom of the flowers in the public gardens. His refuge with his girl, a servant in the house of a baron, has the Lawrencean direction away from the town to the more natural countryside. She is given the outcast potentiality that characterized Paula in "Love Among the Haystacks." By nature she is like a wild animal, and is probably the foundling child of gipsies. Though she is devout and has a crucifix in her room, she is religiously naive and pagan. Fiercely virgin, she is revolted by the vulgar, drunken love-making of the common soldiers and girls. She needs to be in subjection because she is so primitive; but her nature demands an uncommon master. Lawrence supplies Bachmann with a background that meets this requirement. Of farming stock, vitalistically valuable in itself to Lawrence, he has a native breeding, and he has enough money to provide a measure of independence.

As always in Lawrence, relationship brings troubled reactions. She resents being cast out of her less personal world by her responsibility to protect Bachmann, and by the power of his desire and touch. Intercourse brings her peace through loss of consciousness; he finds restoration and completeness.   In keeping with the social-psychological backgrounds Lawrence assigns them, she feels secure again in serving him, and he is liberated, wondering, and happy. But, in a characteristic Lawrencean open ending, they must adventure further into relationship, and stand almost alone against the world. They plan that he will escape to France, and then go to America, where she will join him. When the shame of his fear re-emerges, he can accept and endure it with the vitalistic self-reliance of "What I am, I am; and let it be enough." In the night together that follows, their intercourse is "complete victory and satisfaction." The town—that is, another kind of law than the law of being—is completely gone from their awareness except for the ominous claim of the bugle at the barracks. (The threat of social law to the vitalistically emancipated is always in Lawrence's hearing.) But their only practical hope lies in the aristocratic old baron. He turns Bachmann over to the authorities, but while he is doing so he feels his integrity, vulnerability and helplessness, and the quality of honesty and need in the girl. Having suffered himself, he cannot bear this, and prepares to do what he can for them. Such a sympathetic figure, standing between society and the emancipated, becomes increasingly important in the fiction.

"Once" explores the nature of a vitally powerful woman caught in the escapist behavior of this military world. The situations have an almost surrealistic, at times incongruously humorous, effect in which the values are unfamiliar and almost intangible except as purely libertine.

The narrator had loved her when he was a boy, but was then too middle-class, "green, and humble-minded" to think of making love to the daughter of an aristocrat. When, at eighteen, she had come home from school, she had married a handsome but stupid officer who was boring to her even on their wedding night, and had turned out to be a gambler who ruined himself by embezzling government funds.

The narrator feels that, despite numerous affairs, she has never really loved a man and consequently has almost the soul of a virgin. In wanting to give her more than pleasure, he is in something of the position of the Lawrence who in one side of himself loved the shamelessly sensual but also responded to what he humorously called "the English feel." When she enters his bedroom clad only in a transparent chemise, stockings and shoes, and an enormous feathery hat she wants his opinion of, he laughs at and adores her. He expresses his sense of social-sensual comedy by parading in nothing but hat and gloves. Yet despite her protests that he is lovely so, and his amusement at her saying "Think. . . , if all those Englishmen in Picadilly went like that!" he is relieved to get back into his dressing gown. He loves her for her courage to live joyously, but presses her to admit at least one affair that even he cannot acccept. She recalls one she thinks she may be ashamed of.

At one time, she had a lover she would have married had she been free. But on the fourth morning of boredom because he could not get away from the garrison, she met a vital young officer who mistook her for a cocotte, and made an assignation with him. In extenuation, she says that it was as if "something mechanical, beyond their wills," moved them. When he entered her room, he threw an armful of roses on her. They made love among crushed petals that were almost like blood, and he worshipped her body as if "the gods would envy him." Once, without thinking, he wound a gold chain about her knees, making her prisoner. And she, like Constance later in *Lady Chatterley's Lover*, put roses in his hair.

Her story troubles the narrator. He wonders why she should love a man for the "way he unbuckled his belt," and asks ironically if she preserves this memory as a standard by which to measure the amount of satisfaction she gets from others. She now refuses to admit the shame she had half promised when she began the story. The narrator is tired of such uncertainty in his relationship with her. At the end he gets something of the answer that makes his own position possible. When he accuses her of wanting only sensation, she asks what else, in her situation, she could take. Only when he asks if she has not felt the lack of something in all her loves, does an open "yes" make his heart stand still.

The story has the effect of an uncharacteristic, unresolved sketch. It may be that here Lawrence was unable to transmute the various auto-biographical materials with which he usually began, into his vitalistic art because there was something too intimate and painful about them for him to control. Certainly he could never handle the purely libertine.

One other short story, "New Eve and Old Adam," may belong to this time (1912-14), or a few years later, though when it was posthumously published,[2] it was dated in 1910-11 among the early stories. The evidence for the later date is internal—the struggle for rapport in the year-old marriage of a woman who resembles Frieda and a man who resembles Lawrence, and the Continental setting. The struggle involves alternations of antagonism and rapport resembling those in *Look! We Have Come Through!* The story is so episodic and so unresolved that it resembles a portion of a novel that never got beyond its autobiographical base. Its interest lies in the glimpse it may give of the difference between the relatively raw material of experience and the art Lawrence made of it.

Each feels the other forces submission.

> She crouched between his knees and put her arms round him. She was smiling into his face, her green eyes, looking into his, were bright and wide. But somewhere in them, as he looked back, was *a little twist that could not come loose to him, a little cast, that was like an aversion from him*. . . .The hot waves of blood flushed over his body. But at last, after many months, he knew . . . that *curious little strain in her eyes, which was waiting for him to submit to her*, and then would spurn him again. He resisted her while ever it was there.

She, on the other hand, is in revulsion from his eternal demanding and giving nothing back. This one-sidedness may be partly a result of his bad health. But, she says, she wants a simple, warm man who will love her without all these reservations and difficulties. She calls out to a telephone lineman working outside their window, and she has apparently agreed to an assignation with someone that day.

In this crisis in their relationship, he leaves her and goes to a hotel. He loathes the mechanical unity of his bedroom. Instinct for bodily life makes him want to bathe, but this is barren routine because his mind is occupied. Only when he turns out the lights, is there darkness inside him as well as without. When the power of the elemental male returns

---

2. *A Modern Lover,* 1934.

to him, he feels a horrible claustrophobia, and is better able to understand her wanting to get away from their intimacy to an "easy, everyday life where one knows nothing of the underneath," and living can take its way apart from consciousness. He works out the final justification of individual freedom typical of Lawrence during this period. She wants to be free of him in the deepest sense—she does not want the deeper part of herself to be under the influence of any other being.

When they are reunited, arousal of tenderness temporarily reachieves their rapport, but his mind reverts to her accusations, and he finds the problem too complicated and difficult. Only when she moves to him, in a mixture of triumph and yearning, and touches her hand hesitatingly to his hair, does the blood "strike across his consciousness," and the deadness go out of him. Later he again feels the sense of being dominated. He is something like her "lordliest plaything," and she will continue to take and reject him "like a mistress," though perhaps for that reason he will love her all the more.

The story ends in the separation their reconciliation has only temporarily postponed. She says of him in a letter:

> Your idea of your woman is that she is an expansion, no, a *rib* of yourself, without any existence of her own. That I am a being by myself is more than you can grasp. . . . Your *feelings* have hated me these three months, which did not prevent you from taking my love and every breath from me. . . . You say I am a tragedienne, but I don't do any of your perverse undermining tricks. You are always luring one into the open, like a clever enemy, but you keep safely under cover at all times. . . .

In answer he confesses that without her he is done. But his counter-accusation is that she too will not be able to love anybody except herself.

Frieda Lawrence was quite capable of such a rebellion and such a scolding as this green-eyed wife makes. And one of the paradoxes of Lawrence is that though he championed the unconscious and the insouciant, he was capable of endless analysis of and reservation in relationship, and of considerable violence in asserting not only his independence but his dominance. In his good fiction all this is transcended and resolved through his vitalistic faith, as far as it permitted any finality.

2 🐚

Lawrence's first novel after *Sons and Lovers* seemed crucially transitional to him. He told his editor, Edward Garnett, that he no longer took pleasure in "accumulating objects in the powerful light of emotion, and making a scene of them." His new novel was "the vaguer result of transition." When Garnett objected to the psychology of character, he explained it and defended it by discussing his interest in the theories behind cubism and futurism. He liked that side of these art movements that purged the emotions of old forms and sentimentalities, but he did not like its ultra-scientific and spurious attempts merely to diagram mental states. There was truth in Marinetti's analysis of modern Italy as "a great mechanism." There was a dead stage of civilization and the sensibility that had to be passed through, with everything appraised according to its "mechanic value" and "made subject to the law of physics." And, he said, using the terms of vitalistic paradox, the nonhuman in humanity was more interesting to him than the old-fashioned element that in the past had resulted in characters "made consistent with a certain moral scheme," as in Turgenev, Tolstoy, and Dostoevsky. Consequently Garnett need not look in his new novel for the "familiar, stable ego" of character. He did not care what his woman character felt in the ordinary sense, which "presumed an ego to feel with." He cared only about what she was as a phenomenon representing some greater, nonhuman will. The failure of the futurists was that they looked only for the "phenomena of the science of physics" instead of the "new human phenomenon."

On the personal side Lawrence was here defending the exploration in his fiction of his new experience and direction in his relationship with Frieda. The social-moral experience and fate of Tolstoy's Anna Karenina and Vronsky, and Hardy's Sue Bridehead and obscure Jude were essentially different from their "coming through." As a vitalist he stood beyond both an older view of the validity of individual rights as opposed to institutional law, and the new scientific determinism that gave to psychic experience a logical, schematic validity while robbing it of religious and moral significance and sanction. In *The Rainbow* he was attempting to reintegrate man and the universe in modern terms. When he spoke to Garnett of some greater, nonhuman will he was echoing the terms of his religious consolation to his sister in 1911. The psychic stages through which his characters are now to pass constitute a search for the absolute in a world of disastrous relativity and irreligiousness.

The achievement of such an intention involved many months of revision, in which one novel, the exuberantly satirical *The Lost Girl*, was shelved and his original plan divided into two novels—*The Rainbow* and *Women in Love*. His and Frieda's letters to Garnett carry on a debate over "form" as opposed to "life," and related problems of attitude and tone. She was all for life, equating Garnett's formalism with the restrictions of English society. She and Lawrence, as part of their modus vivendi, carried on a mock fight in which his role was often expressed in the coarse language of the down-to-earth, lower class man. Involved in their fight was what may be called the "rights of woman" theme of *The Rainbow*. Lawrence was, of course, aware that this "fight" was not automatically art. He linked its transmutation into art with the expression of his deepest religious feeling, and this expression is at one point his sole criterion for success or failure. (His description of the manifestations of failure suggests criteria for all his work and may implicate the tone of the early part of *The Lost Girl*, and all of *Mr. Noon*, which he abandoned.)

> All the time, underneath, there is something deep evolving itself out of me. And it is *hard* to express a new thing, in sincerity. And you should understand, and help me to the new thing, not get angry and say it is *common*, and send me back to the tone of the old *Sisters*. In the *Sisters* was the germ of this novel: woman becoming individual, self-responsible, taking her own initiative. But the first *Sisters* was flippant and often vulgar and jeering. I had to get out of that attitude, and make my subject really worthy. You see— you tell me I am half a Frenchman and one-eighth a Cockney. But that isn't it. I have very often the vulgarity and disagreeableness of the common people, as you say, Cockney, and I may be a Frenchman. But primarily I am a passionately religious man, and my novels must be written from the depth of my religious experience. . . . My Cockneyism and commonness are only when the deep feeling doesn't find its way out, and a sort of jeer comes instead, and sentimentality, and purplism.

The first half of *The Rainbow* explores the social, psychic, and religious history of the three generations of Brangwens that produced the modern girl, Ursula, who is the chief character. The second creates Ursula's development through childhood to social responsibility as a school-teacher at seventeen, and, finally, to vitalistic independence and faith at twenty-two when her affair with the modern, social-mechanical man, Skrebensky, fails because he cannot match her religious quest for higher meaning.

The farming Brangwens of the 1840's contain the origin of the problem Ursula must solve. The men are nonintellectual, knowing the "cycles of intercourse between earth and sky," trusting the church for a "larger view." It is the women who look "outward to the world beyond the blood-intimacy." This early, stable way of vitally organized life is gradually walled in by the mines and the town.

The disturbance of vital natures inherent in this situation manifests itself in Tom, Ursula's grandfather. His mother insists that he be educated, but his feelings are dominant, and he learns little in the conventional sense. He cannot grow into sexual fulfillment because woman is the "keeper of conscience and the source of stability." He is obsessed by the consequent failure of his relations with both the good girls and the loose ones. When his mother's death removes his one source of stability, he seeks relief in drunken unconsciousness.

His destiny is relinked with the stability he knows only through women when he meets the Polish refugee, Mrs. Lensky. She has been dominated by the *idée fixe* of her dead husband, a Polish intellectual and patriot who neglected his personal life for political action, only to waste away in exile in England. Her lapses into "long blanks of abstraction," and only occasional attentiveness to life, are the result of this painful impersonal effort. The unconscious, vital side of Brangwen draws her back into life.

Their relationship is a cycle of consummation and happiness, estrangement and uneasiness. Her foreign past "confounds his mind and makes his world a chaos." Her mystic, dark states drive him and her daughter, Anna, nearly mad. Alienated further from her during the self-sufficiency of her pregnancy, he feels like a broken arch, a negative form of the recurrent symbol of integration that gives the novel its title. He can soothe the hysterical Anna by taking her into the natural presence of the farm animals; but she is not freed from anxiety until his relationship with her mother becomes whole. Their reconciliation involves a transfiguration through acknowledgment of selves that religiously transcend his inability to understand her past and her consciousness. Then little Anna, no longer struggling to support the "broken arch" of husband and wife, is free to be a child playing beneath the rainbow of the limited and relative in harmonious relationship with the infinite and absolute.

Lawrence then follows Anna's life to her third generation marriage that mingles the Lensky-Brangwen natures and produces Ursula. Because of her aristocratic, questing Polish background and her stepfather's self-compensatory ambition for her, she becomes absorbed in the ideal of the free, proud lady. At school she resents the moral suasion, and the authority invested in coarse natures. In religion she is indifferent to outward forms, worshipping God in a personal, sensuous way that "includes her family and contains her destiny." She conceives of a husband as someone with whom she will participate in "a mystery" of life and death.

The growth of her relationship with young Will Brangwen, the son of her stepfather's chaotically rebellious brother, is in keeping with this. Most important to Lawrence's theme of a religiously obtained integrity of life is his being a creative man who, stimulated by Ruskin, is interested in church architecture. His great drive is toward the absolute, whether in relationship or in the symbolism of art. The first woodcarving he makes for Anna bears Lawrence's favorite personal symbol of vital resurrection and wholeness, the phoenix. His carving of the creation of Eve suggests the novel's ultimate center in the development of a new kind of woman who, opposing the fatal dualism of blood and mind, physical and spiritual, relative and absolute, will in relationship test the man against her religious intuitions of the life force.

The marriage of Anna and Will is an experimental answer to the whole range of questions that troubled Lawrence. How was the rich if limited nature of the farming Brangwens, imprisoned and dying in the new industrial world, to be given a purposive direction? How could this be done without surrender to the sterility of abstract intellectuality or the religious vacuity of merely mechanical social life? And how could a connection with the aristocratic spirit of religious leadership be established without falling into the old traps of arbitrary power? Finally, how could such a man preserve the relationship with woman that gave him his central stability when that woman, like Anna, was a proud lady who had

her own tendency to lead, and, especially in motherhood, her own vital
self-sufficiency?

For Will and Anna the first passionate isolation in marriage breaks
away the superficial, social surface of life. It is a plunge into the vitalistic
absolute. The return to the social world, relatively easy for her, is a source
of great trouble to him. His demands irritate her, and his self-absorption
seems evil. Yet they are manifestations of his religious-artistic desire for
the absolute. When they visit Lincoln Cathedral, she shares at first his
ecstasy over the symbolism. To him the cathedral is like a great seed.

> Spanned round with the rainbow, the jewelled gloom of the cathedral folds
> music upon silence, light upon darkness, fecundity upon death, as a seed
> folds leaf upon leaf and silence upon the root and the flower, hushing up the
> secret of all between its parts, the death out of which it fell, the life into
> which it has dropped, the immortality it involves, and the death it will em-
> brace again.

The imagery of this vision, so distinctively Lawrencean, creates, through
the analogy of the natural cycle which the cathedral's arched darkness
immediately leads to, the vitalistic experience of a dynamic life force
absolute.

But Anna objects to Will's ecstasy. The sly faces of the gargoyles
suggest to her that the cathedral is not absolute. She interrupts Will's
communion by showing him this lively mockery, and succeeds in destroying "another of his vital illusions." He realizes that outside the cathedral
there are many "flying spirits" that can never be "sifted" through its
jeweled gloom.

In this disillusionment there is, of course, much of Lawrence's predicament. It is fair to say that he was committed to a search for an absolute to
which the skepticism of his wife, his sense of human limitation, and his
quite modern general awareness of the dynamic and relative were opposed. Will, like Lawrence, finds a release from this contradiction by
continuing to love the church as a symbol. In his daily life he relaxes his
will, gives up his attempt at spiritual control of Anna, and lives simply
in their physical love. He realizes that he must face his own limitations
and control the temper rising from his frustration. Yet he hopes that, if

the darkness in him can never unfold into the cathedral-rainbow integration of finite and infinite, perhaps it will in his daughter, Ursula.

In her childhood Ursula must assume responsibility for her sister, Gudrun, whose self-sufficiency and irresponsible detachment briefly foreshadow the failure traced full length in *Women in Love*. Because of their "aristocratic" heritage, they cannot achieve real intimacy with the lower-class boys. They fear being pulled down by petty people. Ursula, dreaming of escape, passes through a romantic, "Idylls of the King" phase that Lawrence humorously contrasts to the bedlam of a house crowded with children. After she is punished by her father during one of his chaotic rages, mistrust and defiance "burn away" her dependence on him. Her romantic interest in nature and in her family's past constitute an "intensely woven illusion" that is also destroyed. For a time she makes a new illusion of school; but if knowledge does not come to her instinctively, she cannot learn. She recoils into contempt and arrogance for which she punishes herself. She feels a need to avoid conflict with authority, fearing the power of "the mob lying in wait to destroy the exceptional person."

In her religious development, she comes to think of sin as something much deeper than rules of conduct. The ordinary idea of sin is only "the jealousy of vulgar people who will allow nothing beyond their narrow selves to exist." To her Jesus is beautifully remote, "shining in the distance like a white moon at sunset." She is terrified when a blood-red moon suggests to her the Calvary, dead Christ side of Christianity. The mythic affirmation of life in Genesis — "the Sons of God saw the daughters of men that they were fair; and they took them wives of all which they chose" — stirs in her a dream of the future, and suggests the mythic content of *The Plumed Serpent*. But the celebration of Christmas brings the family only a brief religious ecstasy followed by the deathliness of winter. The sense of tragedy preceding Easter is so strong that it prevents joy in the Resurrection. But the Christian epic does give some sense of eternity to their inconsequential lives.

At this point of religious dissatisfaction, when Ursula is sixteen, Lawrence places her first love, for Anton Skrebensky, the son of another Polish refugee, the highly refined, cool-natured Baron Skrebensky and his "elusive, ferretlike" English wife. On leave from the Army Engineers, Anton admits that army life is a "toy" life, but thinks war would be a means of doing something important. Ursula challenges this view. His belief that he is serving "the highest good of the community" can give him no vital fulfillment because the highest good now simply means material prosperity. He is simply a unit in the social machine. In a typical counterpoint, Lawrence puts them into contact with vitalistic reality through an encounter with a lower-class family that might be called a Lawrencean holy family. Though the man of the family is a captive of society and knows it, he worships Ursula with both body and soul, gives her a warm, rich feeling, and makes Skrebensky seem "a sterility."

Ursula and Skrebensky act out the limitation of his kind of love in a scene that foreshadows his climactic failure at the end of the novel. She desires, under Lawrence's mystic feminine, life-cycle moon, a vitalistically religious consummation he cannot measure up to. He is "annihilated inwardly," losing his male indomitability.

When, acting on the plane of social relativism, he goes off to the Boer War, Ursula feels helpless and lost. She lapses into a "cold imperturbability" that is disturbed at times by yearning for Skrebensky. Sensually she becomes abnormally sensitive. In this state she succumbs to the corruptness of a passion for her teacher, Winifred Inger. Miss Inger encourages her with stories of women's ugly experiences with men and consequent suffering. Ursula is freed from this attachment by experiencing the inner chaos of such a woman and her provincial intellectual circle, whose anti-religious philosophy that everything good is the product of the human mind, suggests that of Bertrand Russell and the Cambridge group with whom Lawrence quarreled. While outwardly they behave "rationally and tamely" enough, inwardly they are "raging and mad." Half out of concern and half repulsion, Ursula arranges a meeting between Miss Inger and her uncle, who no longer cares about anything and acquiesces in the sterility and desolation of a colliery-industrial area. He believes that the miners must alter themselves to fit the system; an unemployed miner is simply a machine out of work. He and Miss Inger deplore the present state of things only to perversely substitute "inhuman order." Their corrupt marriage at least permits Ursula to leave their aura.

Now, as a schoolteacher, she experiences the man's world of work and responsibility. Relations among the teachers and between them and the children are marred by a spirit of bullying that only a few individuals escape. Yet at best the students must be compelled by the "stronger, wiser will" of the teacher, and this requires giving up the personal self to apply a system of laws. Ursula's initial failure is caused by her attempt to use no compulsion. Only when her "soul hardens enough" that she can cane the boy who is her chief antagonist—a boy with something "cunning, etiolated, and degenerate" about him — is she the master of this man's world. The caning is a violation of self, but she benefits in independence and strength as she struggles between her world of "young summer and flowers" and that of work and responsibility. Sometimes she succeeds in conveying this personal, vital world to her children; but afterward she must work harder to get them ready for examinations. She dreams of a time when she need not teach, but responsibility, as a value, has "taken place in her forever."

In college she at first respects her professors and enjoys their lectures. Because of her love of nature, she particularly likes working in the botany laboratory. But after the first glamour fades, she sees the college itself as like a laboratory, operating as "mechanically as a factory." She turns all her interest to botany, where to her the "mystery of life still glimmers" under the microscope. But her teachers believe that there is nothing beyond their rational knowledge. As Lawrence puts it, they turn their faces inward "towards the sinking fire of illuminating consciousness," and ignore "the vast darkness around them with half-revealed shapes lurking on the edge." What is more, in this metaphor of a campfire, if any man throws a firebrand into that darkness, they "jeer him to death" as an antisocial knave.

At Easter during her last year, Ursula hears from Skrebensky, back from the Boer War and waiting for reassignment to India. She thinks of him as a means of redemption from her disillusionment. Pondering the materialistic view of science while she is working in the laboratory, she has an insight that provides her with an ultimate criterion for testing Skrebensky. Her instructor has suggested that life is a complex of physical and chemical activities resembling those already known. But Ursula wonders what will and purpose lie behind the cellular activity under her microscope. She experiences an "intensely gleaming light of knowledge" that she does not completely understand but which answers her question. Life is not "limited mechanical energy" or merely the purpose of "self-preservation and self-assertion," but a "consummation" of self with the infinite, so that to be oneself is a "supreme triumph of infinity." It is from this vitalistic sense of a higher consummation that she begins her affair with Skrebensky.

They repeat the cyclic experience of the earlier Brangwens, passion followed by sleep, and then troubled awareness of the outer world. Ursula resents the lights shining at night because they "falsify the primeval darkness into the social mechanism." For a time Skrebensky shares her preference but his talk of marriage and her accompanying him to India as a soldier's wife reveals his vitalistically weak, essentially mechanical direction. She wants them to remain as they are. When she becomes restless and insists that they travel, he feels that she is searching for something that is not in him. He experiences the "cold, ashen sterility" of the social world; his sense of not-being is horrible to him, and he drinks to escape it.

In the climactic test of Skrebensky on the dunes by the sea, Ursula marvels at "the blaze" of the moon, which calls to her. She cannot explain to him this vitalistic, experiential corollary of her insight in the botany laboratory — the ultimate consummation, sexual and mystic, of the finite with the infinite. Intercourse under the "great flare of moonlight" becomes an ordeal for him, and he seeks a dark hollow. When she insists on a slope under full moonlight, his desire fails and she is left physically and spiritually cold and dead.

After the consequent break in their relationship, he returns gratefully to conventional life, unable to bear either darkness or the thought of Ursula. He has, Lawrence says, no soul. As a means of screening himself from his failure, he marries his colonel's daughter, and goes on to India.

Ursula lapses into an apathy from which she is shocked by discovering that she is pregnant. Physically she feels fulfilled, and even thinks of expressing remorse to Skrebensky and rejoining him. But inwardly the incomplete consummation that produced the child troubles her until it becomes a madness. Caught outdoors in the rain, she seeks shelter in the ancient wood on the common, and encounters a band of horses. Ironically, of course, the wood is only a modern remnant, and the horses are fenced and imprisoned. In a scene that is a nightmare of vitalistic entrapment and disturbance, the horses block her return to the cultivated fields and the road. In escaping on the other side of a hedge, she falls. The result is miscarriage of Skrebensky's child. Lawrence, of course, emphasizes not her social but her religious, vitalistic emancipation through this "accident." For a fortnight she is very ill, but though her soul is full of pain, it is at last itself forever, in a fundamental break with Skrebensky and his world. Her great need is to break out of the past "like the shoot from an acorn." As she gains confidence in her "new reality," she begins to sleep peacefully. As she convalesces, she sees in the socially imprisoned colliers and the "false, hard confidence" of their women a "painful waiting for liberation." Sometimes she re-experiences the horror of the "social husk," a prison in which all people are going mad. But her religiously grounded hope is stronger, and she sees a rainbow form over the barren land, "making great architecture of light and color, its pedestals luminous in the corruption of the houses on the low hill, its arch the top of heaven." It is "arched in the blood of the sordid people" and will "quiver to life in their spirit." It is Will Brangwen's cathedral of harmony of the relative and the absolute freed from its institutionally, humanly limited form by a natural emblem of the life force and its manifestations.

This theme of the evolution of a tenable absolute from a few experiential clues remaining in the progressive disorganization, in a religious sense, of modern life, is intensely and richly imagined. No matter how extensive a rationale Lawrence gives in his running exposition and key words and phrases, many scenes have the inevitably strange, sometimes even frightening power that must indeed have confused and offended the man who complained to the authorities and set off the book's suppression. The ultimate daring was to concentrate the religious significance in sexual intercourse, and such related experiences as pregnancy. Life as a consummation has devastating implications for familiar modes of behavior. Among these scenes, one may recall Anna's celebration of the meaning of her pregnancy by dancing naked; Tom's frantic effort to right the vitalistic imbalance of his estrangement by an otherwise aimless conquest; his quieting of the hysterical child Anna by taking her among the farm animals, whose natural wholeness establishes a felt circuit of restoration; his death in the flood, which becomes an overwhelming natural requiem for his strong, but tormented nature; and of course Ursula's terrible demand on Skrebensky in the full light of the vitalistic eternity. The vitalistic communion was no more explainable than any other religious experience. It was potentially very terrible in its close approach to the tiger of creation, though it had its lamb of tenderness, too, and its ultimate vision was one of universal harmony.

The novel is not easy reading because of the necessity Lawrence was put to of developing his own metaphors and symbols for a such a revolutionary experience. A reservoir of these lay in the early work — in the "worlds" of town, home, and countryside in which the struggle for fulfillment in love began. The difference of *The Rainbow* does not lie in revolutionary technique, as it does, say, for Joyce between *A Portrait . . .* and *Ulysses*, but rather in the recombination of Lawrence's former materials and methods through his present "vision." The result is a sustained "symphony" of scenes revelatory of religious meaning moving toward an affirmation, a novel of family history developing an apocalyptic revelation.

3 🐚

In *The Rainbow*, however apocalyptic its vision of the future, Lawrence's hope was still centered in England. In *Women in Love* decadence is so far advanced that one must turn away from the scene of eruption of murderous forces in the psyche. The novel does not, of course, deal directly with the war of 1914, but Lawrence revised it as late as 1917, and indicated in a foreword (published posthumously) its incorporation of his wartime sense of catastrophe: "I should wish the time to remain unfixed, so that the bitterness of the war may be taken for granted in the characters." He also indicated that he was not surrendering his hope of a new kind of life based on a new idea but reappraising it.

> This novel pretends only to be a record of the writer's own desires, aspirations, struggles; in a word, a record of the profoundest experiences in the self.
> . . . Any man of real individuality tries to know and to understand what is happening, even in himself, as he goes along. This struggle for verbal consciousness should not be left out in art. It is a very great part of life. It is not superimposition of a theory. It is the passionate struggle into conscious being.
> We are now in a period of crisis. Every man who is acutely alive is acutely

wrestling with his soul. The people that can bring forth the new passion, the new idea, this people will endure. Those others, that fix themselves in the old idea, will perish with the new life strangled unborn within them.

The most significant new development in the novel is the attempt to define a vitalistic relationship between men that will complement that between men and women. To the protagonist, Birkin, the lack of this threatens to make love of woman a destructive, even murderous contest of wills, and the role of men in an industrial society a disintegrative, dangerous instrumentality. In Lawrence's earlier fiction, the antecedent of this development is the bathing scene between Cyril and George in *The White Peacock*, in which Cyril, witnessing George's slow disintegration because of his limited nature, feels that his love for George is the deepest and purest he has ever known. Lawrence's newly intensified interest in such love probably reflects his increasing isolation in marriage and the artist's lonely, often rejected task, and his envy of the comradeship of the soldiers.[3]

Whatever the variety of catalysts, the result is the high point of his art of the novel because here he most successfully integrates the full range of the elusive, complex psychological forces that are his métier, with all the cultural problems that are for him both causes and expressions of those forces. For this reason the novel is perhaps the most difficult one to discuss. Here, only indications of the rich development of psychological experience through clusters of images, and symbolic setting and action, can be made.[4]

Even Gudrun's Nordic name is significant to the developing pattern of cold, anti-life correlatives of disastrous detachment. She responds to northern, alter ego qualities in the mine-owner's son, Gerald Crich — his fair skin and hair glistening like sunshine "refracted through crystals of ice." She feels that his totem is the wolf; his mother must be an "old, un-

---

3. This response is noted by Frieda Lawrence in her *Memoirs and Correspondence*.

4. Rebecca West, in *The New Adelphi*, June-August, 1930, said of the nature of the difficulty: "He laboured under a disadvantage compared with the fathers, in his lack of a vocabulary of symbolic terms such as was given them by theology; in the allegory of the death of the soul which ends with the death of Gerald among the mountains in *Women in Love*, he cannot tell his story save by the clumsy creation of images that do not give up their meaning till the book has been read many times. But even these struggles are of value, since they recall to one the symbolic nature of all thought."

broken wolf." Their affinity is also, in a set of images suggesting the me-
chanics of science and industry, like the field of a magnet, and the electricity Gerald employs in more efficient exploitation of the mines. This
side of their natures is increasingly correlated with the failure of vitalistic,
hence basically responsible relationship in modern society.

Ursula's attraction to Rupert Birkin contrasts sharply. His appeal is
highly physical and warm despite his thinness and pallor. It comes from a
"curious, hidden richness" that awakens her to a "living, tender beauty,"
Lawrence's terms characteristically suggesting a mystic source and a humanly vital effect.

Ursula's rival in her early relationship with Birkin is Hermione Rod-
dice, a modern aristocrat interested in reform who as a woman engages in
"intimacies of mind and soul" with men of capacity, is "nerve-worn with
consciousness," and lacks a natural, robust self. She is capable of taking
the Birkin-Lawrence line that the life of the mind is deathly, but the
paradox of this causes Birkin to tell her that her love of the passions and
animal instincts is "more decadent than the most hidebound intellec-
tualism."

The tendency of such vitalistically disintegrated natures as those of
Hermione, Gudrun, and Gerald toward violence and death is most poignantly developed in the Cain-Abel theme running through Gerald Crich's
story. Birkin, who by virtue of his position as school inspector and intellectual is able to cross class lines freely, experiences the anarchic quality
of the Crich family, and, because of his own revulsions feels greatest rapport with the wolflike old mother, who does not care for most people. But
when she admits that she does not know her own children, he is afraid.
Gerald, she thinks, is the most lacking in personal connection with other
people, and she asks Birkin to be his friend. Birkin is tempted to make
Cain's answer, "Am I my brother's keeper?" He remembers uneasily that
Gerald had in childhood accidentally killed his brother. Birkin's subsequent attempt to develop vitalistic intimacy with Gerald is an attempt to
save him from the modern Cain-curse of vitally, humanly irresponsible
power in love and in society.

For the first half of the novel the setting is the Midlands, and the central source of imagery is the lake, Willey Water, a ubiquitous emblem of
decadence and death.

Gudrun, seeing Gerald swimming there alone, envies his perfect independence, and the man's social freedom that permits it. The Chinese
painting Birkin copies is an artistic corollary of the suggestion of disintegration by the water-lilies growing from the rank ooze of the bottom.
When Ursula and Gudrun go to the lake to sketch the waterplants, and
Gerald and Hermione approach them in a boat, he is to Gudrun her
means of escape from the "cultural slough" of the "underworld, automatic miners" of the region. He has risen from the mud; his whitish-
blond hair is like the electricity of the sky. This impersonal, instrumental
view is countered when Ursula finds Birkin patching a boat and tries to
get him to confess the supreme importance of love. Insisting that love is
not an absolute but only a part of human relations, he uses a vitalistic
analogy to make his meaning clear. When he drops daisy petals on the
water, they veer away on the current as a flotilla, individual related to
individual by a greater power.

Willey Water is the scene of the catastrophe that throws Gerald and
Gudrun, and Ursula and Birkin together in an effort to escape further
disaster. At the water party, both couples act out the difficulty of reconcil-
ing individual freedom and relationship. Alone, the girls bathe happily,
delighting in their childlike freedom. Afterwards Ursula is peaceful and
sufficient to herself, while Gudrun, hearing her sing, feels desolate and
outside of life, and must assert herself by eurythmic dancing to the singing. Her dancing expresses "a will set powerful in a kind of hypnotic influence." When Highland cattle appear, Gudrun is not afraid, as she
usually is. Her dance before the cattle suggests her drive toward irresponsible sensation and power. When Gerald and Birkin appear, she expresses
her resentment of the interruption by running at the cattle and terroriz-
ing them. When Gerald protests, she strikes him in the face, her first
giving-in to the "lust for deep brutality" that he later matches. Immediately following this Birkin interprets the decadence suggested by the
marshy smell of the lake. "When the stream of synthetic creation lapses,
we find ourselves part of the inverse process, the blood of destructive
creation. Aphrodite is born in the first spasm of universal dissolution —
then the snakes and swans and lotus — marsh-flowers — and Gudrun and
Gerald — born in the process of destructive creation."

Later, as Gudrun and Gerald row across the lake, they hear the child's cry of terror signalling the drowning of Gerald's sister, Diana. Gerald's tireless search for her body takes on symbolic proportions. He is "purely instrumental," as if he belongs naturally to dread and catastrophe. At last he must drain the lake to its corrupt bottom, where his sister lies with her arms, in the gesture of love, around the young man who tried to save her.

Lawrence explains the ultimate cause of this catastrophe as the breakdown of the Christian love relationship between miners and owners. The father of the Crich family has based his life on faith in charity and love. This has prevented his dealing strongly with his wife's opposition to discipline of their headstrong children. In managing the mine he has tried to follow the belief that in Christ he is one with his miners, and that to move nearer to God is to come closer to them. His heart has been broken by the "war" between owners and miners, forced on him against his Christian principles by the Masters' Federation, on the miners by the unions' assertion of their rights in the machine. For both sides "the machine became God." Disintegration of relationship involved confusion about equality; the only equality is in "being, not in having or in doing, which are processes." Now death is his only resource for escaping the chaos that is superseding his more organic Christian way.

When Gerald had begun to help his father with the mines, he had found a seemingly positive direction for his rebelliousness. But what he had done was to become the "God of the machine." The will to subjugate matter to his own ends had become his absolute. His position and authority are to him right because they are functionally necessary in perfecting the social, productive machine. Under him the miners become mere instruments, losing joy in life, swearing vengeance, but gradually accepting the new order with "fatal satisfaction." The result has been the paradox of "pure organic disintegration" as far as human relations are concerned and "pure mechanical organization." The inward consequence to Gerald is that he is losing the ability to feel.

Gerald's failure in his relationship with Gudrun, then, is the intimate, human corollary of his failure religiously and socially. His ultimately irresponsible power, gradually reciprocated by Gudrun's nature, results in a shared sadism when Gudrun, taken into the Crich household in the hope that she can guide the detached, ironic child, Winifred, attempts to remove a rabbit from its cage. When the animal fights, and Gerald subdues it with a blow, Gudrun's perverse thrill identifies her with him.

Ursula and Birkin are brought into a very different kind of rapport. Ursula, in revulsion from deathliness and an analytical, bitter Birkin who seems to her tainted by it, wanders at night to Willey Water. Fearing the moonlight, which seems deathly in its paleness, she seeks the darkness of the trees. Birkin, also wandering in despair, appears and stones the reflection of the moon upon the water, alternately destroying it and seeing it regather, and cursing it with the names of ancient sexual goddesses. As a Lawrence mask, Birkin reacts against the moonlight for reasons that lie embedded in Lawrence's associations of it with his mother's death, his early struggles for sexual fulfillment, and his opposition now to the supremacy of the love relationship. When Ursula, dazed from watching, her mind entirely gone, asks him why he hates the moon, his enigmatic answer — "Was it hate?" — contains the conflict between his love and his drive towards a vitalistic transcendence.

He tries again to get Ursula to understand and accept his vitalistic, religious paradox of being. He wants an unknowing, unconscious relationship that is like a natural phenomenon. This relationship cannot be achieved either through the old code of spiritual love and service or the sheer sensuality into which those emancipated from the code tend to fall. The white races (and Gerald and Gudrun) take the sensual way from the direction of their "vast abstraction," which is like snow and ice, a "mystery of ice-destructive knowledge and annihilation." He chooses a way that he here describes as "the paradisal entry into pure, single being, the individual soul taking precedence over love and desire for union . . . a lovely state of free proud singleness, which accepts the obligation of permanent connection with others . . . but never forfeits its own proud individual singleness, even while it loves and yields."

Ursula's opposition to Birkin's ideas surely expresses ironic self-criticism by Lawrence, as well as her limitations. She hates his savior role because she wants him entirely to herself, but she also sees in him the irony of a "wonderful, desirable life-force" ridiculously effaced at times into "a Salvator Mundi and Sunday School teacher," so that he can be "a prig of the stiffest type." His demands upon her are a form of male bullying.

While she is glad, sardonically, that the society that has turned sea, land, and air into "murderous alleys of commerce" has at least been unable to conquer the kingdom of death, she is repelled by Birkin's despondency and ill health, that make him look like an image of a deathly religion.

Later, when Birkin asks her father for her, she rebels against their attempt to "compel her from her own radiant, self-possessed world." At this point of defeat, Birkin turns most intensively to the possibility of a vital friendship with Gerald, almost as if it were compensatory. In the wrestling scene, sometimes pointed to as evidence of the homosexual, the struggle is in part for harmony of psychic opposites — an integration of Gerald's white, northern, disintegrating power with Birkin's dark, unconscious, saving power. It is also an attempt to duplicate for men, without sexuality, the vitalistic communion of touch. When the two discuss the meaning of their experience, Gerald is skeptical of Birkin's emphasis on its profundity. Birkin sees the result of his attempt to achieve blood brotherhood as at least a desirable new freedom and openness between them.

Birkin finally draws Ursula to him and his metaphysic of relationship by taking her away from the cultural values and attitudes that oppose him on a drive into the country, and by getting her to accept three rings that he calls "tokens of the reality of beauty." They suggest the vitalistic unity of two individuals in the life force, though in the context of the Cain-Abel, brotherhood theme the third ring suggests the man and man relationship. By accepting the rings Ursula accepts the man of her childhood religious dream in the preceding novel, The Rainbow, "one of the sons of God." In terms of the vitalistic corollary of the magnetic-electrical imagery of the novel, she establishes "a rich, new circuit of passional electrical energy released from the darkest poles of the body."

His plan is that they leave the decadence around them and find a place where they can share life with a few people who understand. Ursula does not see the necessity of sharing. But together they write their resignations from their jobs as a step in this cultural secession. It is not until they reach Sherwood Forest, emblem of the more natural, vital old England, that they have their sexual consummation.

For Gerald, without a transcendent religious view of life, the relationship with Gudrun becomes supreme. Lawrence makes his obsession with sensuality a fatal social capitulation. He accepts the established order, in which he does not "livingly believe," and retreats to the "underworld of passion" for his life. Gudrun would like the stability in marriage that Ursula and Birkin achieve. But Gerald's failure to make a total break with the world makes it impossible for her to accept him as a husband. As a lover he is only a means of escape.

Birkin and Ursula feel that the Continent, too, is decadent. Only at Innsbruck, high up in snow and cold, do they begin to feel themselves happy in another world. But this world, at first releasing in its non-humanness and purity, is also deathly. Gudrun, however, is exultant when they move even higher up to a place where it is unbelievable that life can continue in the waste of whiteness, silence and cold. Gerald, feeling completely alone, must fight with her "as if with ice and steel" for his sensual fulfillment. At first he is strong enough to achieve her submission, but she longs for the "lonely beyondness" of the snow.

The ultimate meaning of her tendency is revealed to her by Loerke, one of those perverse characters Lawrence could so deftly sketch, who combine decadence with a mastery through will. His name suggests Loki, the Norse god of discord. He is a tremendous coda to the themes of the novel. Through the range of his decadence, he links Bohemian London, the sensual depths there into which Gerald plunged in his relationship with the "Pussum," the African sculpture that is her totem, and the decadence of the men who oscillate about her, with Gerald's role as God of the industrial machine.

Socially Loerke is characterized by chatter, mischievous jokes, and a "blank look of inorganic misery." His homosexual relation with his traveling companion has reached the stage of mutual hatred. As an artist he is doing a frieze for a factory in Cologne, the theory being that places of work must be made beautiful as machinery and labor are beautiful; otherwise men will be so nauseated they will prefer to starve. Art must interpret industry as it once interpreted religion, showing that man is controlled by the machine, and that he enjoys his mechanical motion.

Loerke sees in Gudrun an essentially kindred spirit, and she sees in him the "rock-bottom of life, stripped of illusion." Birkin judges him as the "perfectly subjected being," existing almost like a criminal, who has gone "many more stages in social hatred" than either he or Gerald. Showing them a statuette of a young, naked girl on a great stallion, Loerke takes pride in its having no relation to emotion, just as he had discarded the model, also his mistress, when her figure was gone. Ursula judges the statue as the picture of his stupid brutality. But Gudrun is fascinated as her soul recognizes the "inhuman soul" behind it.

Ursula longs for the "fruitful, humanly warm" south across the mountains, and Birkin takes her away, after reminding Gerald that he has loved him, and being repelled by an "icy skepticism." Gerald's final defeat in his contest of wills with Gudrun is accomplished first by her, and then by her in league with Loerke. First, with "diabolic coldness," she forces from him the truth that he has not really loved her and never will. She is now self-complete and without desire. Only one more "convulsion of his will" is needed for him also to become "impervious and isolate."

She forms an alliance with Loerke. They share a taste for African and Aztec art, the former used earlier in the novel to illustrate the completely sensual modern escape, the latter the death-symbol art out of which Lawrence later struggled to create a positive, vitalistic symbolism in *The Plumed Serpent*. Loerke knows the secret of the power that can now master her. She wants, says Lawrence, "the subtle thrill of extreme sensation in reduction." Gerald does not take this ultimate step because his soul still has some need for "oneness with goodness, righteousness, and ultimate purpose." Interrupting Gudrun's pleasure in anarchic freedom with Loerke, he strikes Loerke, is struck by Gudrun, and experiences a "perverse, voluptuous" desire to assert his mastery by killing her. But he turns away in revulsion and nausea because he realizes he does not really care about her. He sheers off "unconsciously from any further contact."

> He sheered away. Somebody was going to murder him. He had a great dread of being murdered. . . . Yet why be afraid? It was bound to happen. To be murdered! He looked round in terror at the snow, the rocking, pale, shadowy slopes of the upper world. . . . Lord Jesus, was it then bound to be—Lord Jesus! He could feel the blow descending, he knew he was murdered. . . .

His encounter with the crucifix, and his acceptance of a fate he feels to be connected with it, is in part an expression of Lawrence's overwhelming association of the tragic side of Christianity with the defeat in life of his mother, and so many others. The impossibility of salvation is reflexively linked to Gerald's father's broken ideal of Christian brotherhood, and Gerald's rejection of Birkin's vitalistic brotherhood. Even Gerald's denial of his murderous impulse is the ultimate manifestation of his essentially unrelated being, so that nothing remains but collapse and death.

Ursula and Birkin return from Italy to "do what they can." Gudrun cannot grieve. Although she has not violated the civil law, Birkin sees her essential guilt. At the place where Gerald died, he feels the paradox of his nearness to guide ropes to the summit and the slope south "to Italy and life." But he wonders if that way is any longer effective, and feels that either "the heart will break or cease to care." He thinks it possible that God can now do without mankind. In this extremity he turns to vitalistic faith in the life-force itself.

> If humanity ran into a *cul de sac*, and expended itself, the timeless creative mystery would bring forth some other being, finer, more wonderful, some new more lovely race, to carry on the embodiment of creation. . . . Races came and went, species passed away, but ever new species arose, more lovely, or equally lovely, always surpassing wonder. The fountain-head was incorruptible and unsearchable. . . . To have one's pulse beating direct from this mystery, this was perfection, unutterable satisfaction.

Later, in tears beside Gerald's body, he thinks Gerald's loving him would have made a difference.

> Those who die, and dying still can love, still believe, do not die. They live still in the beloved. Gerald might still have been living in the spirit with Birkin, even after death. He might have lived with his friend, a further life.
>
> But now he was dead, like clay, like bluish, corruptible ice. Birkin looked at the blue fingers, the inert mass. He remembered a dead stallion he had seen: a dead mass of maleness, repugnant. He remembered also the beautiful face of one whom he had loved, and who had died still having the faith to yield to the mystery. That dead face was beautiful, no one could call it cold, mute, material. No one could remember it without gaining faith in the mystery, without the soul's warming with new, deep life-trust.

He has Ursula, and they will not despair. But he is still troubled by his want of a friend, "eternal as she and he are eternal." He refuses to believe, with her, that such a love is perverse and impossible.

The novel is a tremendous religious-ethical transmutation of Lawrence's experience — the struggle with Frieda for harmony between two
powerful natures; their friendship with John Middleton Murry and
Katherine Mansfield, in which Lawrence asked of Murry more friendship than Murry was prepared to give; the hazards and indignities of his
intensity and zeal; and above all the unbalancing blow to his sensibility
of the war, which denied the fulfillment he had found, reawakened the
death-drift in him, and stirred in his nature intimations of violence and
madness. It is, in part, as Rebecca West once said, an "allegory of the
death of the soul," taking *soul* in the sense of the sensitive, feeling, profoundly intimate, and life-tending reaches of being. The values that survive are vitalistically based love and belief: love of man as well as woman,
belief in a "timeless creative mystery," a fountainhead of life "incorrupt-
ible and unsearchable." The "northern" natures of Gudrun and Gerald
had lost this connection, and their world had turned to anti-life isolation.
The possibility of returning to the fountainhead had a cultural and geographical direction, south to the Mediterranean and Italy. And this was
Lawrence's direction as soon after the war as he could manage it.

4 🐑

Seven of the ten stories collected in 1922 as *England, My England, and
Other Stories,* contain Lawrence's most direct treatment of the war's effect on life. The other three, which continue his concern with decadence
and strife in relationship in the Midlands, reflect more indirectly the
dark, nightmarish side of his experience, and his resistance and means
of rectification and sanity.

"The Primrose Path" suggests his early manner in the use of a sensitive, rather lost young man as observer and commentator (characteristically identified with Lawrence by his mother's death of cancer). Unexpectedly meeting his blacksheep uncle in London, he experiences the result of chaotic rebellion against coldness in relationship. When his uncle,
a taxi driver, expresses his fierce antipathy to the people in the street — "I
feel like running the cab amuck among 'em, and running myself to king-

dom come" — the narrator feels "curiously understanding. . . . He uses words like I do, he talks nearly as I talk, except that I shouldn't say those things. But I might feel like that, in myself, if I went a certain road." He realizes that his uncle's bullying expresses his uneasy conscience and fear. In a series of scenes, he encounters the dying wife his uncle abandoned to flee to Australia, the young girl he now plans to marry, and the failure in both relationships. The wife, cold of voice and soul, had no chance of achieving a warmer relationship with such a chaos of a man. At the uncle's new home the dilapidated garden and the view of the suburbs suggest the psychic, ethical, and social breakdown Lawrence is dealing with — a "kind of unresolved borderland." The delicate, warmly colored working-class girl whom the uncle plans to marry endures his passion's leaving "her, the person, out of count." When his passion is aroused, it is "life stronger than death in him," overcoming the "death-horror" of his wife's suffering. Such a crude, violent assertion of life, with its incapability of complete relationship, can only end with the girl's rightly coming to hate him, and her leaving him.

"England, My England" expresses Lawrence's acute association of loss of a vitally strong English past and the failure of modern sensibility. It is essentially the story of the failure of a man's relationship to his family because he is unable to assume higher responsibility and action in the world, ending with his becoming a soldier without clear faith in a cause, and the consequent nihilism of his death in battle.

Egbert has tried to link himself with the English past through folk study. He has married a robust, beautiful girl who has the best qualities of the English yeoman past, and he himself is like an archer. But there is a crucial difference between their backgrounds and natures. Her father is the former type of self-reliant man who has, through his energy, become moderately rich and provided houses for all three of his daughters near the southern downs that "preserve so many relics of the past." Winifred's old cottage constitutes a survival of "ancient strength and passion." Egbert, on the other hand, has only a small inheritance, no profession, and only vague hopes of money from his study of ancient literature and music. He is highly bred, and delightful and spontaneous in passion, so that at the beginning of their marriage they forget their dilettante London life in a passion that is consistent with the cottage's long "blood-history." He is happy in the simple activities of repairing the cottage, but is an incompetent workman.

The coming of children accentuates their dependence on her father, and pushes Egbert out of the center of Winifred's interest. But the deeper cause of his being shut out of her life is his failure to be the center of power her father is. He lacks the father's faith in activity, the "will to power," as what keeps a man going.[5]

Egbert's weakness as father and husband is made more than innocuous by his daughter's cutting herself on a scythe he has carelessly left lying about. Treatment of the resulting infection is ineffectual until the old father intervenes. The girl is left with both a bad knee and the psychic mark of her father's irresponsibility — a "queer, baffled, half-wicked" look, and a reckless spirit.

Winifred, conscience-stricken, turns to Catholic penitence and asceticism—the "final tomb" of Egbert's manhood. His reaction is manifested as a decadent desire for the "passion of the cold-blooded snakes, the mystery of blood-sacrifice, and the intense sensations of primeval people" that linger from the past in the marsh near the cottage. When the war comes, he is unable to feel a sense of loyalty and good purpose, but obeys the simple, unquestioning decision of the old father that he should become a soldier.

His agony of hopelessness as he dies of a wound is undoubtedly expressive of one side of Lawrence's feeling during and after the war. "Better the agony of dissolution ahead than the nausea of the effort backwards. . . . Utterly, utterly to forget, in the great forgetting of death . . . to lapse out on the great darkness. . . . Let the black sea of death itself solve the problem of futurity. Let the will of man break and give up." Such a temptation to despair haunts his work with new intensity from *Women in Love* onward.

"Samson and Delilah" is a Lawrencean comedy of the triumph of vital appeal. The setting and the characters, and the resource of male power, come from his wartime sojourn in Cornwall, and the Celts' re-

---

5. In extolling the patriarchal family here, Lawrence is on the defensive against Freudian analysis in insisting that Winifred's admiration of her father is not a father-complex.

tention of mystic qualities. The hero has dark, mindless eyes and the nonstandard speech Lawrence repeatedly opposes to anti-life distance and propriety. Many years after abandoning his family to go to America, he returns to the pub run by his buxom, attractive wife in a mining village. At closing time, he insists he will stay in his own house. She is still his "Missis." Her hostility ranges from an abnormal, frightening anger to reproach, tears, and appeals to the sympathy of the soldiers drinking at the pub. In the midst of a disarming appeal not to be "a brute of a German," she seizes him, and after a vindictive struggle she and the soldiers subduc him with a rope. When he still will not agree to leave, they place him outside with the rope loosely tied so that he can free himself. When he stubbornly returns to the house, she controls her anger partly from fear and partly because of "the beauty of his head and his level-drawn brows, which she could not bear to forfeit." His sensual appeal and laconic flattering argument overcome her sense of being wronged.

Both Lawrence's despair and his lifeward, constructive reaction are expressed in "The Blind Man," one of his most remarkable stories psychologically. The letter to Katherine Mansfield in 1918 mentioning its completion — "the end queer and ironical" — associates it with a reassertion of his belief in "friendship between man and man, a pledging of men to each other inviolably. . . . as eternal as the marriage bond, and as deep;" and with a strong imaginative experience of the inhuman. "On Butterley platform — when I got out — everything was lit up red — there was a man with dark brows, odd, not a human being. I could write a story about him. . . . It seems to me, if one is to do fiction now, one must cross the threshold of the human people." He added that he felt "despair altogether about human relationships."

In the story, his protagonist, Maurice Pervin, blinded and disfigured in the war, lives in isolation in a country cottage with his wife, Isabel. He does not regret the loss of his sight when he experiences the "almost incomprehensible peace" of contact in darkness. This invisible but rich and real world is shared by his wife; but its glamor leaves them at times, and he suffers a depression she cannot bear. Her solution to this and the ennui she sometimes experiences is to try to give him some further connection with the world by inviting friends to visit, though he finds people shallow.

One of her attempts involves Bertie Reid, a bachelor barrister and man of letters who is the psychic and cultural opposite of Maurice. His mind is quick, but his emotions slow. Maurice, of a "good old" country family, has a slow mind but is passionate and sensitive. The story concerns the failure of their attempt at vital friendship in Lawrence's religious sense.

Lawrence assigns Maurice a duality that seems quite autobiographical. He takes profound pleasure in "the immediacy of blood-contact," without the intervention of visual consciousness. The occasional check of this "flow of life" leaves him at the mercy of his conflicts. His duality extends to his reaction to Bertie in Isabel's presence. He is fretful and beside himself "like a child that is left out of the life circle," and at the same time is a powerful man infuriated by his own weakness. On the other hand, Bertie, though kind and chivalrous, is "unable ever to enter into close contact of any sort" because of his shame at not being able to approach women physically. He is "afraid, helplessly and even brutally afraid."

The climactic scene occurs when Bertie, shrinking and nervous in the "wet, roaring night," goes to look for Maurice, who has retired to his world of vital touch. He finds him pulping turnips, a cat rubbing against his leg. The attempt at male relationship of the wrestling episode in *Women in Love,* with its hope of blood brothership, becomes here a pathetic hope of unqualified contact. Maurice worries that Isabel, always alone with him, will find him a dead weight, and also sometimes feels that he is horrible to her. When he asks Bertie to tell him how much he is disfigured, Bertie nervously calls the scar a rather bad one. Maurice asks Bertie to let him touch him so that he may truly know him, and runs his hand over his skull and face. When he asks Bertie to touch his scarred eyes, Bertie's repulsion is overcome by a "strange power." Maurice presses his hand upon his eyes, rocks slowly from side to side, and then exclaims joyfully that they now truly know each other. Essential, vitalistic communion has overcome the antagonisms of consciousness and vital damage. Maurice is filled with "hot, poignant love," the passion of friend-

ship, the passion, Lawrence says, that Bertie perhaps shrinks from most —
that is, more than from the contact with woman. When the two return
to Isabel, she protects Maurice's gladness by taking his hand and saying
that he will be happier now.

> But she was watching Bertie. She knew that he had one desire—to escape
> from this intimacy, this friendship, which had been thrust upon him. He
> could not bear it that he had been touched by the blind man, his insane re-
> serve broken in. He was like a mollusc whose shell is broken.

The realistic grounding of the story, and its psychological development,
are quite rich. Its weakness lies in the disproportion of the barrier to contact in Bertie, to the intensity of Maurice's need. One cannot help feeling that at times Lawrence was bending his metaphysic to the service of
an hysterical experience of loneliness and frustration.

"Tickets, Please" is an ironic psychological comedy of the attitudes
among the girls and men who operated the wartime trams. John Thomas,
the tram inspector, makes love to all the "young hussies," who have the
"*sang-froid* of an old non-commissioned officer." Only Annie scorns him,
until she meets him at a fair, comes into rapport with him through the
fun and abandon, and enjoys his love-making. But she tries to make him
more than "a nocturnal presence" by taking an "intelligent" interest in
him and wishing an "intelligent" response. When he avoids her, she
enlists the help of the other girls in taking vengeance. One night in their
waiting room they try to force him to choose one of them, and attack and
beat him when he refuses. This making of him into a beaten though still
defiant animal, Annie finds a "terrifying and cold triumph." And when
at last he cunningly chooses her, she feels disgust and bitterness; something is "broken in her." Realistically the story is a brilliant objective
vignette of wartime aggressiveness and anarchy. It is also another chapter in Lawrence's parable of the inimical conditions in which the life
force imperfectly asserts itself and is humiliated or broken.

"Monkey Nuts" is a terse vignette of the emotion-paralyzing after-
effects of the war. Albert, forty and a corporal, and Joe, twenty-three and
a private, are stationed after the Armistice at a collecting point in England for hay, timber, and coal. One of the land-girls, Miss Stokes, has

already seen hundreds of Alberts standing in loose attitudes and watching nothing in particular, and a good many Joes, quiet, good-looking young soldiers with half-averted faces. But she likes Joe and tries to attract him. Joe and Albert feel nothing deeply. Joe resists and resents all her advances; Albert is willing to substitute for him in casual love-making, which is what he thinks she wants. When Joe's resentment of the girl becomes upsetting to the pleasantness of their soldiers' camaraderie, Albert advises him to make a decisive break with her. When one day she tries to call Joe away from Albert, Joe jeeringly mocks her, and she is deeply hurt and never returns, as they are afraid she will. Joe, Lawrence says sardonically, is more relieved than he was when the Armistice came.

The technique of "Wintry Peacock" seems anomalous among these rather objective stories in its use of the observer-narrator of the early stories. The peacock's "spiteful, inhuman" behavior is the correlative of the spirit of the young farm wife who asks the narrator to translate a letter addressed from Belgium to her soldier husband, who is expected home that night. He rephrases the letter, which is from a girl who says she has had a baby by the husband and wants to come to England, to protect him. But he is unable to remove the wife's suspicion and antagonism. Like the peacock she loves, her head is "drooped, sinister, and abstracted," and her voice malevolent. At the end she is unreconciled and unloving, though the letter has been burnt without her knowing its contents. She will not admit the human truth that her husband might fall in love while away. The narrator senses her "terrible abstractedness" from people when they are out of her immediate presence. When the husband questions him about how much she knows of the letter, they understand each other. Through the deceit, the husband has won a move in the contest with his wife's peacock spirit. He thinks the Belgian girl may be deceiving him, but he is uneasy about her, and the narrator guesses accurately that she was attractive. Both men are amused at the triumph over the inhuman, anti-life spirit at home.

"Fannie and Annie" is a deft mixture of psychological realism, class comedy, and victory for the vitalistic ethic. Fannie, who as a lady's maid has acquired the genteel sensibility, returns to an industrial-mining town after twelve years to marry an old sweetheart who is a foundry worker. The suspense lies in whether or not she will recoil from the apparent moral and esthetic chaos of the lower class world. The climax is the question of her response to the accusation, made during church service, that the man she is to marry has gotten a local girl with child.

Lawrence uses touches of his most broadly satirical parodic manner, reversing the sentimental author's address to his readers: "Let us confess it at once. She was a lady's maid. . . . Poor Fannie! She was such a lady, and so straight and magnificent." Harry speaks only the dialect. Its effect is hilarious when he sings hymns in the chapel choir. But while his behavior is common, he himself is not. There is, as so often in early Lawrence, something of "a mother's lad about him—warm, playful, and really sensitive." Women like him, and Fannie is really attracted to him. What she rebels against most is his having no ambition. At the crisis of the traditional moral contretemps involving the pregnant unwed girl, when he should be the melodramatic immoral villain or the repentant lamb, and be righteously rejected or forgiven, he and his family are staunchly practical about the slight chance of his being the father among so many candidates. They are not ashamed. And Fannie chooses their way and world.

"You Touched Me" develops the theme of the active raid on the middle-class world by the lower-class man. Here Lawrence's ubiquitous two sisters are the daughters of a pottery owner who is about to die and leave them old maids with fortunes. In an industrial district it has not been easy for such girls to find husbands. The suitable bank clerks, non-conformist clergymen, or even schoolteachers, Lawrence says, have not appeared. An adopted son, Hadrian, on leave after the Armistice, reappears. Originally a charity boy, he had resisted the sisters' attempts to refine him, resented their condescension, which involved calling him merely cousin, and at fifteen had gone to Canada. He is liked by the whiskey-drinking father, who has not forsaken his lower-class origin, and their mutual understanding and leaguing against the women develops into the climax of the story. Matilda one night accidentally enters Hadrian's room and, thinking he is her ill father, touches his brow. This touch is the catalyst of his scheme to get the father to make her inheritance dependent on her marrying him. When after much resistance by the sisters, who think he wants only the money, she capitulates to the vital response to her touch that motivates his cunning, the father feels that at last relations are right. This Lawrencean variation on the old middle-class moral theme of the mercenary struggle over an inheritance, has something of the pattern but none of the rich symbolism of "The Fox."

"The Horse Dealer's Daughter" is a memorable, beautifully wrought development of Lawrence's vitalistic death and resurrection theme, resembling the earlier "Love Among the Haystacks." Fanny is the only unmarried daughter in a family that is breaking up because its once lucrative horse-dealing has failed. The physically handsome but ineffectual sons cannot get her to make one of the proper choices — to go to her sister's, become a servant, or enter nurse's training. The young doctor friend of the family is disturbed by her impassivity and the danger expressed in her eyes. Knowing only coarse, brutal men, she has continued to live only in the memory of her dead mother, whom she loved. Enacting a familiar Lawrencean trauma, she feels at her mother's grave, contact with a world of death more real than her life. The doctor, seeing her there, senses in her a power that delivers him from his "fretted daily self." When she attempts suicide in a pond, he rescues her from "the hideous, cold water," carries her to the house, removes her clothes, and wraps her in a blanket before the fire. Her resurrection from death in life is accomplished by his full commitment to her. When she revives in nakedness, she feels that she is loved and is transfigured and triumphant. Through her touch he is drawn from his professional impersonality and fear.

> She shuffled forward on her knees, and put her arms round him, round his legs, as he stood there, pressing her breasts against his knees and thighs, clutching him with strange, convulsive certainty, pressing his thighs against her, drawing him to her face, her throat, as she looked up at him with flaring humble eyes of transfiguration, triumphant in first possession. . . .
>
> Her hands were drawing him, drawing him down to her. He was afraid, even a little horrified. For he had, really, no intention of loving her. . . . Her eyes were now wide with fear, with doubt, the light was dying from her face, a shadow of terrible greyness was returning. He could not bear the touch of her eyes' question upon him, and the look of death behind the question.

With an inward groan he gave way, and let his heart yield towards her. . . . He never intended to love her. But now it was over. He had crossed over the gulf to her, and all that he had left behind had shrivelled and become void.

It is characteristic of Lawrence that the "happy ending" is complex, containing their fears both of the world outside their rapport and of the risks of commitment. This existential honesty, and the inobvious, unforced creation of a correlative natural symbolism, are the mark of his best work.

The themes of this second collection of stories, except for "The Blind Man," resemble those of the earlier short stories. Technically, as one might expect, the stories are on the whole more mature, particularly in tone and diction. The preciousness of the earlier young narrator is gone, while the sensitive feeling for hurt, unfulfilled natures is continued, as in "The Horse Dealer's Daughter." Such "war" stories as "Samson and Delilah" and "Monkey Nuts" achieve an almost classic modern realism in the objectivity of point of view and tone, and the informality of diction adapted to characters and situation — what Joyce called the deliberate "meanness" of style in *Dubliners*. Thus the opening sentence of "Monkey Nuts" — "At first Joe thought the job O. K." But the farthest reaching development is in combined narration and analysis which deftly sustain a characteristic Lawrencean irony — the compounded muddle of relationships leading somewhere to a showdown. The effect is achieved by using in analysis the jargon and the clichés with which the characters themselves would express their sense of their problems. Thus the effect of the coming of a child on the relationship of Winifred and Egbert in "England, My England":

After the child was born, it was never quite the same between him and Winifred. The difference was at first hardly perceptible. But it was there. In the first place Winifred had a new center of interest. She was not going to adore her child. But she had what the modern mother so often has in the place of spontaneous love: a profound sense of duty towards her child. Winifred appreciated her darling little girl, and felt a deep sense of duty towards her. Strange, that this sense of duty should go deeper than the love for her husband. But so it was. And so it often is. The responsibility of motherhood

was the prime responsibility in Winifred's heart: the responsibility of wife-
hood came a long way second. . . .

Egbert was out of it. Without anything happening, he was gradually, unconsciously excluded from the circle. His wife still loved him, physically.
But, but—he was *almost* the unnecessary party in the affair. He could not
complain of Winifred. She still did her duty towards him. She still had a
physical passion for him, that physical passion on which he had put all his
life and soul. But—but—

Such ironic reiteration of, and hesitation on, key phrases, is an instru-
ment with which the mature Lawrence plays variation after variation on
his theme.

5

Composition of the short stories, ranging in time from 1914 to 1922,
was interspersed among a really staggering number of projects for a man
so troubled and so often ill. Driven hard by economic as well as spiritual
necessity, Lawrence finished *Twilight in Italy,* and produced the text-
book *Movements in European History;* the periodical version of *Studies
in Classic American Literature,* which he hoped would gain him a live-
lihood lecturing in America; *Psychoanalysis and the Unconscious; Fantasia of the Unconscious;* and *Sea and Sardinia;* as well as poetry, other
essays, and the fiction being discussed here. These years were a time of
furious reassessment and redirection.

During the postwar phase of this, Lawrence wrote three novelettes
which, with the exception of a few of the short stories, are the most perfect and rich examples of his work in the short forms. His novels now
tend to take on the more episodic form inherent in their exploration of
new places and conditions of life. The novelettes are more unified in
their fusion of sardonic realistic insight with vitalistic salvation.

"The Fox" reflects Lawrence's surrealistic sense of psychic disorder in
the wartime world. The fox that raids the farm of two dilettante girls who
maintain an anti-life alliance suggesting the intricacies of lesbianism, has
a mesmeric appeal to the repressed, distorted vital self of the one, and a
fatal antagonism to the other as the agent of such distortion. The fox is,

in a sense, the totem of the lower class man who breaks up this unholy alliance. The conventionally predatory and evil animal and man have the cunning and ruthlessness required to achieve the vitalistic reversal of values and relationship.

Banford and March, nearly thirty and manless, have gone to the farm with the dilettante notion of acquiring leisure for reading, cycling, painting on porcelain, and cabinetmaking. Banford is small, thin, delicate, and nervous, with no "unconscious power" of empathy. March is the Lawrencean woman of vital potentiality, looking almost like a young man in her work clothes but having a woman's face, wide dark eyes, and a way of "lapsing into unconscious reverie." The realistic basis of the vitalistic drama is the girls' inability to apprehend and shoot the fox that raids their chickens.

March is deterred by a mysterious rapport with the fox. When he unexpectedly and slyly confronts her one day, she falls under his spell, and later looks for him in "strange mindlessness." The twenty-year-old soldier who in 1918 comes to the farm looking for his grandfather, who once lived there, is immediately identified by March with the fox. Lawrence parallels their physical appearance, their sly way of gaining their ends, and their dark, submission-inducing power, and gives the man another of his marks of mystic, unconscious power, a Celtic Cornish origin and way of speaking. As part of the pattern of alienation of such power, Lawrence also makes him a runaway to Canada as a youth.

Banford's perverse suspicions of men are overcome for a time. She consents to his staying for a few days because her natural warmth and sympathy are freed by a sisterly relationship, and he is efficient at the farm work that is defeating them. He is the completely unidealized, lowerclass Lawrencean man in the development of his relationship with March. He first thinks of marrying her after he suddenly sees the farm as a good thing to possess, and senses a means to this in her vulnerability to him. Only after he has apprehended her as a woman when she wears a dress for the first time and he touches her in an embrace, does Lawrence give him what might traditionally be called "love" for her. And this is keyed very low as a sense of male responsibility. He knows that if he goes to her with a frank proposal of marriage, she will respond with her usual attitude of ridicule of men and their tomfoolery. He must approach her as a hunter stalks the deer. Only his "fox" side, taking her unawares, in her unconscious self, can compel her. In conversation, it is not his argument but the soft, rhythmic power of his Cornish voice that draws her to darkness "as if she were killed."

Banford's antagonism increases in ratio to his success with March. She succeeds in restraining March with the practical and moral arguments of their class. March must not lose her self-respect. She doesn't know what she is letting herself in for. He is only a "beastly labourer," cold, selfish, an "awful little beast."

Angered and, in a sense, defeated, by overhearing this judgment, he makes the fox a curiously *alter ego* victim by hunting it. Alone in the night with his gun and the barking fox, he feels that the situation is an expression of the littleness and tightness of an England that doesn't give the fox a chance, and thinks of the fox as the last of its kind. Awakened by his shooting the fox, March later has a dream that nightmarishly mixes her waking concern for Banford with the fox's vital power and death. Banford is dead, and March can find only the wood-box in the kitchen for a coffin. Then she is unable to find anything to cover her with and must use the fox skin, "a ruddy, fiery, unfunereal coverlet," as if Banford were consumed in flames. Her response to the dead fox next day refers back to her also dreaming that the fox's brush touched her face and burned her mouth, and to the man's "quick brushing kiss" that seemed to "burn through her every fibre." Lawrence's passion for life, and acute sense of loss of it, modulates every phrase and is felt in the characteristic intensives *lovely, great, full, delicate, wonderful, splendour.*

> It was a lovely dog-fox in its prime, with a handsome, thick, winter coat; a lovely golden-red colour, with grey as it passed to the belly, and belly all white, and a great full brush with a delicate black and grey and pure white tip.
>
> "Poor brute!" said Banford. "If it wasn't such a thieving wretch, you'd feel sorry for it."
>
> March said nothing, but stood with her foot trailing aside, one hip out; her face was pale and her eyes big and black, watching the dead animal that

was suspended upside down. White and soft as snow his belly: white and soft as snow. She passed her hand softly down it. And his wonderful black-glinted brush was full and frictional, wonderful. She passed her hand down this also, and quivered. Time after time she took the full fur of that thick tail between her fingers, and passed her hand slowly downwards. Wonderful, sharp, thick, splendour of a tail. And he was dead! She pursed her lips, and her eyes went black and vacant.

Finally, seeing the skin nailed on a board, March thinks of the fox's death as a crucifixion.

The climax of this vitalistic tragi-comedy of errors comes when March, left alone with Banford, reverts to her, and Henry receives a letter full of her responsibility to and love of Banford, who makes her feel "safe and sane." Feeling that all human society is opposed to him, he gets twenty-four hours' leave from an understanding Cornish captain, and arrives at the farm just as Banford and March are trying to fell a fir tree, with Banford's ineffectual, jeering father as an onlooker. Quite properly, he offers to help by giving the final blows to the tree. Banford stands just where the tree, if he gives it the right touch, will hit her. In a concession to conscience and fair play, he has already warned of the danger, and been disagreed with by the father. In his final hunted fox's cunning he warns Banford in a tone that he knows will imply to her that he is being falsely solicitous. When she refuses to move, he fells the tree and kills his enemy in a struggle for survival in which the murder is vitalistically ethical.

After this climax, Lawrence characteristically places what seems an anticlimax — Henry's continued struggle for rapport with March. In the sense of complex realism this is a strength, for the Lawrencean conflict could never be fully resolved as long as the old values persisted, as long as Lawrence did not oversimplify, and as long as he was self-critical. The resulting ambiguity sometimes leads his readers to accusations of inconsistency when what he is doing is quite consistent with the conditions of his theme. In "The Fox" nothing in March has changed. The vitally powerful man wants to make her "just his woman," and hopes that taking her away from the England that has so "stung him with poison" will accomplish this, but he is not at all certain.

Lawrence's exposition at the end expands from March to an essay on

the world, with a deliberately repetitious semantic toughmindedness
ringing changes on the key value terms planted in March's consciousness.

> She still felt she ought to *do* something, to strain herself in some direc-
> tion. . . . And she could not quite accept the submergence which his new
> love put upon her. If she was in love, she ought to *exert* herself, in some way,
> loving. She felt the weary need of our day to *exert* herself in love. But she
> knew that in fact she must no more exert herself in love. He would not have
> the love which exerted itself towards him. It made his brow go black. No, he
> wouldn't let her exert her love towards him. No, she had to be passive, to
> acquiesce, and to be submerged under the surface of love. She had to be
> like the seaweeds she saw as she peered down from the boat, swaying
> forever delicately under water. . . .
>   And she had been so used to the very opposite. She had had to take all
> the thought for love and for life, and all the responsibility. Day after day
> she had been responsible for the coming day, for the coming year: for her
> dear Jill's health and happiness and well-being. Verily, in her own small way,
> she had felt herself responsible for the well-being of the world. And this
> had been her great stimulant, this grand feeling that, in her own small
> sphere, she was responsible for the well-being of the world. . . .
>   Poor March, in her goodwill and her responsibility, she had strained
> herself till it seemed to her that the whole of life and everything was only
> a horrible abyss of nothingness. . . . That is the whole history of the
> search for happiness, whether it be your own or somebody else's that you
> want to win. It ends, and it always ends, in the ghastly sense of the bottomless
> nothingness into which you will inevitably fall if you strain any further.

"The Ladybird" is a complex parable of the deathly psychic effects
of the war, and develops for the first time in the short fiction the leadership theme that culminated in *The Plumed Serpent*. Like many of his
contemporaries, Lawrence tends to fill the cultural vacuum caused by
his anti-traditional, vitalistic position with more esoteric materials. His
native, natural metaphorical imagery of bird, beast and flower is supplemented by ancient symbol. The mythic patterns of his youthful experience — night and day, darkness and light, unconsciousness and consciousness, death and resurrection — are reinforced by his readings in
anthropology and theosophy.

The realistic grounding of the story is sensitively worked out. The failure of the older generation of English aristocrats, Lord and Lady Beveridge, is due to a familiar Lawrencean disparity of means and situation. Her combination of the best of the tradition of idealism and humanitarianism means that she cannot cope with the barbarism of the war, and the decline of this tradition is reflected in her loss of social prestige. He, retaining the force and passion of his "primitive border race," is thwarted both by her idealism and by modern vulgarity. They have lost two sons in the war. Their daughter, Lady Daphne, whose husband, reported missing in the near East, had turned up wounded and a prisoner of the Turks, and has returned with a scar that marks a vital psychic trauma, is the Lawrencean heroine saved from total hopelessness. Her illness, which destroys her beauty, is the psychosomatic Lawrencean one of divided being, caused by her wishing to be like her mother while she has the spirit of her father.

The mother, refusing to be swept into the "general vulgar hate," visits a German prisoner-of-war hospital and finds there, near death, an old friend of the family, Count Johann Dionys Psanek. Through his vitalistic connection with death and eternity and the power of resurrection, he becomes the means of healing to the neurotic suffering of Lady Daphne and the trauma of her husband. Both must submit to his power and thus, in a sense, to his leadership.

The details of the story are unified by their ultimate reference to the central death and resurrection symbol of the ladybird and Psanek's concomitant power. Lady Daphne's split between mental consciousness and blood consciousness and the consequent deadening of her vitality are suggested by her eyes, a "fiery, animal blue-green made cold and glaucous," and by her blondness and the whiteness of her skin. Psanek — dark-eyed, dark-haired, and dark-skinned, his hair low on his forehead — looks like a survival of a primitive central European race. To prevent himself from succumbing to the deathliness of hate and violence, he has turned from his "modern, monkeylike social self" to the ancient ways of his family. The symbols of the secret society, probably Rosicrucian, he once joined as a diversion, have become meaningful to him.

The first link between him and Lady Daphne had been a thimble bearing the heraldry of his family that he had given her when she was seventeen. Now between visits to him at the hospital, she uses it in making shirts for him. This bond between them is lost when she conscientiously turns from their rapport to concern for her returning husband. The husband regards the thimble conventionally as a mere curio. At its base is a serpent, an earth-symbol of the source of being, and possibly an underworld, death symbol. On its top is a bug, a Mary-beetle, a ladybird, or the Egyptian scarab, depending on the degree of conventional literalness in the beholder. Through the Egyptian myth of the beetle's creation of the world by rolling a ball of dung, and in combination with the serpent, the thimble is allied to such other Lawrencean vital integration, resurrection symbols as the plumed serpent and the phoenix.

Psanek's name is translated *outlaw,* and contains an anagram, perhaps not deliberate, of *snake.* He has decided that the only solution to the vitalistic imbalance that has had such traumatic effects culminating in the war, is to attack and destroy the world created by men, in what amounts to a vitalistic nihilism of return to the source of life.

Daphne's trauma and the night-death-Psanek way to renewal of life are very complexly counterpointed — her sympathetic love and cold green eyes to a vitalistic opposite like the wildcat "when in the night the green screen of its eyes open" though its love may be savage; her white love like moonshine, her husband's penchant for calling her a moon-goddess (Astarte, Venus, Cybele, Isis), distastefully mixing lust and adoration, to Psanek's dark independence, unidealistic recognition of the reality of hate, singing of old folksongs in the night, and her submission to his power in death, as if he were an Egyptian king-god.

Though the leadership theme is developed in conversations between the husband and Psanek, the entire story emphasizes submission to a greater power. All of the characters belong to an hereditary aristocracy, English or Bohemian, and all have found that way of organizing life ineffectual. Daphne has been attracted to vital lower-class men, particularly to an "impudent, ruddy-faced, laughing" gamekeeper, but accepts (and apparently Lawrence with her) the gulf between her highly de-

veloped being and the "unconscious" classes. Psanek and her husband
engage in a love-democracy versus power-leadership debate. To the husband love is the opposite of will, which is purely autocratic, as the Kaiser
was. To Psanek, the Kaiser was a mountebank who had no conception
of the sacredness of power. He believes in "the sacred duty to shape the
destinies of other men," a duty that cannot be fulfilled until men will-
ingly put their lives in the hands of a man whose "soul is born able" to
direct them.

This idea of submission to the superior soul, with its Carlylean and
Nietzschean overtones, is to become an increasingly important Lawrencean theme. The continuous opposition of the woman in Lawrence's fiction
to this power-leadership program, biographically related to Mrs. Lawrence's disbelief in his colony idea, is foreshadowed by Daphne's dislike
of Psanek's idea. Her rapport with him comes only when he appeals to
her through ritual and symbol, and she becomes "the night-wife of the
ladybird," entering into a state of peace and virginity which makes her
husband sympathetic and ashamed of his lust. Only when she seems like
a sister does he "see clearly and feel truly" about their relationship. They
agree to abide in this love without sex which is the ultimate realization
of his belief in ideal love, and the inactivity demanded by his war trauma.
Psanek can be her lover, because he is, in a sense, the priest of the vitalistic source, in the death toward which the divided being and the thwarted
vital need of Daphne tend. Psanek, in keeping with his role as the man
with a divine mission, goes his way. But, he says, he and she will always
be "king and queen on the other side of death," so that she need never be
"afraid of life." Their vitalistic rapport is eternal as the life force, in the
midst of death and living-death, is eternal.

The power of this story depends not so much on a clear understanding
of, and belief in, Psanek's dark way, as on the sense of its inevitability
as an ultimate resource after the failure of all other ways. This sense is
developed and sustained by the tonality of analysis and narration in
which a brutal irony rises from mimicry of the accents and diction in
which such traumatized people might express their values and their reaction. Thus the opening paragraph:

How many swords had Lady Beveridge in her pierced heart! Yet there always seemed room for another. Since she had determined that her heart of pity and kindness should never die. If it had not been for this determination she herself might have died of sheer agony, in the years 1916 and 1917, when her boys were killed, and her brother, and death seemed to be mowing with wide swaths through her family. But let us forget.

And thus Daphne, thinking of Psanek's attitude toward her:

> He said her eyes were like jewels of stone. What a horrid thing to say! What did he want her eyes to be like? He wanted them to dilate and become all black pupil, like a cat's at night. She shrank convulsively from the thought, and tightened her breast.
>
> He said her beauty was her whited sepulchre. Even that, she knew what he meant. The invisibility of her he wanted to love. But ah, her pearl-like beauty was so dear to her, and it was so famous in the world. . . .
>
> What then would the Count's love be like? Something so secret and different. She would not be lovely and a queen to him. He hated her loveliness. The wildcat has its mate. The little wild-cat that he was. Ah!

The same technique of exploratory commonplace diction is sometimes used in expressing Psanek's serious meaning. But at climactic moments the tone changes to that of the rhythmic, rather Biblical language Lawrence used when he was most intensely serious about his religious feeling. Thus Psanek's reassurance of Daphne:

> "Listen," he said to her softly. "Now you are mine. In the dark you are mine. And when you die you are mine. But in the day you are not mine, because I have no power in the day. In the night, in the dark, and in death, you are mine. And that is forever. No matter if I must leave you. I shall come again from time to time. In the dark you are mine. But in the day I cannot claim you. I have no power in the day, and no place. So remember. When the darkness comes, I shall always be in the darkness of you. . . . "

"The Captain's Doll" is an example of Lawrence's vitalistic comedy, with quite serious, even shocking overtones of the consequences of vital failure. It too uses a central symbol, not of animal or mystic power, but of the anti-life of the marriage code that reduces the male to a travesty of vital power, a process that can be reversed only by refusing the trap of love and service, by reasserting honor and obedience as terms of the woman's vow, by rejecting postwar, fatalistic pleasure-seeking, and by assuming the male's proper role of adventurer into the future and creator of a new life.

Stationed in Austria after the war, the Scottish Captain Hepburn has a rather extraordinary kind of affair with a refugee German countess, Hannele. Supporting herself by making and selling dolls, she makes one of him, for amusement, that captures his "finished" social self.

> It was a perfect portrait of an officer of a Scottish regiment, slender, delicately made, with a slight elegant stoop of the shoulders, and close-fitting tartan trousers. The face was beautifully modelled, and a wonderful portrait, dark-skinned, with a little, close-cut dark moustache, and wide-open dark eyes, and that air of aloofness and perfect diffidence which marks an officer and a gentleman.

The first part of the story consists of his middle-class English wife's efforts to claim his doll-like self from the intrinsic self involved in his relationship with Hannele. A part of this intrinsic self is a carelessness about the personal, human factor that Hannele cannot bear. Hepburn suggests the Lawrencean mystic, vitalistic hero in his "curious, dark, unseeing" eyes, the "mindless power" of his voice, and the Celtic otherworldliness of his Scottish origin. His night, moon, cat self is viewed rather comically when his wandering about on the roof disturbs Hannele's sleep.

> She tapped softly on the window-pane. He looked round like some tomcat staring round with wide night-eyes. Then he reached down his hand and pulled the window open.
> "Hello," he said quietly. "You not asleep?"
> "Aren't *you* tired?" she replied, rather resentful.
> "No, I was as wide awake as I could be. *Isn't* the moon fine tonight? What? Perfectly amazing. Wouldn't you like to come up and have a look at her?"
> "No, thank you," she said hastily, terrified at the thought.
> He resumed his posture, peering up the telescope.
> "Perfectly amazing," he said, murmuring. She waited for some time, bewitched likewise by the great October moon and the sky full of resplendent white-green light. It seemed like another sort of day-time. And there he

straddled on the roof like some cat! It was exactly like day in some other planet.

This amateur astronomy situation is the occasion for his telling her that he is returning to his wife because he doesn't "want to hurt her feelings," and wants her "to get what pleasure out of life she can." When Hannele asks what *he* feels, and his answer is "I don't consider I count," she feels that he is "a sort of psychic phenomenon like a grasshopper or a tadpole or an ammonite. Not to be regarded from a human point of view. No, he just wasn't normal. And she had been fascinated by him!"

The tactics of Hepburn's wife when, before he can join her, she campaigns against Hannele, satirically create a sense of the contemporary chaos into which the love-service ideal of marriage has fallen. She had first written to his superiors to intervene and then come to claim him in person. The doll becomes the center of contention. She herself is like one of Hannele's dolls with her "lardy-dardy" middle-class English, her well-dressed complacence, and her "curiously crumpled" face that reveals her vital failure. Thinking that Hannele's vivacious, roguish friend Mitchka is the other woman, she attacks her by talking with Hannele. First she veils her attitude in moral indifference. Her husband's slip is simply part of the general wartime moral deterioration, and need not be taken very seriously. The wives are primarily to blame, and even she herself has flirted a bit. To illustrate how much worse the situation could be, she tells of an acquaintance whose husband brutally scolded her for not meeting him when he was arriving home late because of a casual affair. She is thankful that her husband has always lived up to his promise on their wedding night that he would devote himself to making her life happy. Now she is not jealous, and she does not believe in "stripping wounds bare." She thinks that Hannele's friend is charming and impulsive, but she and others like her are dangerous to "the English husband away from home." After this preliminary, she reveals the fist behind her reasonableness. She intends having the British authorities expel this woman who menaces her possession, if she does not capitulate. She wants not only the man back, but the doll that represents him as a servant of woman, in love.

Hannele is even more confused about Hepburn at this point. He is two men—the doll who made the vow to his wife, probably in a "ridiculous bedroom scene," so that his magic is a swindle; and, when she recalls his "presence," the attractive, spell-casting man. Deciding that the latter is his true self, she refuses to give up the doll.

The wife's death by falling from the hotel window is a rather subtle example of Lawrence's vitalistic "murders." Realistically it is attributable to her proneness to vertigo, vitalistically to Hannele's defeat of her social self and her inability to measure up to Hepburn, to whose astronomy her vertiginous inability to look at the moon is linked. She has also been destroyed by her own duality of self, as Hepburn sympathetically explains to Hannele. She, too, had a touch of otherworldiness, and he is happy for her that her "fairy Irish soul, revealed in her eyes," is released from "some great tension" and is free of the "social cage."

Immediately after her death, Hepburn feels that there is no life for human beings outside the social cage. He retreats from all relationship, settles his children—in a Lawrencean gambit taking his daughter from a convent and putting her in a jolly English school—and drifts, tired of love and adoration in relationship. At last seeking Hannele again, in Munich, he sees his doll for sale in a shop window. It now represents his rejection of his true self in deserting Hannele, and his consequent discard. Returning to buy it, he finds it has been sold to a painter who has used it as part of an abstract still life—twice-removed from real being and purpose. He buys the painting as if to prevent further distancing of himself from Hannele and life.

In Austria he finds Hannele about to marry the Herr Regierungsrat, a "witty, gallant old Roman of a man" whose bigness and carelessness are based on the postwar "indifference and hopelessness that fatalistically laughs at itself," and whose chief attraction to Hannele is that he makes her feel like a "queen in exile." Hepburn wins her from this "false exaltation" during a holiday trip to a glacier. Their realistically rather ludicrous drive to the foot of the glacier with a party of tourists, and the stages of the climb on foot past restaurants and people until Hepburn surmounts the dangerous ice, leading a few others, while Hannele remains behind frightened and concerned, is, nevertheless, a triumph over the doll-death of subservience to love, and an experience of the extreme non-humanity of the ice that need not be repeated. It leads to a very human comedy of reconciliation. As they return to the social "cage" below, Hannele and he argue his insistence on honor and obedience rather than love above the noise of the car. Later on he sums up the doll metaphor in explaining the cause of his opposition to love, and again he gets in answer her challenge to male dominance.

> " . . . If a woman loves you, she'll make a doll out of you. She'll never be satisfied till she's made your doll. And when she's got your doll, that's all she wants. And that's what love means. And so, I won't be loved. And I won't love. I won't have anybody loving me. It is an insult. I feel I've been insulted for forty years: by love, and the women who've loved me. I won't be loved. And I won't love. I'll be honoured and I'll be obeyed: or nothing."
>
> "Then it'll most probably be nothing," said Hannele sarcastically. "For I assure you, I've nothing but love to offer."
>
> "Then keep your love," said he.
>
> She laughed shortly.
>
> "And you?" she cried. "You! Even suppose you *were* honoured and obeyed. I suppose all you've got to do is to sit there like a sultan and sup it up."
>
> "Oh, no, I have many things to do. And woman or no woman, I'm going to start to do them."

Hepburn plans two "moves to the future" that Hannele must concur in. He will go to East Africa to join a man who is "breaking his neck to get three thousand acres under control"—Lawrence's colony idea. And after a few more experiments and observations, he will do "a book on the moon," the latter phrase an amusing corollary of Lawrence's defense of his "moonshine" at the beginning of *Fantasia of the Unconscious.*

While Lawrence's mood in "The Captain's Doll" is dominantly "comic," and while there is considerable self-criticism in the characterization of Hepburn and the forceful statement of Hannele's position, the story comes from his intense conviction of the hopelessness of life in postwar Europe, the absolute necessity of making a new, religiously oriented start in self-chosen exile, and the precedence that male leadership in such an effort must take over love and marriage. His own wife's opposition is heard in Hannele's argument. It had begun to be heard quite clearly in Ursula in *Women in Love,* and it continues to provide him with the major challenge of his theocratic-tending vision.

6 🐟

Though a diary note records Lawrence's beginning of *Mr. Noon* in May of 1920, the technique and mood are so like the early part of *The Lost Girl*, one wonders if this, too, was not revision and expansion of earlier work. His saying very little about the story in his letters, and his telling his agent that it might be cut as much as he liked for serialization, suggest that Lawrence did not think very highly of it. He abandoned it after finishing Part I, which was published posthumously.[6] There was an urgent reason for abandonment in the demands on his interest and energies of *Aaron's Rod*, which, following his dominant present tendency, explored his recent personal experience in postwar Italy, the chaos of contemporary political and intellectual life, and his belief in the necessity of vitalistic leadership. In comparison *Mr. Noon* looks like a potboiling bit of fun that did not come off. After a realistic comedy of manners beginning, the tone becomes more and more extravagantly burlesque, and the old-fashioned asides to the reader more flagrantly mocking, until at the end the whole illusion collapses.

> Oh, *Deus ex machina,* get up steam and come to our assistance, for this obtuse-angled triangle looks as if it would sit there stupidly forever in the spare bedroom at Eakrast. Which would be a serious misfortune to us, who have to make our bread-and-butter chronicling the happy marriage and the prize-taking cauliflower of Emmie and Walter George, and the further lapses of Mr. Noon. . . .
>
> Is our prayer in vain? We fear it is. The god in the machine is perhaps too busy elsewhere. Alas, no wheel will incline its axis in our direction, no petrol will vaporise into spirit for our sakes. Emmie, and Childe Rolande and Mr. Noon may sit forever in the Eakrast bedroom.
>
> Well, then, let them. Let them go to hell. We can at least be as manly as Walter George, in our heat of the moment.

Three more paragraphs promise a second part about Mr. Noon, an elopement, and a *decree nisi;* but the "go to hell" seems overwhelmingly final.

Lawrence was working with the characteristic elements of his vitalistic parable. He begins with a marriage, uneasily based on intellectual in-

---

6. *A Modern Lover,* 1934.

terests, in which the wife of forty, forgetful of her youthful "spooning" past, is unfulfilled, and then introduces a potential savior in the person of Mr. Noon. Intellectually Noon is so brilliant in mathematics and music that he might have continued at Cambridge on a fellowship. But he is unexpectedly unambitious, and has returned to his Midlands home to teach and devote himself to the nocturnal life of spooning more or less accepted by the people as a prelude to marriage. He sees no relationship between this and the perfection of music and mathematics.

> "Mathematics is mathematics, the plane of abstraction and perfection. Life is life, and is neither abstraction nor perfection. . . . Life is incompatible with perfection, or with infinity, or with eternity. You've got to turn to mathematics, or to art."

Lawrence's gambit with this rather smug dichotomy is to involve him in farcical contact with the absolute side of local mores.

A former male spooner who is now the father of a grown daughter, catches him in intercourse with his daughter, relentlessly hunts down his identity, and reports him to the school authorities. Summoned before them for a hearing, he resigns before they have the chance to discharge him. The girl herself has fled to a friend's house in a neighboring village with a "stomach ache." She is worried over what her fiancé will think of her escapade because she may lose the chance of marriage. Noon is talked into a sense of responsibility for her by the wife of the intellectual, though in the promiscuous chaos of spooning it might be hard to determine paternity. He arrives at the girl's sanctuary just in time to form an "eternal" triangle that is beyond his mathematical powers. He finds her fiancé and her in sentimental rapport, aided and abetted by a cozy young couple with a baby.

> The course of their true love was as plain as a pike-staff. It led to a little house in a new street, and an allotment-garden not far off. And the way thither, with kisses and the little plannings, was as sweet as if it had led to some detached villa, or even to one of the stately homes in England. It is all the same in the end; safe as houses, as the saying goes. Emmie was now taking the right turning, such as you have taken, gentle reader, you who sit in your comfortable home with this book on your knee. Give her, then,

your blessing, for she hardly needs it anymore, and play a tune for her on the piano:

> The cottage homes of England,
> How thick they crowd the land.

Or, if that isn't good enough for you:

> The stately homes of England
> Are furnished like a dream.

The potentially serious vitalistic counterplot to this involves Noon's relations with the intellectual husband and wife, who admire his gifts, and do not seriously condemn his playing with life, though she thinks he is cruel to the girls. The socialist husband, agnostic and sensually tolerant, receives Lawrence's favorite epithet for sensual dilettantes: something of a Christ with a touch of the goat. His reading consists of the rather unlively *The New Age* and *The New Statesman*; he enjoys teasing the girls going by to church. His wife and he seem an ideal couple, but he is always "slightly forcing her attention," and while she is pleased because this keeps her from feeling lonely, she also feels she will go mad with irritation.

Noon is clearly her potential Lawrencean vitalistic rescuer, but here, too, Lawrence's tone is not entirely serious. Noon and she meet in the natural setting that characterizes Lawrence's serious approaches to fulfillment. They walk together in the park of an abandoned hall in late winter, the neglected ponds and gardens and the late winter season of half ruin, half early flowers constituting his familiar setting for cultural and vital decadence. When she challenges his advanced view that marriage is a matter of mutual freedom, and tells him from her mature experience that he will think differently later, he is moved by her "strange, changed, almost uncanny" face and her intensity. Lawrence's development of this sounds irresistibly like burlesque of his own, as well as romantic, seriousness. She is

the soft, full, strange, unmated Aphrodite of forty, who had been through all ideal raptures of love and marriage and modern motherhood, through it all, and through the foam of the fight for freedom, the sea of ideal right and wrong, and now was emerging, slowly, mysteriously, ivory-white and soft, woman still, leaving the sea of all her past, nay, the sea of all the extant human world behind her, and rising with dark eyes of age and experience, and a few grey hairs among the dark; soft, full-bodied, mature, and woman still, unpossessed, unknown of men, unfathomed, unexplored, belonging nowhere and to no-one, only to the unknown distance, the untrodden shore of all the sea of all the unknown knowledge.

Noon's feeling for her and this lofty potentiality is destroyed when a disagreeable-tempered heifer charges her, and his unheroic saving of her involves his undignified retrieval of his coat. After this, she seems to Noon only a shattered, elderly woman whom he pities. And she suffers a self-conscious, humiliated revulsion.

Poor Noon is completely frustrated by the imperfect perfections of life. The lively, undemanding girl has made it smoothly into marriage, and the wise middle-aged Aphrodite has collapsed. If Lawrence thought of a development in the second part that would make Noon the vitalistic rescuer of the latter—the elopement and *decree nisi* he promised—he may ultimately have felt there was nowhere to go after such an outburst of farce.

7 🐦

The Lost Girl, completed and published in 1920, was begun at the same time as *The Rainbow* and *Women in Love* in early 1913, and laid aside in favor of them. The technique of the first part is very different from that of those novels, and most of the later work. Witty, satirical chats with the reader burlesque that archaic novelistic manner and may reflect the exuberance of his gift of mimicry, the not very delicate mockery that was one side of his early relation with Frieda, and the "jeering" he told Edward Garnett he could fall into when he was not his religious self. In such later work as "The Ladybird" this tone of satirical attack had been modulated into irony that never violates the distance from the reader, or the underlying seriousness. When he returned to *The Lost Girl,* after, one must remember, the suppression of *The Rainbow* and some years of severe poverty, with *Women in Love* unpublished, he seems also to have hoped it would be a means to greater popularity. In December 1919, just before beginning revision, he told his publisher,

Martin Secker, that it would make "a perfect selling novel." After revision he wrote ironically to Catherine Carswell: "I think it's quite amusing: and quite moral. She's not morally lost, poor darling." Then, from nonmoral Italy, he was much less sure of the novel's effect in his comments to Secker:

> Being out here, I find it good—a bit wonderful, really. But when I get a sort of "other people" mood on me, I don't know at all. I feel I don't know at all what it will be like to other people. Somehow it depends on what centre of oneself one reads it from. I wish I could get it serialized—in England too. One *must* make some money these days; or perish.

Whatever the reasons for the early comic tone, it is clear that Lawrence could present his vitalistic reversal of values with as much thought-provoking comic blandishment as Shaw, when he chose.

In the first six chapters Lawrence traces Alvina Houghton's growth from childhood to her young woman's failure to find happiness and a really significant place in the world. Paralleling her failure is her father's failure as a person and as a business man. His decline begins with his inheritance of a prosperous dry-goods business in 1880, the year to which Lawrence assigned his native Midlands' industrialization in *The Rainbow*. In a business sense, his failure originates in his stocking unusual fabrics and styles to which industrial Woodhouse prefers mediocrity. Instead of accepting this reality, or effectively rebelling, the father turns to a life of fantasy. Lawrence's satirical comment on him is "Sad indeed that he died before the days of Freud." His wife is left alone in the monstrous, dark mahogany, Houghton matrimonial bed. Heart disease resulting from nervous repression eventually kills her.

The morale of the home depends on the governess, Miss Frost, who judges the father as lacking in human feeling, and in crisis takes "the human line" strongly and generously. Order in the shop is maintained by Miss Pinnegar, who is loyal and unselfish in her way, but lacks Miss Frost's humanity and forthrightness, and eventually judges Alvina's behavior harshly and rigidly from the middle-class code, dubbing her a "lost girl." In this disintegrated family situation, Alvinia's womanliness is defeated step by step. Lawrence gives her as a sign of vital potentiality his mark of the rebel, a quality of irony and mockery that alternates with the good-humored straightforwardness Miss Frost teaches her.

Her first Lawrencean choice comes at twenty-three when she is attracted to a man who is physically very vivid and alive. Miss Frost revokes his influence by making the attraction a question of choosing between sensuality or the loving heart—the dichotomy required by her old-fashioned idealism.

Out of purely random resistance, Alvina decides to become a nurse. During training she seems to thrive, but her hard nurse's quips conceal her basic hysteria. She is profoundly shocked by her experience of what Lawrence calls "the human social beast" in the lying-in hospital and in the slums. In her father high-mindedness has reached a point of pathetic but anti-human quixotry. In her it is stretched beyond the breaking point.

She fails as a nurse in Woodhouse because the people cannot afford her and cannot think of her, a Houghton, as a nurse. After her mother's death, she moves into her room with its massive, immovable bed that suggests the defeat from which Alvina is to be saved. The power that can save her is partially revealed in the miners, who seem to have another kind of knowledge than that encouraged by her training. It is humiliated and subjected in these "slaves toiling in an underworld," but it is "ponderous and inevitable." Sensing that this power, if unleashed, would be "disastrous in an era of light" in which it has no master, she feels that what is needed is a "Dark Master" from the underworld (an echo of Psanek of "The Ladybird").

Almost in panic for fear of becoming an old maid, she again attempts relationship with a man from her provincial English world, Arthur Witham, the plumber, who has a touch of vital potentiality in his physical attractiveness. But, working for his own self-importance and power through money, he cannot achieve a real connection with her as a person, and fails the Lawrencean test of touch. Her realization of the importance of this causes Alvina to break with his brother, Alfred, whose education and rise in the world give him an "inhuman, half-cultured abstraction" that makes his courtship a travesty of feeling.

Turning once more to the solution of work, Alvina thinks it would be better to "be a slave outright" and so at least in contact with "the whims and impulses" of human beings, than to serve some "mechanical routine of modern work"; and Lawrence marks this turning point in her life with a little essay against ordinary people and fates.

> Now so far, the story of Alvina is commonplace enough. It is more or less the story of thousands of girls. They all find work. It is the ordinary solution of everything. And if we were dealing with an ordinary girl we should have to carry on mildly and dully down the long years of employment; or, at the best, marriage with some dull schoolteacher or office-clerk.
>
> But we protest that Alvina is not ordinary. Ordinary people, ordinary fates. But extraordinary people, extraordinary fates. Or else no fate at all. The all-to-one-pattern modern system is too much for most extraordinary individuals. It just kills them off or throws them disused aside.
>
> There have been enough stories about ordinary people. I should think the Duke of Clarence must even have found Malmsey nauseating, when he choked and went purple and was really asphyxiated in a butt of it. And ordinary people are no Malmsey. Just ordinary tap-water. And we have been drenched and deluged and so nearly drowned in perpetual floods of ordinariness, that tap-water tends to become a really hateful fluid to us. We loathe its out-of-the-tap tastelessness. We detest ordinary people. We are in peril of our lives from them: and in peril of our souls too, for they would damn us one and all to the ordinary. Every individual should, by nature, have his extraordinary points. But nowadays you may look for them with a microscope, they are so worn-down by the regular machine-friction of our average and mechanical days.
>
> There was no hope for Alvina in the ordinary. . . .

Ironically it is her father's last speculative endeavor to retrieve the family fortune by engaging in a déclassé cinema venture that provides her means of escape. The showman promoter of this venture, Mr. May, at first seems vital as well as comical in his rebellion against his wife's vegetarianism and Fabian eugenics. But in his intimacy with Alvina he avoids physical advances, liking the "angel and the angel-mother" in women, and despising what Lawrence has him vulgarly call "coming-on-ness."

Alvina enjoys being déclassé in her life as pianist at the cinema. She is interested by the lack of moral squeamishness and the oddity of the stage performers, particularly the Japanese tattooed man, who has an irresistibly Lawrencean serpent around his loins and an eagle on his shoulders, emblems very close to the plumed serpent of Mexico. Like the miners, he suggests the danger of a masterless unleashing of the vital, unconscious force with his frightening look of "toadlike lewdness."

Alvina's salvation through the Red Indian, Natcha-Kee-Tawara troupe apparently owes something to both vaudeville and Lawrence's interest in the psychology of nationality and region. It is handled with an amusing mixture of realism and symbolism. Artistically the troupe are fairly nondescript purveyors of melodrama. The symbolism lies partly in the nature of their brotherhood. Their nationalities range to the north and south of mid-Europe: Max, German Swiss; Louis, French Swiss; and Geoffrey, Alpine French. Cicio, as an Italian the most southern, is the Lawrencean alien man of vitalistic potentiality. The leader of the four young men, holding them together despite their different natures, is an older, Continental European woman who, with considerable ambiguity later on, is called "Madame." Their act farcically allegorizes Lawrence's reconciliation of the white, northern consciousness with the dark, southern one, the modern disintegrated culture with the primitive but more vitally powerful one, when the white prisoner, freed through the compassion of the Indian wife, Kishwegin, kills the bear, and kneels hand-in-hand with her beside her dead husband's body—on the vaudeville level the triumph of love and the white man over primitive danger.

The remainder of the novel develops Alvina's relationship with Cicio. This becomes such a complex exploration of the cultural and psychological difficulties inherent in the relationship that the characteristics of Lawrence's most serious work supersede the extravagance of his comic beginning. Cicio is not only accused of evils that are merely cultural stereotyping; he contains real limitations. The question becomes: Are his passional, vital virtues great enough to make Alvina's rebellion, quite real suffering, and exile worth it all?

Even in the brotherhood of the troupe, Cicio is something of an outlaw, impolite, inconsiderate, and aloof. But Alvina feels that he has an instinctive good-naturedness. She knows that only the conventions of her culture make his expressing himself best in gesture and grimace seem "childlike and stupid." His animal, catlike self does frighten her at times, but when she contrasts the colliers, tramping gray and heavy to see the troupe's parade, with the vividness of Cicio trotting softly on his horse "like a flower on its stem," she rejects the Woodhouse attitude that the troupe are mountebanks while "the utilitarian town is eternal."

The conventional pessimistic expectations of Cicio are confirmed within the troupe when he, insulted, attempts to knife Max. The northern Max calls him a dirty "Eyetalian" who understands nothing. The fight seems also to illustrate a real problem of lack of *esprit* in Cicio as Lawrence weighs the value of his individuality against the dangers of anarchy.

When Cicio visits Alvina on the day of her father's death, the first invasion of the house by her deliverer coincides with the dissolution of her last family tie. She now feels a "dark flicker of ascendancy" in him. Her "soul" sinks from her, and she can answer his subtle questioning by acknowledging that she loves him. But even the Madame's cosmopolitan experience questions the feasibility of their relationship. She questions Cicio sharply about his intentions and warns Alvina that she knows these "wandering Italian laborers" and their conceit when they have a chance to rise in the world. She sketches for Alvina the social problem of being the wife of an Italian laborer in England, and even finds in his last name a bad sound that "sends life down instead of lifting it."

At the funeral it is Cicio's turn at the game of cultural criticism. To him the English are barbarians. The working class are all "raw angles and harshness," like their weather. Even Alvina, grave, pale, pinched, and reserved looking, is part of the uncongeniality of the scene, and only his obstinacy keeps him near her.

When Alvina rejects the stereotyped, anti-life plans the village would make for her, and joins Cicio, and the troupe as pianist, she is given a feast of affiliation. She is a white daughter, sister, and wife adopted into the dark way. Given a new name arrived at through a polylingual, perhaps ribald gamut—Vaali, Viale, Le Petit Chemin, L'allée, and finally apparently an affirmative Allaye—she becomes an intimate member of this disreputable international league.

The Englishwoman fated in her culture to become an old maid, feels at first like a slave in sexual intercourse with Cicio, though she is aware of his "lustrous, dark beauty." In public she is offended by his giving her no attention. Working reluctantly at cooking and sewing for the troupe, and seeing in a blowsy landlady one possible outcome of her rejection of respectability, she moves further into revulsion, excludes Cicio from her room, and decides to return to Woodhouse. Cicio, accompanying her, must make a second conquest of the English way.

Miss Pinnegar brings to bear on Alvina an outraged sense of propriety emotionally reinforced by invocation of the memory of the dead father. Her final moral judgment is that Alvina is a lost girl. Her final sophistry is that Alvina's living in an unmarried state makes it hard for her in Woodhouse. Cicio's disappointed reaction to the news that debts will probably take the house from Alvina supports Miss Pinnegar's suspicion that he is merely mercenary, and Lawrence explains his attitude as a "fundamental instinct of the meaningless of material prosperity" disturbed by his boyhood poverty and overlaid by his little education, which makes money and independence an *idée fixe*.

Even Mr. May's quasi-liberal values are offended when he learns of Alvina's traveling with the troupe in an unmarried state. When he calls this white slave traffic on the Madame's part, Cicio drives him from the house. The final triumph of the Tawara brotherhood over the Houghton-Woodhouse past is Alvina's sexual fulfillment with Cicio in the marriage bed in which James Houghton had so disastrously failed her mother. The last Woodhouse pressure upon Alvina comes through her lawyer, who will salvage something for her out of the indebtedness of her father's estate if she will stay. Though Alvina renounces both the material and moral claim, her association of money, prestige, and love is so strong that she feels she will be humiliated when the troupe learns she has no fortune. Respectable Woodhouse, defeated at direct moral and economic suasion, employs detectives to inquire about the brotherhood's sleeping arrangements. When the resulting tension darkens Alvina's relations with the troupe, Cicio contemptuously views her hopeless feeling as part of an habitual "can't."

Alvina's separation from the troupe because of her desire to be alone and free reflects the Lawrencean revulsion into sheer individuality. For a time she is happy in manless freedom as a nurse. But the conventional world soon traps her through her acquaintance with a bachelor physician of fifty-three, to whom she becomes the object of his fantasy of a cozy marriage in which he can be proud of his wife and his house. Her rejection of him is made difficult by his temper, a manifestation of the instability of a personality based on "social bullying and human denial." When he collapses into abject apology and a plea for forgiveness, she can only pity the "hysterical child under the authoritative man."

Lawrence creates her counter-reconciliation with Cicio through an incident that sardonically extends their cultural, psychological conflict. One of the opponents of Alvina's marriage to the doctor is Mrs. Tuke, who is herself caught between two ways and worlds. Her head, with its dark eyes, arched nose, and black hair, is like those on "lovely Syracusan coins." About to have a child, she admits that neither her flesh nor her mind wants it. She is particularly tormented at night, when she begs Alvina to stay with her, and studies the blood-red stone in her ring as if reading something. On one such night they hear Cicio playing his mandolin in an appeal to Alvina. Mrs. Tuke is fascinated, and asks her husband, who hates emotional Italian music, to come into the house so as not to frighten away the singer. At the end of one song, with its "clamorous, animal-like yearning," she follows the serenade tradition by asking Cicio to enter to take his rose. When he will not, she sends Alvina to him and is thus the means of *rapprochement*. The beginning of childbirth pains for Mrs. Tuke coincides with this *rapprochement;* though she cannot herself participate in it, she is released from her not caring, and insists on seeing the reality of Cicio's yearning for his woman. Her husband comes to her simply because her cries have disturbed him in his study. Though she is fond of him, she cannot stand his presence, feeling herself the victim of a life of machinelike responses.

Yet even she eventually regards Alvina's attraction to Cicio as a dangerous atavism. It is highly significant Lawrence, if frustrating to the reader who expects a conclusive reconciliation, that Alvina now runs away from both the insufficient doctor and Cicio, with whom she has promised to go to Italy. She seeks the ultimate Lawrencean release from the conflict of relationship, isolation in nature. She sits on the cliffs above the sea, and walks on the moors, in perfect, "almost paradisal" liberty, turning back towards human relationship only when the weather becomes bad and she dreams that her first, youthful fiancé reproaches her for arriving too late to board their ship. Cicio overcomes Alvina's recurrent doubt and revulsion only by exercising a "snakelike, mesmeric" power, as if he is "the possessor of sensual secrets"—a ritual aspect of vitalistic extinction of consciousness. Through it she experiences a "nonchalance as deep as sleep" but, in Lawrence's endless extension of the conflict with consciousness, so dark and sweet that she feels it must be evil.

After their marriage, Alvina sees in Cicio's pale, northernized cousin in London the disintegration of the vital man that can be accomplished by her culture. He patronizes the fallen Alvina but is jealous of Cicio's "stealthy, leopardlike pride." When they leave for Italy, Alvina notices the eagerness of Cicio's Italian friends to embrace and kiss the man who is taking the "dark way" of return, so that he is "the one victor" over the north.

On the steamer, Cicio's strangeness gives him a "wistful nobility" that for the time being places him beyond all ideas of class inferiority. England, across the "wintry" water, looks like "a coffin slowly submerging." Alvina is happy when they reach southern France, half Alpine, half southern, but Cicio is distressed by her hopeful anticipation of Italy. The rest of the novel explores the difficulty both for the English sensibility and southern, vital power in an Italy that contains its own decadence and, in Cicio's remote mountain home, primitive, soul-killing conditions.

One kind of misuse of the vital Italian nature by the northern world is seen in Cicio's uncle, who in his youth had been an artist's model in London, and recalls being painfully posed for a crucifixion scene. With the money earned in such perverse use of his magnificent body, he had built a big house in the mountains that is now womanless, run-down, and cheerless. The journey from Naples to this house takes on mythic proportions in the movement away from civilized conditions of life (a movement repeated in "The Princess"), from bus to cart to climbing on foot. It places Alvina at a catastrophic opposite pole to England. The region itself is inimical to life, as if it lay too far back in the vitalistic evolutionary scale, or, better, were a triumph of sheer chaotic savagery over the life force. It is one of those "negative localities that refuse a living culture," and convey a sense of "ancient gods who knew human sacrifice." Alvina's soul is tortured by this, and her happiness is very like despair. The people are like "lost, forlorn aborigines," and seem to need a higher being to serve. During the season of rain and sleet, the place becomes horrible to Alvina. The natives keep themselves alive by "constant, dumb, elemental work," but Alvina lacks this resource, falls ill, feels that she will die here, and thinks of escape to England or America. She re-experiences the power of Cicio's love, but after she discovers that she is pregnant, living makes almost too great a demand on her, and she wishes for a continuous state of unconsciousness of her surroundings.

Such a situation is hardly either a primitivistic or vitalistic happy ending. At Christmas the native music evokes the "magic of the untamed heathen past," but Alvina also recognizes the peasants' mutual distrust. By contrast there is in the northern soul something "free, touched with divinity." Yet Cicio's uncle's story reminds her of the perversity of that soul, as does the insulting letter she receives from her jilted English doctor. Watching Cicio talk with their neighbors, she realizes that he has none of the English sense of home, his "active, mindful self" belonging in the piazza with the men, yet she is indignant at his unwillingness to engage in a discussion with a woman. When spring brings lovely mountain flowers, she feels that to keep her sanity she must shun human intercourse and keep to the open air. But at times even the flowers repel her with their suggestion of a cruel pagan world. Even the cultivation of the grapes seems a degrading worship.

Then the war begins. Cicio's resolve to volunteer seems at first a cruel triumph over her. But she clings to her knowledge of his love, and sees that his decision is based on his "essential hopelessness of spirit." He wants to take her away, but cannot. She rallies him from his sense of doom with a vitalistic affirmation. If he does not return from the war, it will be because he does not want to. He responds with the anti-fate, fighting, Lawrencean position: he will come back to her—be damned to them all—and they will go to America.

The novel that started out in 1913 as a high-spirited satire of the ordinary fate of the English girl—vitalistically degrading marriage, spin-sterhood and a routine job—endèd in 1920 in escape to an almost hopeless opposite situation. Italy here is not the wonderfully nonmoral environ-ment Lawrence so welcomed on his first visit during 1912-13, when he and Frieda were in the early phase of their relationship, but Picinisco in December of 1919, shortly after his war-long wish to leave England was realized. He wrote of it to a friend:

> It is a bit staggeringly primitive. You cross a great stony river bed, then an icy river on a plank, then climb unfootable paths, while the ass struggles behind with your luggage. . . . The village 2 miles away, a sheer scramble no road whatever. . . . Withal, the sun shines hot and lovely, but the nights freeze: the mountains round are snowy and very beautiful.
>   Orazio is a queer creature—so nice, but *slow* and tentative. I shall have to dart round. . . . If the weather turns bad, I think we really must go on, to Naples or Capri. Poor Orazio!

Though his indication of unfavorableness is here the casual one of the traveler, Picinisco was a crisis in Lawrence's personal search—for health, for healing of his own deeply wounded being, for a new world and life. Most of his postwar experience of Italy went into his next novel, *Aaron's Rod*, where it is explored in the more complex terms of his conviction of the need of religious leadership, developed during the war, and partially dramatized in "The Ladybird."

8

Aaron's Rod is Lawrence's last novel before he left Europe in the exile compelled by his revulsion. The character who represents him and the postwar move to Italy that was his preparatory step is Rawdon Lilly. The man whose possible redemption through Lilly the novel explores, the miner Aaron Sisson, leaves a situation in England not unlike that of Lawrence's father, though his flute playing gives him a classless, creative potentiality the father did not have.

Like Ursula of *The Rainbow*, and Birkin of *Women in Love*, Aaron can make no compromise. In profound revulsion against the status quo of the labor movement and marriage, and the postwar heritage of destructiveness, he commits the unpardonable sin of abandoning his family (he does provide them with an income), experiences step by step the decadence that extends outward from his village origin, and encounters the theory of power and leadership Lawrence was working out as a means of ordering such chaos. Under attack as the central cause of chaos is the love ideal.

His decision to leave his family is made during the first postwar Christmas season. The peace has only resulted in a new atmosphere of menace because of the release of inner tensions. His wife reproaches him for caring about the colliers, who simply want more money and will probably callously vote him out as secretary of the union. The quarreling of his daughters over the Christmas tree ornaments is part of the postwar cultural discontinuity and release of tension. Millicent, getting the blue ornament which has lasted unbroken from Aaron's childhood, perversely wonders how much abuse it can stand, and throws it wildly until it smashes. When Aaron plays sixteenth century Christmas music, its mood of peace is contradicted by his maddened exasperation. His playing of rapid, brilliant Mozart is a means of escaping the family dissension and releasing his feelings.

In the crowds of Christmas shoppers Aaron senses a "neurasthenic desire for excitement" as an outlet for hostility. When he shops for candles and candy, he finds little because of continuing shortages and rationing. His revulsive mood is intensified at the pub. The landlady is a passionate, attractive woman, but loves intellectual discussions, and sets the men to arguing over the labor problem. Aaron feels even more strongly what Lawrence calls his secret malady—a "strained, unacknowledged opposition to his surroundings," an "irrational, exhausting withholding" of himself. He would like to feel his senses "flow into darkness," but is in a "cold, white fury." He sees in the Hindu doctor's argument the same perversity as the landlady's—benevolent words concealing an intention to destroy the man in one. "Modern good will is righteous bullying." The landlady's benevolence breaks down when she angrily blames the doctor for causing Aaron's refusal to stay after closing time.

Wandering aimlessly in the darkness, Aaron comes upon the young, upper-class people who are celebrating the season at the home of one of the partners in the colliery firm. Out of their post-dinner, bored, nervous talk of happiness, they have sought excitement in lighting with candles a fir tree outside the house. The scene is strongly ironic. One of the girls begins a ritual dance in worship of the tree, against the anachronistic background of a pit-bank on fire and the panting of machinery. The flames of the candles do succeed in giving a "perpendicular aspiration" to the night, and Aaron appears just as the scene is becoming harmonious. This vitalistic harmony is broken by the hysterical laughter of the young heir to the mines, Jim Bricknell, who is in the stage of intoxication which gives no release from "maddening self-consciousness." This is the first of a series of contacts between Aaron and these money-and-prestige-possessing young people, who offer him the popular freedoms of the Twenties.

In London, after leaving his family, Aaron puts his flute to a best practical-choice use in the orchestra at the opera. Here the young people of the Bricknell party begin to patronize him. Josephine is a woman of vitalistic potential in her foreign, dark look, attributed to her having some American Indian blood, and her awareness of the sham of life in *Aida*— the makeup, the fat women, the eunuchlike tenor. The conversation about her turns on whether she should leave her husband and live with Scott, with whom she has carried on a nervous affair based on "soul sympathy and emotional excitement." Her husband is willing to have them try such an arrangement because he thinks it cannot last long. At this point Rawdon Lilly's Lawrencean judgments of decadence, mingled with sympathy for rebels, begin. He is sarcastic about the relationship of such an affair to eternity, and at the same time is concerned that they should not, by rashly unconventional behavior, put themselves at the mercy of the world. His antagonism to Jim Bricknell rises from Jim's making love of woman the supreme value. When Aaron joins the group, Jim takes great satisfaction in having captured one of the common people, and exults in the idea of a revolutionary victory by Labor. Lilly, on the other hand, believes in the necessity of a revolution in relationship. Love has become a vice illustrated by Jim's simultaneous desire to be loved, and delighted anticipation of violence. The anti-love theme is developed in the failure of relations between Josephine and Aaron. When she asks him what his reasons for leaving his family are, she does not get the expected answer, that he is seeking the love he could not achieve with his wife. Rather, he says, he had felt forced to love when he no longer felt love; he is at a "center of indifference." Josephine is in the nihilistic stage of the love ideal. Though she tells herself that she wants to marry and feel sure of something, she really would like "a great upheaval." Aaron, frightened by this nihilistic desire, takes her cold hand in his "warm, living" grasp—Lawrence's ritual of vitalistic salvation from decadence and death—but refuses the "love game" of a kiss he does not want.

Jim Bricknell's incapability of vitalistic relationship is revealed during his visit to the Lillys.[7] Jim argues that Christ is the "finest product of Western culture," love and sacrifice being the supreme values. Lilly takes the Lawrencean position that one does not want "crucifixion *ad infinitum*"; he opposes the subjection of feeling to an abstract principle. When Jim's belief in love manifests itself in increasing intimacy with Lilly's wife and an assignation with a "nice" girl who will "do anything he wants," Lilly has it out with him. When Jim strikes him, Lilly sees in the blow the "maudlin deliberateness" that comes from hysteria. Jim's insistence that he really likes Lilly more than any other man he has known, gives his behavior a Judaslike perverseness. The scene is not, however, an unambiguous triumph for Lilly. Tanny's reaction is that Lilly should be willing to realize how his criticism may make people feel. Lilly will admit no fault, but she has the last word (saying what Frieda probably said): "You shouldn't try to make a little Jesus of yourself, coming so near to people, wanting to help them."

Lawrence now brings his two vitalistic protagonists together—Aaron, the inarticulate but creative lower-class man in revulsion from the love ideal; and Lilly, who, having replaced that ideal with a counter-concept, may be able to guide him. The action is symbolic of vitalistic death and resurrection, and brotherhood, from the beginning. Lilly, defeated in the relationship with Jim, and alone while Tanny is away, watches from his room the draft horses that bring produce to the market, and the spontaneous play of the brawny porters and the page boy they tease. Seeing

---

7. The situation probably reflects, again, the troubled friendship with Middleton Murry.

Aaron, partly drunk, partly ill, collapse on the pavement, he brings him to his room. Aaron's illness is essentially psychosomatic. Having finally given in to loving Josephine, he has been broken by the thought of his wife and children. Lilly laughs at his concern over what is not active infidelity but his seduction by Josephine. Restoration comes through the Lawrencean ritual of vitalistic brotherhood. Massaging Aaron with oil, he works "mindlessly" in a "sort of incantation" until the spark returns to Aaron's eyes and he falls into a healing sleep.

Pondering the ultimate possibility of guiding Aaron, Lilly experiences two doubts—Aaron will turn on him as Jim has done; Tanny is right in saying that he merely wants power over people. His answer to the second is that a "bit of healthy, individual authority" is better than the "mob power" of contemporary politics, and the "immolation of the individual for the public good." The remainder of the novel explores the consequences of this decision for authority. Aaron is both attracted to Lilly's ideas and sceptical, so that, with Tanny, he forms a strong testing of the necessity and beneficence of a vitalistic aristocracy, soon to be fully developed in the theocratic hierarchy and ritual of *The Plumed Serpent*.

Lilly reflects the advent of this American direction and symbolism in Lawrence's imagination when he feels that he would have loved the Aztecs and the Red Indians because they possessed the "living pride" with which he wishes to replace his sense of defeat and fear of betrayal. Contemporary society exists for children and their "sacred mothers." Life is given to men for a greater purpose than their present instrumentality, but it is now impossible for them to stick together without feeling criminal and betraying one another by "groveling before a woman."

Aaron agrees with Lilly's view of love and women, but ridicules his Lawrencean belief in the efficacy of new places. Lilly will be no more free and content in Malta than in London. "You're no more than a man who drops into a pub for a drink, to liven himself up a bit. Only you give it a lot of names, and make out as if you were looking for the philosopher's stone, or something like that." Lilly's defense is that this is not quite true: a new place does bring out something new in a man, and he believes that one may ultimately come into possession of his own soul, as the Buddhists teach, without, like them, ceasing to love as well as to hate. Despite his emotional outbursts, he feels that he is learning patience and peace. "You learn to be quite alone, and possess your own soul in isolation—and at the same time, to be perfectly *with* someone else." Aaron challenges this as "word-splitting" that he cannot understand. In implicit rebuttal Lawrence creates such a relationship after they stop talking and Lilly prepares the evening meal. Coming from the same district and class, he says, they feel an "almost uncanny" understanding of each other and at the same time a "brother-like hostility" that is not antipathy.

Lilly tries to explain his meaning further by a vitalistically symbolic analogy with Aaron's flute. While to Aaron the flute is a means of earning bread and butter, it is to Lilly Aaron's rod, capable of putting forth scarlet runners like those he imagines must have issued from the rod of Moses' brother, as a bond between them. When Aaron does not respond, Lilly reassures himself through myth by reading the "fantasies of Frobenius about Atlantis and the world before the flood," when the ideal and action, the spirit and the flesh had not been sundered.

A characteristic bit of Lawrencean strategy is the introduction, in the person of a soldier suffering from the trauma of war, of evidence of the need Lilly preaches. The voice of this man, even in casual conversational, is the anguished one of a man who has "seen and experienced too much of death" and does not know where to turn. Lilly wishes such men would wake up from an experience that he thinks, in the Lawrencean denial of psychological determinism, took place in "the automatic sphere as dreams do." He wants to get out of what he calls the "dream helplessness of the mass-psyche, that makes men base and obscene," as it had during the war since no man "awake and in possession of himself" would have used poison gas. When Aaron suggests that it is the wide-awake men who invent and use gas, and asks where they would be without it, Lilly tells him to get out. He will have no friends who do not fundamentally agree with him on such a point. Modern man can be saved only by "breaking the old ways of life without letting the pride and courage of life be broken." When Aaron leaves he knows that he does not intend to "obey" Lilly's "call to his soul," and even feels rather superior to his wordy, unworldly acquaintance.

Lawrence now develops Aaron's experience to a point at which he may be better able to understand Lilly. Finding himself, back in London, at loose ends, he revisits his home in the Midlands. In his wife's voice he hears the sickness of the strain between them. In a moment of "roused exposure" when she weeps, she is beautiful. But when she tries to gain his admission of wrong during their embrace, half rousing his passion and half horrifying him, and he will not betray himself by professing remorse he does not feel, her appearance of love is changed into passionate hate. Aaron turns away from home and England in final independence.

He is brought still closer to Lilly's position by experiencing the post-war decadence of Italy and the Englishmen who live there. At the house of the wealthy Sir William Franks, he has an experience and makes a judgment that resemble Lawrence's in postwar letters. Sir William and his lady know that the obsequiousness of their guests is only homage to success in making money. Even his decorations for war-work were prob-ably given primarily because of the money he contributed. He disap-proves of the dependence of Aaron, and Lilly, whom he knows, on Providence, advising "Providence plus a bank account." Lilly's working when the spirit moves him, without calculation of the market, tempts Providence. Sir William had, in his youth, taken his spirit in hand and harnessed it to "the work of productive labor." His attitude towards Lilly forces Aaron to take sides for the first time in his life, and by defending Lilly, to move a step nearer him.

Lady Franks views Aaron's having left his family as criminal selfish-ness. Aaron first defends it on Lawrencean vitalistic ground, as a reaction that was as "inevitable as birth or death." Then he makes a somewhat un-Lawrencean concession, since he knows he may some day need her help, by suggesting that there may be suffering and repentance beneath his defense, and so making her feel that she is getting on with her work of restoration of woman "to her natural throne." Afterward, leaving the house and entering the natural surroundings of the garden, he feels like a bird escaping a trap. As he looks at the Italian countryside with its "fear-less, violent city" of Novara, his "sleepy English nature" is startled into awareness that he must "wake from pathos, tragedy, and spasmodic pas-sion," and take on the responsibility of a new self.

At this point, after the experience of female dominance in the scene with Lady Franks, Lawrence turns to the extended exposition that links his technique to the older English tradition, and writes a long "essay" on the horror of the female will, and of men's yielding to it.[8] The passage does contribute a certain grounding to Aaron's now being able to explain the causes of his cultural and moral default. His wife's hatred had originated in her realization that beneath his manifest love he "withheld the central core" of himself. He realizes now that he had never intended to yield himself entirely because his being is pivoted on "isolate self-responsibility." This realization, and his decision to abide by it, is, in Lawrence's vitalistic symbolism, like the emergence of a "dark, night-lustrous chestnut from the green ostensibility of the burr."

In Milan Aaron begins his experience of a postwar religious and political chaos so complete that compromise is impossible. The beautiful cathedral no longer holds attention. It, and the money-based villa life of the Franks, are contradicted and threatened by the radical mob in the streets. As far as getting at the heart of the problem is concerned, the action of the Carabinieri is both brutal and stupidly ineffectual. The chaos is further explored when, cultivated by two aristocratic young Englishmen, Aaron experiences the social comedy of their friendly efforts to bridge the class differences of an Italian train while maintaining their insular aloofness and feeling of superiority.

Only the magic of Florence, in the south, makes Aaron forget his anger and the humiliation of his poverty. He feels Florence to be one of the world's "living centers" when he sees the statue of David and, nearby, the naked men of Bandinelli. When these statues were created, men had been at their "intensest, most naked" pitch, at the beginning of a new world. Since then they have become "puling and apologetic." Feeling himself at the beginning of a new life, Aaron believes that the "one, great manly quality" is fearlessness, though it is, perhaps, too "acrid" in a world that now contains "little worthy of challenge."

At this point of potentiality for the Lawrencean renaissance, Aaron

---

8. One wonders if this comes from a compulsion to explain and justify that may have originated in his discussion of his work with Frieda, who felt no compunction about challenging such views of women. Her situation was acutely involved.

re-encounters Lilly, but, in the endless convolutions of Lawrence's awareness of the difficulties of vitalistic salvation (and, surely, the possibilities of development of various thematic elements), he becomes involved in an affair with the Marchesa del Torre, an American woman from the Southern states who suggests, on the satirical, anti-love level, a "modern Cleopatra brooding Anthony-less." As a singer who has deliberately given up her career, she represents on the philosophical-religious level, the Lawrencean trauma of the vital, creative, willess self. Lawrence's handling of her salvation through Aaron is extremely ironic. The distinction of one kind of love as anathema, and another as salvation, becomes quite tenuous. The disruptive element, as from the beginnings of Lawrence's fiction, is the individual's, particularly the man's, revulsion from what seems an absorption of being.

Aaron's playing for the Marchesa metaphorizes this problem. Unlike the chords and harmonies, "sounds all sticking together," that the Marchesa dislikes, the notes of his flute are single and free. They express no human emotion, intention, or meaning, but are "wild like a bird's singing." The Marchesa feels that she has glimpsed "sunshine and pure air" through a "wall of emotions" and a "ghastly atmosphere of must-be." In a characteristic Lawrencean counterpoint of "social" betrayal to such an experience of equipoise in relationship, Aaron's pocket is picked by a gang of soldiers (as was Lawrence's). He resolves never to expose himself again in absolute trust of his fellow humans.

This latest revulsion is connected with the difficulty of intimate relationship by the conversation of Argyle, Lilly, Aaron, and the Marchesa's husband that follows. When Lilly attacks the assumption of mastery by modern women, the husband confesses that his wife has never loved him when he has taken the initiative. She has reversed the old way, with its insistence on the innocence of women before marriage so that "they should not begin the imposition of their desire" and "take men for their use." Only Lilly is not purely negative and satirical. His solution has been to remain in contact with his wife and friends but to know that he is essentially alone. Aaron, hearing the "simple amiability" of Lilly's laughter, realizes that he does succeed in "asking nothing and imposing nothing." Though he feels insulted by Lilly's way of "placing the gift of friendship quietly back in the giver's hands," he knows that he can depend on him for help so long as he does not break the "intrinsic isolation" of Lilly's soul.

Aaron now experiences in his relations with the Marchesa her tendency to take the initiative in love and use men that her husband had spoken of. He is terrified in the midst of desire, and knows that he must keep the power to recover himself. She relaxes her "druglike tension" and softens with a "womanly naturalness" only when she hears the music of the flute, which is a male voice, calling and half commanding her, telling her something, and soothing her soul to sleep. But even this makes Aaron wonder in still greater terror what she is going to ask of him. When the challenge of the flute frees her voice so that she sings again, pure and unhampered as she had always wanted to, the two voices of the music—a simple French love ballad—complete Lawrence's imaginative definition of vitalistic relationship. In intercourse Aaron recovers "the splendor of male passion-power and godliness." But there is no terminus to interference with such pure relationship. Even the problem of the displaced husband is "a thorn" in this latest flowering of Aaron's rod. The next time he and the Marchesa meet he is unable to cast his spell, and in passion she is small, childish, almost like a younger sister, and in "some strange way" against him. Out of his revulsion from this, he writes a challenging letter to Sir William Franks that is really a letter to himself. Lawrence calls it an expression of Aaron's greatest, or innermost truth: "I don't want my Fate or my Providence to treat me well. I don't want kindness or love. I don't believe in harmony and people loving one another. I believe in the fight and nothing else. I believe in the fight which is in everything. . . ."

Aaron's position represents one major aspect of Lawrence's way of experiencing life, as Lilly's has come to represent another. Both find a harmonious relation with woman impossible (though Lilly talks of remaining in contact while knowing he is essentially alone), an impossibility connected with female domination that is destructive of "male passion-power and godliness," or, in Aaron's latest experience, resembling Paul Morel's in *Sons and Lovers,* a somewhat incestuous weakness and passivity that is also devitalizing. But at this point in the novel Aaron is at the extreme individualistic, almost nihilistic position that rejects all claims of relationship for the fight in everything, a meta-phor that seems to link his feeling with the evolutionary life-death struggle inherent in vitalism. Lilly, on the other hand, seems a serene projection of the side of Lawrence that was the teacher, the dogmatic friend, and the Salvator Mundi to whom Ursula had objected in *Women in Love.* What he now preaches to the extremely intransigent Aaron is the subordination of one's being to the higher being that can be found in some men. The love and leadership problem, as it develops, contains a dualism that Lawrence seems unable to reconcile except in a very short-range way, the revulsions continuing relatively endlessly.

Recalling Lilly's saying that one must possess oneself, Aaron refuses to follow his instinct to hate the Marchesa, and avoids her. He experi-ences his greatest happiness alone in the Tuscan countryside of ancient cypresses, where his soul seems to leave him and go back to a "lost, subtle world they commemorate," a world in which men had other ways of knowing and feeling. When this isolation is exhausted, he returns to the Marchesa, and in intercourse achieves a deeper "obliviousness"; but he is caught again in the conflict between his desire for the "magic feeling of phallic immortality" and the "blight of his central life" the sexual relationship brings. He feels that she uses him as a "magic im-plement in her terrible priestess-craft," so that he is "God and victim" in one (perhaps a feeling of reversion to a lower point on the evolution-ary, religious scale).

Aaron retains but one tie with the past and his culture, the flute, and this is taken from him violently. Wandering alone at night, he encoun-ters the political violence of the city, three men bent over a body in a "tableau that is both medieval and modern." At a cafe he encounters Lilly and, worried about leaving his flute in his overcoat pocket since it may be stolen, settles into conversation about the violent Socialist demonstration the day before. Lilly rejects the economic and political solution of Socialism. It may be the "logically inevitable" next step, but in action it is essentially perverseness and criminality sanctioned by all the old ideals—liberty, brotherhood, the sanctity of human life, public-spiritedness, self-sacrifice, and unity and unanimity.[9] When he is

---

9. The position here regarding the perversion of idealism in revolutionary violence and nihilism resembles that in Albert Camus' *The Rebel.*

pressed to say whether his alternative is not nihilism, he answers in exasperation that after "sufficient extermination" people will elect a "healthy, energetic slavery." He follows this angry extreme with a whimsical smile and the admission that he really believes that "every man is a sacred, holy individual, never to be violated." He then propounds the Lawrencean theory, resembling vitalism's idea of the superman, that the "life-issue of inferior souls" must be committed to the "responsibility of superior souls."

His point about socialism's ultimate criminality is illustrated by the explosion of a bomb in the cafe. Aaron and he are unhurt, but the flute is broken. Aaron's reaction is to feel that with it the "reins of his life have slipped from his grasp." Lilly simply says with insouciant faith that the flute is a "waterplant that cannot be killed." (Again the attitudes of the two Lawrence "masks" seem to express his cyclical hope and despair.)

At the end of the novel, Aaron's rebellion has been brought the full road Lilly, and in a sense Lawrence, had already taken—the Midlands mining region; London and the Bohemian world with its moral anarchy; Italy with its expatriate, rich, English materialists, its rebellious but ineffectual Bohemians, and its violent political anarchy. He reviews his journey in a surrealistic Lawrencean dream of disaster in the love relationship that is worthy of Kafka. It begins in an underworld country in which the men are cannibalistic, the children uncared for, the women isolate and gray, and extends over a lake on which stakes marking the course strike his arm three times because he does not heed the warnings of the boatman—most overtly Aaron's three attempts at love with his wife, Josephine, and the Marchesa. As he draws near a lake-city (suggesting Mexico City), he awakes and only remembers seeing an idol that he identifies as the Phoenician sexual goddess, Astarte, whose image Birkin had stoned in *Women in Love*.

Aaron has no plan. His only attachment is to Lilly, of whom he is still critical, making what seems to be reflexively, among the masks, Lawrence's self-analysis. Lilly gives himself in friendship at first, then withdraws and reveals a basic indifference and an arrogance that "leaves his friends to their limitations." Yet Aaron feels that it would be better to yield to the mastery of such a nature, devilish as it seems, than to woman or to society. In a last encounter with Lilly, he experiences the other man's oscillation between north and south, his desire to seek "a new life-mode on another continent" yet his revulsion against seekers, and his inner peace when, in the countryside, his face has the "odd, distant look of some animal, awake and alert yet perfectly at one with its surroundings."

Lilly preaches to him that there are two great urges in life, love and power, and attacks him as one of those moderns who have "the love urge to which hatred and the violence of criminals and anarchists is the inevitable recoil." To avoid such neurasthenic reaction one must abandon the love urge and "develop the egg of one's own soul into the phoenix." This state of oneness of being, associated with resurrection of life, can only be developed by "never betraying or denying the Holy Ghost within." Love and passion, if Aaron must have them, must be understood as a life means, not a goal.

By continuing to criticize Lilly, Aaron calls up in him (and Lawrence) all his powers of self-justification. If, since we are not alone in the world, we must love and hate, we need not fix on one of these modes. If the power-urge seems dangerous, it need not be the "Nietzschean will-to-power, but a dark, living, fructifying power, not seeking any fixed state, but urging the displacement of the old and the inception of the new." Since there must be "someone who urges and someone who is compelled," there must be submission; but this need not be "a slave's submission to foolish and arbitrary power, but a deep, rich submission by women and men to the power-soul in the individual man."

Despite this stubborn devotion to the vitalistic leadership idea, Lawrence was not ready to create the necessary submission. When Aaron asks the overwhelming question toward which his whole relationship with Lilly has been tending—"And whom shall I submit to?"—Lilly is consistent with his paradox of freely chosen submission, and replies, "Your soul will tell you." Aaron does not reach the Promised Land. Neither does the Lawrencean Moses, Lilly. But the latter has fully imbibed the Old Testament theocratic lesson of the necessity of submission to the Lord and his prophet. And Lawrence was to reincarnate this prophet in the midst of the contemporary social-political-religious struggle in Mexico, and in the very teeth of the democracy to the north.

3. Search for a New World

TO USE so severe a term as "exile" for Lawrence's departure from Europe in 1922 is to acknowledge the extremity of the response he made to his cumulative awareness of anti-life forces in contemporary civilization. The real, and imaginatively relived and interpreted experiences that contributed to this, have been traced in the preceding chapters. During his youth in the Midlands he had encountered blocks to the élan vital at all social levels, though most intimately and crucially among the miners. A life of pathos and martyrdom resulted for the exceptional woman of moral integrity, and a compensatory, crippling love for her children. Escape from these dooms required a bitter, difficult struggle for intellectual and sexual independence, and a painful breaking of ties. The ordeal of omnipresent deathliness could be passed through only by means of a sweeping reversal of values. Lawrence's intellectual justification of this reversal resulted from the growth of his earliest religious intuitions of transcendent unity into a reconciliation of science and religion by a form of vitalism, and the characteristic vitalistic ethic— whatever frees or enhances life in the vital, quite physical sense, is good; whatever diminishes or damages it is evil. Though Lawrence achieved sexual fulfillment and marriage, the problem of life-giving independence in relationship continued. His intense examination of the nature and quality of relationship resulted, in *The Rainbow*, in a religious vision of harmony of the relative and the absolute, the creature of society and the godman, or godwoman, of the life force. Then came the cataclysmic threat of the anti-life of war, and the need to assume some responsibility for an intellectual leadership that would make itself felt in the political sphere. This responsibility was interfered with, or so he felt, by the relationship with woman, in which possessiveness and the modern tendency to make sexual or love relations the supreme value were ubiquitous. Men, responsible for the world, must establish a brotherhood as profound as the vitalistic "ideal" for marriage. His attempt to realize this relationship failed, though the hope remained. As he surveyed, from such an imaginative, "unrealistic" point of view, the contemporary means of organizing life, in England, on the Continent, and in democratic America, he disapproved of all, and began to elaborate his idea of a new kind of aristocracy, or leadership, that might realize his vitalistic and theocratic vision of life.

During the postwar years of 1919-22, Lawrence restlessly considered the means, and the justification, of leaving Europe altogether. Beyond the problem of supporting himself and Frieda, and maintaining his frail health, there was the question of whether his departure would not amount to evasion of responsibility for taking part in the struggle at home. Essentially his vision of life had nothing to do with contemporary politics and economics, other than to appraise their effects on the vital integrity of the individual. He seemed to withdraw, to renew his attacks on what he saw as decadence, and to vacillate. As always he preferred living in rather remote, uncomfortable, even unfavorable places, like Sicily, where the poverty and violent struggle to live moved him to translate Verga. Sicily also represented a Mediterranean end of Europe, between East and West.

Here, in the preface of *Fantasia of the Unconscious,* as the fruit of his reading in psychology, anthropology, geography, and theosophy, and of the experience already explored in his fiction, he proclaimed his belief in an ancient world in which "men lived and taught and knew, and were in one complete correspondence over all the earth . . . from Atlantis to the Polynesian Continent." They had a universal science, by which he meant "a science which proceeds in terms of life and is established on the data of living experience and sure intuition," unlike modern objective science, which is concerned "only with phenomena as regarded in their cause-and-effect relationship . . . mechanistic functioning and apparatus of life." After destruction of this civilization by glaciers and a world flood, some of its people "degenerated naturally into cave men, neolithic and paleolithic creatures, and some retained their marvelous innate beauty and life-perfection, as the South Sea Islanders, and some wandered savage in Africa, and some, like Druids or Etruscans or Chaldeans or Amerindians or Chinese, refused to forget, but taught the old wisdom, only in its half-forgotten, symbolic forms. More or less forgotten as knowledge: remembered as ritual, gesture, and myth-story." The great myths, he said, "now begin to hypnotize us again, our own impulse towards our own scientific way of understanding being almost spent."

In his very early work Lawrence had touched on myth in the wistful feeling of his disoriented characters for the Celtic, Druidic past of England. Out of realistic materials—the ordinary functions of washing and bathing, the miners' emergence from the underground, and the cycles of nature in the countryside—and out of the analogy of Christian ritual, he had created patterns of death and resurrection that had mythic overtones. In such late work as "The Ladybird," *The Lost Girl,* and *Aaron's Rod,* Old Testament story and myth had been supplemented by Egyptian, and American Indian, ritual and symbol. Now, in 1922, he was ready to use more consciously and elaborately such clues to perennial vital renewal. Here was a way to give his philosophy of the blood consciousness, once only intuited, a history and a sanction, a hierarchy and a pantheon. In these terms, his postwar exile was not merely nervous flight, or response to fortuitous invitations like that of Mabel Dodge Luhan to Taos, New Mexico. It was also a search, limited by the failing business of his American publisher, and his need of free-cost housing and firewood, but tirelessly directed toward finding a place in which his vision of integration could be realized.

As he hesitated in Sicily, another direction and attitude toward life were suggested by his American friends, Earl and Achsah Brewster, who were going to Ceylon to study Buddhism. Lawrence expected little from the spirituality of Asia, but, he said sardonically, he hoped to gain some inner peace before approaching modern America. The route East, via Ceylon, Australia, and the South Seas to San Francisco, afforded him a rather complete contrast of contemporary ways of life, and encounters with the clues to the ancient, pre-flood culture that he had sketched in *Fantasia.* The climate in Ceylon was bad for his health, and the physical squalor underlying the spiritual exaltation repelled him.[1] Australia represented primarily the utterly new, to which one might yield himself as to a dream existence, materialistic democracy, and economic strife. The South Sea Islands, which he knew through Melville's missionary-troubled Typee, the name he sometimes used to refer to his projected colony, he found lovely but contaminated by white civilization. From modern, white American San Francisco, he hurried to New Mexico and his last clue, the one on which, supplemented by what he found in Mexico, he founded his major work from 1922 to 1926.

Lawrence's first stay in Taos, through the fall and winter of 1922-23, was a time of assimilation of Indian ritual and way of life, and of rather violent reaction to the complicated personal and cultural situation represented by Mrs. Luhan and her circle. He wrote exploratory essays on the Indian question containing ironic comments on the mixture of politics and ideal motives, a few poems for *Birds, Beasts and Flowers,* and made an abortive attempt to write a novel based on Mrs. Luhan's revolt against modern culture in her marriage to an Indian. Such a union suggested a still more radical integration of psyches and cultures than the kind he had been exploring. A significant factor in the quarrel between the Lawrences and Mrs. Luhan that ended the novel project, was Lawrence's friendship with the Danish artists Knud Merrild and Arnold Götzsche. When Mrs. Luhan snubbed them, he cultivated them all the more, and they were the Lawrences' companions during the winter at Del Monte ranch. They seem to have represented to Lawrence the possibility of the male brotherhood so consistently denied him, in his life and fiction, to this point. In physical vigor and integrity of character, they resembled the English farmers who had so appealed to him in his youth. Artists, and self-reliant young men exploring a new world, they gave new hope of establishing a community that would show the way out of contemporary decadence.

There followed a strenuous effort by Lawrence to find in Mexico

---

1. His not visiting Africa was perhaps a matter of availability of money and ships, rather than lack of interest though in *Women in Love* African sculpture represented an extreme of sensuality at one pole of the advance and regress of civilization.

a place where they might found the nucleus of his community. He made his first visit to Mexico, from March to July 1923, without them; but he wrote to them constantly of his search and his hopes. His first companions in Mexico were Witter Bynner and Willard Johnson, out of whose personalities and disagreement with his views he wrought satirical characters for the opening of *The Plumed Serpent*. Bynner and he engaged in a debate over the virtues of democracy and the imperatives of leadership that may have intensified Lawrence's development of a hierarchy, dominantly religious but necessarily political also, as the Quetzalcoatl movement came to power in the novel.

Meanwhile certain of Lawrence's English friends were urging him to return, and Mrs. Lawrence's concern for her children, and disbelief in his community project, pulled in that direction. John Middleton Murry was particularly urgent, offering Lawrence a co-editorship of *The Adelphi*, or a collaboration that amounted to that. For a time Lawrence planned to go back. He wrote despondently to Merrild of the chances of establishing a life in common in Mexico, citing as one obstacle the possibility of further revolution. But as the Lawrences journeyed to New York, he felt an increasing revulsion, first against the United States, then England. The ensuing separation, when Mrs. Lawrence went to England alone, might well have ended in a complete break. Lawrence's comment on the situation in his letters is largely philosophical, but charged with strong emotion involving his fight for male dominance in their relationship and a jealousy of Murry for which there was, or was soon to be, good reason. Murry was the real-life equivalent of Gerald in *Women in Love*, and Lawrence's disappointment at failing to achieve a profound relationship with him was most bitter. Mrs. Lawrence liked and defended Murry. Whether her relationship with him before this latest crisis was intimate or not, is unclear; but that it became so now on her return to England is certain. To avoid oversimplification, it must be understood that despite their differences, sometimes manifested violently, Mrs. Lawrence's "belief" in his work had been essential to Lawrence's achievement from the beginning. Her disbelief in his leadership, community project had introduced in his work new conflicts and, perhaps, new extremes of dogmatic argument and vicarious victory. To lose her would have been to lose his means of fulfillment, to resign his original commitments to woman and marriage, and to end an essential, if painful, modus vivendi in the literal sense.

Lawrence now did a remarkable thing for a man whose health was so frail. He joined Merrild and Götzsche in Los Angeles, and then with Götzsche made the difficult journey down the west coast of Mexico, his intention being to look again for a place for the colony. Merrild did not go because he felt that he had to choose his own way of life; Lawrence was essentially wise, but too dominant. His feeling probably reflected the reaction of many of Lawrence's friends as they contemplated life in the new community.

By November in Mexico, Merrild and Götzsche report, Lawrence was distraught to the verge of insanity without Mrs. Lawrence. He capitulated to the extent of going to England; but he seems to have had little intention of remaining. He offered Murry essays containing aggressively anti-Christian themes that Murry objected to, and accused Murry of lacking the courage to attack root and branch the evils of contemporary culture. The fiction of this period—such short stories as "The Last Laugh" and "The Border Line"—takes revenge on a decadence that attempts to claim the wife, and reclaims her in the name of the Lawrencean vision. Murry figures as the antagonist and victim.

Lawrence returned to America with Mrs. Lawrence and one friend and follower willing to give up the old life, Dorothy Brett. Other friends pledged themselves to join his colony; but none ever did, though some, like Catherine Carswell, always vigorously championed him. Murry confessed rather vaguely to a betrayer's role, and thereby increased Lawrence's scorn. The effect of the episode was to confirm Lawrence's disgust with Europe, and, perhaps, to make him still more uncompromising, if that was possible so late in his stand.

Back in New Mexico and Mexico, Lawrence's American experience now bore fruit in the short stories of *The Woman Who Rode Away* volume, and the final draft of *The Plumed Serpent*, completed at Oaxaca from November 1924, to February 1925. Toward the end of this major effort, Lawrence collapsed in what was first thought to be malaria, but turned out to be a serious tubercular breakdown. After difficulty with the immigration authorities over readmission to the

United States, he returned to the New Mexico ranch and recovered a modicum of health. Though he lived some four years longer, this illness was apparently the beginning of his decline. The strength with which he had so stubbornly fought his cultural battle, and the accompanying personal one within his marriage, was waning.

I

In *Aaron's Rod* the answer to the question of choice of a leader had been "Your soul will tell you." The major theme of *Kangaroo* is the testing and rejection of fascist and socialist leadership by the Lawrencean soul of Richard Somers. The fascist program echoes some of Lawrence's views, so that the lonely creative man who also desired to be a man of action confronts the application of his poetic vision in finite, political form. The sustained experience permeating this testing is the nausea caused by all-pervading hate and lurking violence in modern life, and the necessity of freeing one's soul from them.

Somers resents Australian familiarity of manners and proletarian independence. Authoritiless, the country is on the verge of anarchy. The so-called freedom may be a relief after the tensions of Europe, but the vacant landscape, and the litter of bungalows and tin cans scattered for miles, are terrifying. In the bush he has a sense of the aborigines waiting for ultimate revenge. In the settlements work and play are without inner meaning. Unlike the silent, involuntary communication between the common people of England, relationship among the Australians is based on the code of "you put yourself aside, and I'll put myself aside." The consequent withholding of self makes men "go blank."

Such "conservative" responses form a realistic critical counterpoint to the growth of Somers' relationship with Jack Callcott and the Diggers' political organization. It is ironic, even comic, Lawrencean self-revelation that Callcott's animalistic lovemaking in front of others is rather shocking to the Somerses. His bluff concept of male friendship, expressed in the Australian slang "mates" or "pals," presents Somers with a qualitative problem. Somers' other Australian friend, one of Lawrence's favored Celts, the Cornishman William James, is mainly concerned with the economic depression of Cornwall and is deprecatory of the Celtic magic Somers values, though he exhibits a restless, vague desire that is perhaps a Celtic residue.

Somers' interest in Callcott's political activity is opposed by Harriet. To her his desire to do something for his fellow men is only "nervous obstinacy and self-importance." He does not really like people, and always ends by hating them and falling back on her. The Callcotts and Trewhellas are only common street-people, without the potentiality he imagines them to have. Somers admits that "the roots of his life" are with her, but, in Lawrence's familiar metaphor of the vitalistic dynamic, he wants a "new shoot in the life of mankind." She argues that he should accomplish this in his writing, as he does already. He insists that he is cut off from being "a man among men."

When Callcott sounds out his view of honor and trust between men, and Somers answers that he trusts him, there is a bit of the Lawrencean ritual of brotherhood through touch in Callcott's putting an arm around him and pressing him close. But when they discuss politics, Somers expresses his view that fundamentally most Australians care about nothing, and admits that he himself does not care about politics. Pressed to say what else there is to care about, he can only answer that he cares supremely about something he cannot express exactly. The scene in which Calcott fully explains the political program of the Diggers is created with Lawrencean vitalistic comedy. The intrinsically human limitation is played against the resounding ideal, and both are dwarfed by nonhuman nature. Callcott must awkwardly shout his explanation above the "eternal sound" of the sea. Both men look like "pilots in a storm." They agree that democratic politics is merely vote-getting, and that discipline and obedience are needed. The socialists' world-workers idea plays into the hands of the "tyrannies of the various nationalisms." After this agreement on the deficiencies of contemporary politics, Callcott pledges Somers to secrecy. Lawrence calls it a "tense moment" when Somers looks at the sea, thinks of "his own everlasting gods," and feels the other man's body next to his. Callcott's secret is a veterans' organization with a fascist program of action. Elaborately organized, cell upon cell, they are ready to seize power whenever there occurs either the revolution that the reds talk about or the social-economic disaster that the conservatives hopefully anticipate. Somers' mistrust is caused not by the plan itself but by the "that's-how-it's-got-to-be dryness, sharp and authoritative," of Callcott's voice.

When Somers is introduced to the leader, and dictator-to-be, whose comical nickname, "Kangaroo," is derived from his portly, pouchlike stomach, and from his benevolence, he at first finds him irresistibly attractive. Kangaroo contains an "almost pure kindliness embodied in an ancient, unscrupulous shrewdness," so that he knows how to deal with "mean, barren people," and he has also the capacity for "physically warm love." He has read Somers' essays against democracy and used his ideas. He thinks that for sixty percent of the people education is useless; but he wants them to have full lives "as even slaves have had" under certain masters. He talks in quasi-Lawrencean terms of the sacredness of life, dynamic nature, and the necessity of obedience.

> If a man loves life, and feels the sacredness and the mystery of life, then he knows that life is full of strange and subtle and even conflicting imperatives. And a wise man learns to recognise the imperatives as they arise—or nearly so—and to obey. But most men bruise themselves to death trying to fight and overcome their own new, life-born needs, life's ever-strange new imperatives. The secret of all life is in obedience: obedience to the urge that arises in the soul, the urge that is life itself, urging us on to new gestures, new embraces, new motions, new combinations, new creations. . . . Man again needs a father—not a friend or a brother sufferer, a suffering Saviour. Man needs a quiet, gentle father who uses his authority in the name of living life, and who is absolutely stern against anti-life.

The "steady loveliness" of Kangaroo's "warm, wise heart" makes Somers feel abashed because of his own impatience and rages. Yet he is mistrustful. His ultimate refusal of Kangaroo's fascism expresses not only a revulsion from the violence of political action, but from what he experiences in every aspect of contemporary life, and now acutely in his encounter with the enveloping, paternal love of Kangaroo—the masking of hate and ultimate violence to the individual.

Somers is also offered the other major revolutionary program of modern times, militant socialism. The socialist leader, Struthers, appeals to Somers' working-class origin and love of the people, and stresses the "constructive spirit" in men. Though Somers is put off by something in Struthers that "bears down on him in the way a snake approaches a bird," he is moved. What essentially attracts him is the possibility that a "great new inspiration of belief in the love of 'mates'" might be achieved. But Struthers' program, though godless, is based on Christ's teaching to love one another, and Somers' reaction to this is expressed in terms of the vitalistic mystique in which all Lawrence's Christian, social rejections end.

> It all seemed so far from the dark God he wished to serve, the God from whom the dark, sensual passion of love emanates, deeper than the spiritual love of Christ. He wanted men once more to refer the sensual passion of love sacredly to the great dark God, the Nameless, of the first dark religions.

Chapter XII, "The Nightmare," sometimes singled out as an example of Lawrence's carelessness about structure, can be seen to have a very important function, if the novel is viewed not as an a priori sequence of judgments, but an exploration of new situations in which old traumas make themselves felt, and even break through to conscious appraisal. The preceding chapter, refusing both Struthers and Kangaroo, ends with an experience of Kangaroo's menace when his benevolent power is rejected:

> For a moment Somers was afraid of him, as of some great ugly idol that might strike. He felt the intense hatred of the man coming at him in cold waves. He stood up in a kind of horror, in front of the great, close-eyed, horrible thing that was now Kangaroo. Yet, a thing, not a whole man. A great Thing, a horror.

Here Lawrence appraises his wartime experience as if to understand the totality of causes of his fear and recoil, so that his final stand will have a fully experiential foundation. He recreates the humiliation of the examinations and rejections for service, the terror of the Zeppelin raids on London, the indignity of suspicion in Cornwall, and the subsequent harassment by the police. Hatred had developed in him to counteract his terror at seeing "a criminal marked out by society for annihilation." For a time the terror and hatred had been relieved by a new sense of sweetness and humanness in the heart of Shakespeare's England; but in his native Midlands the "alien spirit of coal and iron" was dominant, and he had vowed "never again to be at the disposal of society."

> Detail for detail he thought out his experiences with the authorities, during the war. . . . Till now, he had always kept the memory at bay, afraid of it. Now it all came back, in a rush. It was like a volcanic eruption in his consciousness. . . . Since he had been in Italy the fear had left him entirely. He had not even remembered it, in India. Only in the quiet of Coo-ee, strangely enough, it had come back in spasms: the dread, almost the horror, of democratic society, the mob. . . .
>
> Richard faced out all his memories like a nightmare in the night, and cut clear. He felt broken off from his fellow-men. . . . So be it. He was broken apart, apart he would remain.

As Lawrence did, Somers turns to the nonhuman and the nonsocial birds, beasts and flowers. What he loves is the *look* of Australia, "that marvellous soft flower-blue of the air, and the sombre grey of the earth, the foliage, the brown of the low rocks: like the dull pelts of kangaroos."

This preference recurs as a motif throughout the book. When Somers is in this phase, which might be called vitalistic communion, even Harriet recedes from his life. Yet she commands his attention as the strong critic of both his ventures into action and his withdrawal. From her, and from bits of undoctrinaire, ordinary experience, come moments of self-criticism for Somers-Lawrence. He finds in anecdotes of Australian life in the newspapers, a "laconic courage of experience" which makes him feel like kicking himself for wanting to join in revolutions or reforms, or struggling with the "soul" and the "dark god." He is "a preacher and blatherer," and hates himself for it.

Eternally for Lawrence the climactic tension was between the absolute of his religious experience and the relativity of personal relationship. Kangaroo, convalescing from a wound received in a political brawl, accuses Somers of killing him by refusing him love, and dies. Somers denies guilt as "a matter of simple sanity"; yet the question of loyalty through love is crucially important to him. When he first argues with Harriet that he must develop his friendship with Callcott, he dreams of a woman whose face, resembling the faces of Harriet and his dead mother, reproaches him for betraying her love. He relieves his sense of guilt by saying that neither of them believed in him, and by concluding that such dreams are only a "revenge which old weaknesses take on the victorious healthy consciousness." Yet this being haunted by the mother, and by the woman who had taken her place nearest him, this possibility of betrayal through his vitalistic and reformist denial of the centrality of love, troubles much of his work, and is implicit in all of it. Maturity and sanity required a constant, often tortured attempt to reconcile the conflict of the boy's dependence with the man's independence, the isolation of married love with the responsibility of the world's work, personal love with redemptive higher aims.

At the end of the novel Somers defends himself from Kangaroo's accusation that he is the enemy of civilization by saying that the one thing he is not the enemy of is "the deep, self-responsible consciousness in man." It is, in fact, what he means by "civilization." He admits that he has made a fool of himself and encouraged great risks for others, but he has quit in time, that is, before the step leading to violence.

The novel contains Lawrence's most direct and involved assessment of the value of extremist political action. There is evidence in his letters that radical socialism in postwar Italy had occasionally appealed to the actively angry, nihilistic extreme of his disgust. But his central tendency had always been to go his own way, pushing forward his exploration of the possibilities of his dark, blood, vitalistic organization of life. He had been forced largely to invent the means of experiencing this. When he left Europe, he had had in mind places where there might be clues to a prehistoric civilization that had realized what he intuited. But in Australia there was no recourse to myth and ritual. *Kangaroo* is transitional, an incompletely imagined and episodically loose attempt to fill the vacuum of travel, and maintain continuity of experience. Lawrence's more organic intensity and richness of metaphoric image, and symbol, were not to reappear in the longer form until *The Plumed Serpent*.

2

By the end of June 1923, at Lake Chapala in Mexico, Lawrence had completed a first draft of his major American work, *The Plumed*

Serpent. Then, after going as far as New York, he decided not to return with Mrs. Lawrence to the past in England, went to the West Coast, and journeyed down into Mexico in a stubborn final attempt to realize his hope of a colony, with Knud Merrild and Arnold Götzsche as a nucleus. During this time of stress and exhausting travel he revised *The Boy in the Bush,* a novel by an Australian friend, Molly Skinner, in the hope that she might get it published. Between early September in California and mid-November 1923, in Mexico, he completely "recreated" her book, making what he called "a rather daring development, psychologically."

As he turned away from the past in defiance, and explored wild, new country, he was in something of the position of the hero of the novel, a young Englishman working out his destiny in the Australian bush. Whatever the locale, here was another chance to develop imaginatively the present nature of his stand against contemporary culture. The task may also have diverted him from the trouble of his separation while at the same time reflecting it.

Jack Grant loves his Australian mother and is indifferent to his English father. While the mother is, in terms of social convention, "the dearest thing imaginable," she feels that there is "no fence between sin and virtue." Her feeling expresses Lawrence's vitalistic synthesis of civilization and nature. The distinction between the two is as if sin were "the unreclaimed bush" and goodness only "the claims the settlers have managed to fence in." There is more bush than settlement, and one is as good as the other; they serve different ends. The good life consists of always "having around your claim the endless wilderness." Though the bush does contain a devil, it is "a wild and comprehensible one," unlike the "more frightening tame devil" of the settlements, manifested in drunkeness, greed, and foolish pride.

The young heroines and heroes are differentiated by their vitalistic and social potentialities. Monica has a daredevil quality but tends to dominate. Mary has softer, more womanly qualities but is submissive to convention. Jack, and his antagonist, Esau, broadly represent Lawrence's two kinds of power: the vitalistic, and the anti-life. Monica finds in Jack softness, warmth, and a masterfulness that is "more animal than human." He is like a "centaur with its nonhuman power and its

wisdom of hot blood-knowledge." She feels that this denies her something, and is attracted by Esau's "fixed, hard, exciting will."

Jack also expresses Lawrence's "conservative" awareness that tradition
and society are stabilizing as well as anti-life forces, and that there is
danger of disintegration and death in rebelling against them. Midway
in the novel, he makes a hazardous horseback trip across Australia that
must have afforded Lawrence a poignant parallel to his journey into
Mexico. Jack feels that in England there was a "strong pivot" for life.
He has rebelled against the "fixed hold over everything" in England,
but likes the looseness and carelessness of Australia only up to the
point at which it becomes crazy and frightening. The possibility of disintegration is rapidly expanded into the Lawrencean religious imagery
that expresses the crisis of two deathly extremes. Either the "dim white
god of the heavenly infinite" or the "great black Moloch of the living
death" must prevail. Jack, traveling the "dark road," wants to be a
"proud Lord of Death . . . , fighting his enemies and taking his woman until the last, black embrace of death."

When he returns, more resolute because of this journey, Jack finds
that Monica has had a child out of wedlock, ostensibly by an ineffectual,
conventional man who is willing to take care of her, but actually by the
irresponsible Esau. He kills Esau and flees into the bush. There, lost
and dying, he thinks again of the power and dignity of nonconformity
in life as depending upon mastery in death. He will not go into "the
black halls of death as a scavenger servant," like Esau, or "a sort of butler," like his father. Rescued by Mary Ellis and her brothers, he passes
through a long Lawrencean illness during which he loses his "softness
in the other-world of death" and brings back some of "the relentless
power, and the inevitable touch of mockery," that belongs there. He
resembles closely the fighting side of Lawrence that had been forged by
crucial experiences of death.

When he claims Monica, she must accept, as the Lawrencean heroine
is usually reluctant to do, his never belonging to her. His "doomlike"
quality takes away her own "strange, fascinating female power," but
at the same time makes her feel saved, since her power has brought her
"a nothingness like madness" in her relationship with the social man
who offered to help her.

Jack's subsequent search for gold becomes the Lawrencean search for the means to make a place on earth for a few "aristocrats-to-the-bone." When news of an inheritance brings him to the city from the isolation he prefers, his return resembles Lawrence's impending return to England, where he claimed his wife and returned with her and Dorothy Brett to the new world. Re-encountering Mary and her softer potentiality, Jack makes the proposal, which she refuses, that she come with him as a second wife. His sanction for this is his being faithful to "what stirs within him." His God tells him to go his own way and "never be frightened of people and the world." He wants "to pitch his camp in the wilderness with the two brothers and with wives, to go like Abraham under the sky, speaking to a fierce, wild Lord, and to have angels stand in his doorway."

On his return journey to the wilderness, he is overtaken by a young woman who has overheard his views of marriage, and has the kind of fearlessness that is developed through dread of the social world. Gone even further in rebellion than he, her "uncanny, hardly human quality" makes her a "real borderline being." The spark of revenge in her might, through Jack, be "kindled into a natural sun," its resistance and aggressiveness turned into vitalistic wholeness. They agree that she will join Monica and him, and he rides away confidently through the wilderness in which he had once been lost.

Though, of course, the novel is not basically Lawrence's, his development of the meaning of situation makes it irresistibly an expression of his fears and resolution as, refusing to return to England, and separating from the woman on whom he had once staked his future, he encountered the quite real hazard of his pioneering journey into Mexico. The controlling concept and its central symbol carry through his next short stories—the existence of a psychological and cultural borderline having certain geographical analogies, and of borderline beings who are potentially capable of crossing over from death into a new way of life. The demarcations are between civilization and nature; between man's perverse, incomprehensible behavior and nature's unambiguous and strengthening hazards; between the weakness of lack of commitment to the fight to avoid decadence by making new communities, and the pride and strength of the vitalistic soldier in the face of both inward

and physical death. In Lawrence's imagination the Australian frontier
had become the borderline situation of contemporary culture.

3 🐚

The short stories that followed *The Boy in the Bush* reflect Lawrence's relations with Frieda, John Middleton Murry, and Dorothy
Brett at the time of his brief return to England late in 1923. Frieda and
Murry had been intimate since her separation from Lawrence. The
failure of Murry's plan for a peaceful collaboration with Lawrence on
The Adelphi no doubt reflects Lawrence's personal feelings over the
affair with Frieda, but the lines of Lawrence's argument are consistent
with his imaginative and philosophical stand. When Murry, from what
may be described as a love as supreme value position, objected to Lawrence's articles on the ground that they would only make enemies, Lawrence's reply was that this was exactly what he wanted to do; he hated
the slime of the "all the world's my friend" attitude.

The essays Murry printed—"The Proper Study of Mankind," "On
Being Religious," "On Human Destiny," and "On Being a Man"—are
strong expressions of Lawrence's rejection of traditional values in favor
of religious renewal from what might be called the vitalistic "reservoir."

In "The Proper Study of Mankind" he metaphorizes his conception
as a voyage down the stream of knowledge to the sea of the "God
mystery." The subjects of man's relation to man, to himself, and to
woman have been exhausted; in those areas there remains only the
literature of perversity and the playboy attitude. The new literature
must penetrate to that point "where the first and greatest relation of
every man and every woman is to the Ocean itself, the great God of the
end, who is the All-Father of all sources. . . ."

In "On Being Religious" he speaks of the true believer as referring
himself "back to some indefinable pulse of life in him," beyond goodness, love, or being made more tolerant. He is attracted by the idea that
the important thing is what God does with one, which is to use him as
"the thin edge of the wedge"; he thinks he might believe in such a God
"if it looked like fun." God has had enough of "sighs, supplications,
prayers, tears and yearnings," and, as if on a "great strike," has left

heaven empty. He is dynamic, shifts his position in the cosmos, and sends new saviors.

> . . . we go in search of God, following the Holy Ghost, and depending on the Holy Ghost. . . . We hear His strange calling, the strange calling like a hound on the scent, away in the unmapped wilderness. And it seems great fun to follow.

"On Human Destiny" makes essentially the same points, with greater emphasis on a cyclical decline and renewal of civilization. Most men, knowing that "our civilization has got to smash," take the coward's attitude of living their own lives while "waiting for the slow accumulation of circumstances." What is needed is a minority, like the Christians after the fall of Rome, to keep the knowledge of God alive.

> The exquisite delicate light of ever-renewed human consciousness is never blown out. The lights of great cities go out, and there is howling darkness to all appearances. But always, since men began, the light of the pure, God-knowing human consciousness has kept alight. . . .

It is not an impossibly long step from these conceptions to the Lawrencean comedy of "The Last Laugh," with its creation of Pandemonium in London. At midnight in Hampstead (where the Lawrences lived during the London visit), Lorenzo (his friends' familiar Italianate name for him) says goodnight at his door to a man and a girl (who seem to be portraits of Dorothy Brett and Murry). When he ironically calls the snow-covered scene a new world, the girl is interested and laughs. The other man, a malicious mixture of pagan and Christian, calls it merely whitewash. The story involves his being proved wrong by the return and revenge of the Pan spirit of vitalism.

The man, according to his mixed nature, is the first to hear the Pan laughter, while the girl, after adjusting the hearing-aid that is her badge of dependence, can hear only his laugh. A young policeman, reassured that her companion is not drunk, accompanies them in search of the source of the laughter, and gives conventional assistance to the girl, who has always held herself aloof from physical contact. When, as her metamorphosis begins, she sees the man she has always known she will see one day, her companion and the policeman cannot see him. The former is diverted from the Pan search by a woman who has come out to see who has mysteriously knocked on her door, explaining that one is always expecting something wonderful will happen. As for the choice of man, anyone she can like will do. When her companion takes the love direction by entering this woman's house, the girl is able to remove her hearing-aid. Freed of her relationship with him, and in touch with Pan, she feels new pride, power, and surety. At the moment at which she is no longer afraid of the policeman as a man, snow begins to fall and the air is full of "strange, unheard" voices saying "He's come back! Aha! He's come back!" When they come to a church, the doors of which are open so that the wind, snow, and voices blow through it, and she hears the laughter for the first time unaided, Lawrence's vitalistic renovation of relationship and religion is complete.

At her house the girl permits the "tame-animal," frightened policeman to warm himself at the fire while she goes to bed. Next morning, gay and laughing, she learns from her disapproving housekeeper that he is lame and still there. She thinks of her relationship with her companion of the night before as a "ridiculous, overly self-serious" love in her mind. He, when he arrives, says of the change in her that it has left her without a soul. The policeman, they find, has developed a curiously clubbed foot, like the paw of some animal—obviously a Pan change. The man, unable to see how all this could have happened, hears the laugh again, apparently, according to the Pan legend, has the fatal experience of seeing Pan by daylight, is stricken with the realization that he has made a "final fool" of himself, and falls dead, a victim of vitalistic revenge.

"Jimmy and the Desperate Woman" satirizes the perverse, escapist motives and feelings that characterize the eclectic, compromising intellectual. (Its portrait of Jimmy suggests Aldous Huxley's Burlap in *Point Counter Point*.) Jimmy, editor of a highbrow magazine, has the dual nature of the man in "The Last Laugh." When he is most himself, his face is a "pure Pan face," but in his own opinion he is a sort of martyred saint, and women think of him as a vaguely fine man who needs a woman to look after him. One wife having tired of this protective role, he decides to find a simple, uneducated girl to whom he will be only "fine and strong."

His opportunity comes when a miner's wife sends in a poem which grimly, antagonistically reveals her husband's hardness. Her probable desperation appeals to Jimmy, though she does not sound like the "nestling, unsophisticated rustic type." On his sentimental journey to see her, he encounters for the first time the ugliness of the industrial country and the hostility of the people. Though he is frightened by the wife's appearance of a woman who is "holding her own against Man and Fate," he is excited by a gamble in which he cannot lose very much, and asks her to live with him. All of Lawrence's sardonic insight into the miners' feelings is contained in the scene in which Jimmy settles the question with the husband, whose independence and harsh, fighting voice contrast with Jimmy's weakness. The miner has decided that he is only made use of both at the mines and at home. He does not want his wife "opposing him and making his child oppose him," and he is having an affair because "someone must give in to him." When the wife, out of sheer reaction, accepts Jimmy's proposal, the miner turns hard and stoical, and gives his permission. Though Jimmy fears her hardness, he hates the other man's superiority and can perversely triumph over him through her. He will manage her by becoming "apologetic and pathetic."

The best of this group of stories is "The Border Line" because of its combination of Lawrence's immediate involvement in a contest for relationship with his prophetic awareness of resurgent barbarism in Germany, and his sense of the urgency of achieving a new strength to survive this. The situation involves the crosscurrents of nationalistic as well as vitalistic sensibility that were most poignantly familiar to Lawrence through his marriage. The identity of Frieda is only slightly concealed in the central character, who is the daughter of a German baron and has not been altered racially by fifteen years of marriage to an Englishman. Departing from Paris on her way to Germany, where her second husband is working, she is reminded by the Gallic sensuousness of the men, of her first husband, Alan, one of Lawrence's superior Celts, a captain in a Highland regiment, and an astronomer, like the hero of "The Captain's Doll." They had stopped living together because of their "mutually unyielding pride," and she had fallen under the spell of Alan's friend, Philip, whose "look of knowing" and "impression of secrecy," along with conveyance of a "sense of offering like that of a loving dog," made him interesting to women. Philip had loved Alan, calling him a real man who never let himself be carried away. Alan had had an "indifferent tolerance" and "occasional contempt" for Philip, who was too much on the "wrong side of the border."

The issue is essentially the same as that in the *Adelphi* essays—the precedence of contemporary crisis and the man's responsibility to be engaged in the fight to preserve the essential core of civilization, over the love relationship. In "On Human Destiny" this preservable core was "the exquisite delicate light of ever-renewed human consciousness," and, in the same passage, "the pure, God-knowing human consciousness." In "The Border Line," it is simply "the human flow."

> She only wanted to alter everything, to alter the past, to alter all the flow of history—the terrible flow of history. Secretly somewhere inside herself she felt that with her queen-bee love, the queen-bee will, she *could* divert the whole flow of history—nay, even reverse it.
>
> But in the remote, realizing look that lay at the back of his eyes, back of all his changeless husband-care, she saw that it could never be so. That the whole of her womanly motherly concentration could never put back the great flow of human destiny. That, as he said, only the cold strength of a man, accepting the destiny of destruction, could see the human flow through the chaos and beyond to a new outlet. But the chaos first, and the long rage of destruction.

Philip's view that the war was a "colossal, disgraceful accident," and his noncombatant's advocacy of humanity, truth, and peace, had been soothing to Alan's wife, and she had married him after Alan was reported missing in combat. At first she had found their relationship pleasant and voluptuous. Then she had realized the difference between being married to a "ceaseless born fighter" and a "cunning, subtle equivocator," and had felt degraded.

Now her train enters the Marne country, composed of "centuries of corpses," a border country where her present life seems illusory and deathly, and at Strasbourg the cathedral, where her spirit once "soared aloft," suggests the "eternal blood-creature ready to crush" decadent idealism and let the "blood move erect once more." In this realization of nihilistic danger, she encounters Alan and feels once more the "restful, thoughtless pleasure" of the woman who moves in the "aura of the man to whom she belongs." She wonders why she had fought against this pleasure that dispels the "nervous modern horror of the world" from her body.

They part, and she continues her journey, through the "dreary neutrality" of the occupied zone. In unoccupied Germany she feels the "barbaric undertone of the white-skinned north, beneath its waning civilization." Walking in the snow-covered forest, she realizes how quickly the world would "go wild if catastrophes overtook mankind." Realizing that Philip is impotent in such a crisis, she feels with relief the strong presence of Alan, meets him, and re-experiences his passion. In the reaction pattern of such a vitalistic ghost story, Philip becomes seriously ill, and persuades her not to leave him. But at midnight Alan enters, loosens Philip's clinging hands so that he dies like a thief, and draws her away in the passion of a husband come back from a long journey.

All the characteristics of the successful Lawrence short story are here: the ironic semantic play, especially at the beginning on the death of the "Somebodies with a capital 'S'" in the war, and the continued existence of "many little nobodies and a sufficient number of little somebodies"; the sustained sardonic tone and the complexly interwoven psychological and cultural satire of the long initial exposition; the use of the central metaphor or symbol; and the development of all previously broached implications in the scene and dialogue of present time. The border country is history with its dead who do not walk, a lesson in recurrent crisis, and a place where the vitalistically brave—dead, missing, or alive— have the only rightful claim in relationship.

4 🐚

When Lawrence and Frieda returned to New Mexico in the spring of 1924, the tension in his life and in his fiction between higher purpose (calling for male dominance and leadership) and relationship with woman continued. He had broken with Murry and killed him off in his fiction. Arnold Götzsche had gone back to Denmark, and Knud Merrild was working at an independent career as a painter in Los Angeles. His only follower from England was Dorothy Brett, whose presence antagonized Frieda. In Taos Mrs. Luhan's strong will again complicated his personal life and challenged his values. It is little wonder that the three stories he wrote at the ranch that summer—"St. Mawr," "The Woman Who Rode Away," and "The Princess"—center on the problem of the unfulfilled modern woman.

In "St. Mawr" his central character is a culturally displaced young woman, Lou Witt. An American educated in Europe, she does not quite belong anywhere. Despite the failure of her affair with Rico, son of an Australian baronet, who, underneath his superficial attractiveness, can be spiteful and detestable, she has married him. Her mother, who has arrived at the age when "the Adam in man is more important than the social tailoring superimposed on him," would have preferred that she marry one of the "great, evil porters at Les Halles." The marriage has become a sexless tension of wills. Out of this situation the story develops the discovery of a regenerative vital power, rejection of contemporary European and American culture, and exile to a difficult new environment for the effort of self-integration and vital relationship. The central symbol of regenerative power is the outlaw stallion, St. Mawr. Although he has already killed two men, Lou purchases him because, when the essential power of his free being comes through to her, her soul is filled with an "ancient understanding," and she cannot bear the superficiality of her human relationships.

Two men of vitalistic potentiality are contrasted to Rico. Geronimo Trujillo, of mixed Mexican and Navajo blood, nicknamed "Phoenix" because, wounded during the war, he has been salvaged by Mrs. Witt, moves through the story as servant and groom with a "dark, implacable" quality of male power that is enslaved and resentful. The other groom, Lewis, a Welshman, is a continuation of Lawrence's intuitive, mystic Celt who rejects the contemporary world, and is like Phoenix, an enemy in the "white camp." In moments of intensity he lapses into the social impropriety of dialect. His eyes suggest those of a wildcat, and his bush of beard and hair contrasts with the smooth face of Rico, which is prepared for merely "social purposes."

The first movement of the story is to a rebellion by St. Mawr against vitalistic enslavement by his rider, Rico. Even his falling on his back in the struggle with Rico is a carrying out of the idea that the modern world saves life in the name of the ideal and at the same time "undermines the natural creation." This perversity has erupted into violence twice in our time, Lawrence adds, in Germany, and in Russia, and the only salvation is to withdraw from "the mass" and become a consciously creative nihilist. Lou must decide whether St. Mawr's dangerousness represents the evil vengeance of the slave (suggesting Nietzsche's slave morality), so that he should be destroyed or gelded, as Rico insists after the animal has permanently lamed him, or a purely vital struggle for freedom. Lawrence extends the moral implications of the vitalist's nihilistic position in Lou's comparison of Phoenix with St. Mawr. Phoenix is cruel and aloof, has "the peculiar courage of an inherited despair," and takes a grim satisfaction in a fight. This is not enough, and the hope is that such a man may at last turn to a "greater heroism."

Mrs. Witt, Lou, Lewis, and Phoenix circumvent Rico's judgment that St. Mawr should be gelded or destroyed (felt as society's opposition to the life force) by stealing him and taking him to America. During this maneuver Lewis's relationship with Mrs. Witt expresses the vitalist's criticism of modern love when she, with her combative notion of give and take in marriage, does not respect his body. Lou understands his *noli me tangere* response because of her own experience of sensual disrespect and violation. The timing of the journey to America, in autumn, is poignantly expressive of Lawrence's imaginative connection of that season with his experience of decadence (coinciding with his September birthday). These seekers of life must, like him, go south, away from what is felt as the "arctic horror" and the nervous tension of the "now irreligious north." Only in the Gulf of Mexico (in a passage that resembles Hemingway's making that place a life value) do they encounter the "marvelous beauty and fascination" of nature. On a Texas ranch, St. Mawr is easily ridden, and abandons his *noli me tangere* vitalistic defense by making advances to a ranch mare. Here the story leaves him, and loses the means of unity through a central symbol that marks Lawrence's best work in the short forms.

The human problem could hardly be solved by the *deus ex machina* of relaxed equine relations in Texas. There Lou tires of the "mechanical energy of making good" and the "duty to feel good" that characterize modern, white America. In Santa Fe she and her mother are depressed by the tourist atmosphere. One possibility for Lou is a relationship with Phoenix, who, sure of himself now on native ground, feels that money is her only advantage. She feels that he would faithfully stand between her and the world, but that his private actions as a "predative, alien-blooded male" would have no connection with her. She would not be his "real female counterpart" as is the "soft" Indian woman who attracts him. Contemptuous of her straightforwardness and sexual incompetence, he is ready to trade his sex for her money and social privileges. Marriage between such racial and cultural opposites becomes realistically impossible very near the time Lawrence was accomplishing it through symbol and ritual in *The Plumed Serpent*.

Lou's strongest desire is for relief from nervous tension and "recovery of her soul," that part of the Lawrencean cycle, religious in its pattern, that rejects the world and human relationship. Her place of retreat is a ranch resembling the Lawrence ranch near Taos. Lawrence explores the possibilities of her success in such a place in a long passage that achieves the most sustained and powerful imagery in the story. The history of the ranch is one of human failure against the wilderness, extending from a restless Eastern schoolmaster who was looking for gold, to a trader and his wife who introduced irrigation and modern conveniences. The trader had been defeated by the cost, and a "mysterious malevolence fighting against the will of man." His wife, an idealistic New Englander, had at first thought the beauty at the ranch "pure, absolute beauty." But she had been forced to conclude that in such a place there is only "intense life with an undertone of savage sordidness," and, when wintery November came, she was glad to leave the ranch for a "more human" home in the village. Her belief in a world "ultimately all for love" was dead. In keeping with Lawrence's evolutionary vitalism, Lou is simply "new blood in the ancient human effort to over-

come the half-sordid savagery of the lower stages of creation." Two
things persuade her to continue this effort. She must now "keep to herself," since relationship has not brought the "meaning and mystery that
penetrate her soul." And though she feels at the ranch a "wild spirit
that will hurt her and wear her down," it is "bigger than men and their
religion." Her final comment expresses the sardonically minimal choice
of such a cultural exile. Her mission in the wilderness saves her from
cheapness. If the ranch only aids this, it is a good buy.

"The Woman Who Rode Away" begins with characteristic Lawrencean awareness of decadence, and then develops a newly formal and
ritualistic vision of the necessity of death of the modern will, particularly
woman's will. Through the achievement of this death, the dark, vitalistic sensibility, anterior to Western civilization, and still existent among
the Indians, is freed. Cowboy and Indian melodrama is transformed
into an inexorable, rather terrifying vitalistic resurgence that contrasts
with the creatively directed revolution in *The Plumed Serpent*. The
setting in the wilds of the Sierra Madre suggests one of Graham
Greene's visions of such hells—the naked, ugly mines in the midst
of lifeless isolation; the town with its church but the dog whose corpse
lies unheeded in the market—all "deadness within deadness." Life here
is so lacking in organic meaning that the effect is surrealistic. The mining engineer husband is intent on the main chance of silver, regards
his wife as an analogous precious object, and is at the same time a
squeamish idealist who hates the physical side of life. The wife is a
California girl who had thought such a marriage would be an adventure.

> At thirty-three she really was still the girl from Berkeley, in all but
> physique. Her conscious development had stopped mysteriously with her
> marriage, completely arrested. Her husband had never become real to her,
> neither mentally nor physically. . . . Only morally he swayed her, downed
> her, kept her in an invincible slavery.

Her escape and fatal adventure are precipitated by the remark of one
of their young gentlemen visitors that behind these blank hills live
Indians who practice wonderful old religious mysteries. She is overcome by a "foolish romanticism," the feeling that it is "her destiny to
wander into the secret haunts of these timeless, mysterious, marvelous

Indians." Her journey, begun over the protests of her son and a servant, is from the first an exertion of her will. At first she feels a "strange elation" and ignores the signs that forebode death. But as she nears the Chilchui country, she becomes vague and disheartened, and from the moment she meets the Indians on the trail she and her white will become impotent and destined for sacrifice. At the same time the style changes to the rhythmic, parabolic manner in which Lawrence creates his psychological-religious experiences of the necessity of death before the vitalistic resurrection.

Her preparation for sacrifice is directed from a kiva-like structure by a very old cacique. When she refuses to change to new clothing, guards hold her while two old men slit her clothing with knives and remove it, and her hair is loosened. When the cacique delicately touches her breasts, body, and back with his moistened fingertips, she winces as if death itself were touching her, but does not feel ashamed. After this first ritual of purification and consecration, she is given new, flower-embroidered clothing and led away to an imprisonment in which she is treated with impersonal solicitousness. From time to time she is given a pleasant-tasting drink which is also an emetic. Its effect is a "soothing languor," and a heightening of perception so that she feels she can distinguish "the sound of evening flowers unfolding." During this purification and renewal, she is attended by a young Indian whose presence never makes her self-conscious or sex-conscious, though she sees that in some other mysterious way he is "darkly and powerfully male." At times her contentment is broken by uneasiness at the loss of her own kind of will and power.

As the days grow shorter, her will revives, as if this northern white characteristic belongs to the season of coldness and death. When she is permitted to witness the dance that precedes her sacrifice, Lawrence is explicit about the meaning of his parable.

> Her kind of womanhood, intensely personal and individual, was to be obliterated again, and the great primeval symbols were to tower once more over the fallen individual independence of woman. The sharpness and the quivering white woman was to be destroyed again. . . .

The costumes of the dancers suggest the vitalistic harmony of relationship she lacks: the men, with their red, yellow, and black over white, the fire of the daytime; the women, with their black, the spaces between the stars at night—complementary in activity and spheres of consciousness.

As the solstice approaches with its symbolic aptness for a nadir of white civilization, she feels an increasingly heightened mystic acuteness, as if she were "diffusing into the harmony of things." She will take a message to the sun, who will return to the Indians when he sees "among the Indian women the moon that has been held back by the white woman." Her preparation for sacrifice involves her perceiving the "intense, fundamental sadness, the grimness of ultimate decision, the fixity of revenge, and the nascent exultance of those that are going to triumph." Lawrence leaves her upon the altar before the old cacique, who, with upraised knife, awaits the moment when the sun will strike her through the ice.

In "The Princess," the last of this summer's stories, the woman has a double heritage of withdrawal from vitalistic human relationship, Celtic and New England. She has been given her title of Princess by her Scottish father, one of those "gentlemen of sufficient means" who formerly wandered about, "never arriving anywhere, never doing anything, and never definitely being anything." He had taught her that there is in everyone a demon self that does not care about anyone else, though in modern times the demons of people have become "dwindled and vulgar." The result was that even as a child she had been as "impervious as crystal." In maturity this quality had caused violent antipathy in men. In Rome a cabman to whom "the phallic mystery was still the only mystery" had been revolted by the "blasphemous impertinence of her sterility." At thirty-eight, virginal and looking ten years younger, she has come to a dude ranch in New Mexico with her nurse, to whom she has transferred her passion for her father.

Here men hint at marriage and receive only sardonic ridicule. Only one intrigues her, the guide Romero, whose Spanish family, once owners of the ranch, have been defeated by the white man, the failure of sheep-raising, and the inertia of life on the desert. He is waiting either to die or to be "aroused into passion and hope." The Princess, seeing the "spark of pride and dauntlessness" in his eyes, thinks, in her antivitalistic schizophrenia, that his demon is one of her father's sort, though she also senses in him a "subtle, insidious male kindliness."

Romero's disastrous attempt of relationship with her is made during a journey into the remote mountains that places them in the essential crisis of Lawrence's vitalistic position—human sexuality, tender but stripped of all external, social aids, asserting itself against enormous odds. The ascent is marked by increasing wildness until nothing is left but mountains "empty of life and soul." The Princess is frightened by the "anti-life," and Romero becomes strange and ominous to her, the "nonhuman demon" of himself. At the shack that is their destination, she feels "crushed by the shadow of night" and is frightened by a bobcat. Dreaming of snow, she desires warmth, protection, and loss of self, but at the same time wants the "intactness and freedom" from the power of others that is her "deepest impulse." She calls to Romero, and he takes her into his arms, but his animal warmth seems to "annihilate" her. Regaining possession of herself, she offends his sensual male pride by wishing to go back at once. Romero identifies her attitude with the "spirit of doing a man down" that he feels in his situation as a Spanish American, and forces her submission. In reaction to the horror and pain caused in him by her "stony resistance," he determines to hold her prisoner until she wants to be with him.

By the values of the culture that enslaves him, Romero is guilty of abduction and rape. When two Forest Service men appear in search of her, his fate is sealed by her final inability to like being with him. He is hunted down as the Princess watches, her "spirit hard and cold," her "heart unable to melt." The "will to never love any man" is fixed within her. Her response to her share in this vitalistically unjustified death is to testify that Romero fought because he was a demented man who had shot her horse from under her. When she leaves the ranch, she is "the Princess and a virgin, completely intact," though her hair has grayed and she is slightly crazy.

Lawrence called these three stories "sad" stories. From the intensely felt position of his vitalistic ethic, they are at times sad to the point of tragedy because of the fateful nature of the struggle. While he had long been aware of the savagery latent in nature, the life situations in New Mexico and Mexico were even more immediately frightening than those in England or on the Continent, and his wartime sense of the urgency of the struggle to preserve and advance civilization was reinforced and extended. Man must become not only an indomitable revolutionist and fighter but a Promethean hero-god who could recontact the life force without reverting in the evolutionary scale of civilization. This is plainest toward the end of "St. Mawr," but is felt, more atmospherically, in "The Woman Who Rode Away" and "The Princess."

The tendency to regard Lawrence's novels after *Women in Love* as a falling off, runs the risk of playing down his quite great achievement in the shorter forms. "St. Mawr" will stand comparison with his best work, though it is "imaginatively" broken in the middle by the disappearance of its central symbol of vitalistic awareness and rebellion. "The Woman Who Rode Away" is a considerable *tour de force* in its combination of psychological realism with myth and ritual. "The Princess," the slightest, least richly developed of the three, contains perhaps the sharpest social-psychological insight.

5

Lawrence's major American effort, the novel *The Plumed Serpent*, had been interrupted by his separation from Frieda in 1923, when he decided to return to Mexico rather than try England again, and was not completed until the fall and winter of 1924-25 at Oaxaca. Gestation of its materials had begun during the war years when, in his desperately felt need of a new place as well as new direction, he began to read studies of the North and Central American Indian, and to tentatively identify Indian animism and ceremonial with his vitalistic, potentially theocratic vision. In *Aaron's Rod* he had tested his reliance on the judgment of the individual soul against his concomitant conviction that leadership was required by the limited nature of the cultural underdog. He had sweepingly and savagely rejected the modern tendency to substitute the love relationship for responsibility to make a better world, and he viewed modern democracy's emphasis on equality as an anarchy of wills and an insult to vitalistic individual integrity. It is true that in *Kangaroo* he had rejected fascist and socialist solutions of the problem of disintegrated white culture, but this meant that there was nothing left for him to do, as long as he clung to the prophet-leadership idea, but to work out imaginatively his conception of a religiously organic culture, testing it against the dangers of politics and its most crucial and perennial critic, Frieda.

Many aspects of New Mexico and Mexico encouraged him to make such an attempt. Though he had concluded that it was impossible for white civilization to turn back to the Indian way, the animistic religious orienting of life in ceremony and dance was a means of re-experiencing the evolutionary vitalistic continuum. In Mexico the sacrificial aspect of the ancient religion, though frightful and frightening, might be transformed into punishment that served the higher vitalistic law. The Indian, especially in Mexico, resembled the cultural underdog of the English Midlands and Italy in his subjugation, since the conquest, by the same forces—the spirituality and idealism of Platonism and Christianity become ineffectual as well as repressive; and the materialism of modern social and political philosophies, that made men instrumental to the social-industrial machine. Ideological and political revolution had created a partial religious vacuum in Mexico by the closing of the churches. Most important for the fabrication of a meaningful fable was the Mexican myth that suggested cyclical religious renewal. The Indian had mistaken the Spanish conqueror for the fair, bearded god Quetzalcoatl returning from the East to which he had retired and become the evening star. In a place and time of crisis for the dying white god, Lawrence could imaginatively realize through a return of the true Quetzalcoatl, his own religious-social ideas. A rich source of ritual and symbol existed in his experience in New Mexico of ceremonial dances, carried on in quite loose connection with the church, that moved him profoundly, and that he could interpret in terms of his felt need, with some support from anthropological explanations. In Mexico there was an abundance of astronomically based symbolism of cosmic and human vitalistic unity—evening star, morning star, the moon that in "The Woman Who Rode Away" returned among the Indian women; and most pervasively the plumed serpent. Its associations with his experience of the close connection of death and life, underworld and sky, vital power and aspiring direction, ranged back to the underground of the mines and the natures of the miners; the natural imagery of his experience of inward death and resurrection; the arch connecting earth and sky, blood and spirit, in *The Rainbow*; and the Egyptian snake-beetle underworld and upperworld symbolism of "The Ladybird." Aztec sun worship fitted his earlier sense—for example in *The Trespasser*—of sun and day as male power and action to which the moon of the woman became acquiescent and untroubling. Besides this there was the diversity of the international scene to which Lawrence was so sensitive in the Mexican complex of Indian, Spaniard, Mexican of mixed blood, and English and American tourists and settlers. The handicrafts in the markets; the landscape's contrast of fecundity with arid waste; the mixture of privilege and poverty; the emphasis on male pride; and the omnipresent awareness of death, all contributed to the development of his theme.

Lawrence's potential leaders of a vitalistic revolution had always had to face the opposition of the woman. It could not be achieved without her acquiescence, subjugation or conversion. This is why Kate Leslie becomes the central character of *The Plumed Serpent*, vacillating between her white, European reactions and the dark, vitalistic way of the Quetzalcoatl movement and her marriage to the Indian Cipriano.

At the beginning Kate is already in rebellion against the values of modern life. In Mexico she fears the ancient sacrificial spirit and the violence of contemporary banditry and revolution, a reaction that represents Lawrence's own violence-abhorring English sensibility. The foreboding that fills the novel is in this way accounted for realistically. But psychologically and religiously it expresses the hazards of the vital resurgence Lawrence desired. As he put it in one of the too frequent explanatory passages,

that which is aboriginal in America still belongs to the way of the world before the Flood, before the mental-spiritual world came into being. In America, therefore, the mental-spiritual life of white people suddenly flourishes like a great weed let loose in virgin soil. Probably it will as quickly wither. A great death come. And after that, the living result will be a new germ, a new conception of human life, that will arise from the fusion of the old blood-and-vertebrate consciousness with the white man's present mental-spiritual consciousness. The sinking of both beings, into a new being.

Again and again Kate recoils from this fusion and is reassured. As she journeys to her first meeting with Don Ramón, the prophet-leader of the movement, after her removal from the modern horrors of Mexico City, she feels, in the "seething" light of the lake with the blue-ribbed mountains beyond, that she is swallowed by "some grisly skeleton." She fears the boatman as if he were a "half-being with a will to disintegration and death." But a sense of "peace and power" descends on her from "the potent air," and she feels that she is wrong to be afraid, since such men contain no "fixed evil." At once her apprehension of the scene changes to a sense of vividness and richness. This alternation between revulsive fear and vitalistic trust provides the basic rhythm of the novel.

At Sayula, Kate witnesses the singing and dancing of the men of Quetzalcoatl, and receives a leaflet bearing one of the poems by Ramón which serve as the propaganda and the hymns of the new religion, and sustain Lawrence's fable: the passing of "Jesus the Crucified" back to the womb of the vitalistic cycle of gods and civilizations, and the return of wholeness and fulfillment through his brother, Quetzalcoatl. Kate also discovers that Ramón's wife Carlota, a devout Catholic, is opposed to the Quetzalcoatl movement, and becomes partially leagued with her, through her own revulsive skepticism. Ramón withdraws from their hostility by darkening his room and praying until he has "broken the bonds of the world" and is "free in the other, mindless strength." Preparing himself for sleep, he takes care not to disturb the "poisonous snakes of mental consciousness." When on awakening he hears the voices of the women still talking, he resorts again to "black, mindless" prayer to dispel "the sense of opposition" and his anger.

At his hacienda Ramón has turned the crafts and arts to service of the new religion. A smith forges the symbol of an eagle inside a seven-pointed sun. Ramón's pose for a sculptor suggests the gestures of Indian dance, and possibly other mystic emblems of universal harmony, his right hand reaching to the sky, the left toward the earth. The pose has ritualistic efficacy; when the sculptor assumes it, his face takes on an expression of "peace in noble, motionless transfiguration." The symbol of the eagle within the sun, suggesting the outer world, day activity and power of the male, appears again on the serapes worn by the men of Quetzalcoatl. Ramón summons them to services by beating an Indian drum, and they sing together in the "strange, blind, infallible rhythm of the ancient barbaric world." When he prays, he uses the symbolism (suggesting theosophy) of the snake of the "coiled cosmos, out of whose sleep worlds arise and are gone as dreams," and emphasizes the *now* in a dynamic flux, the moment of intense being. When he preaches, he uses terms that differentiate his concept of leadership from the dominant and possessive. Their leaders will be "lords and masters among, not of, men." To them everything— "property, land, love, life, peace, sorrow, loss of strength, and death"—is part of the vitalistic flow. Nothing is theirs; it is "with them." Another of his prayers suggests the rain dances of the New Mexico Indians when he appeals to the serpent of the earth to send life into feet and ankles, and, raising his right arm, invokes the eagle of the sky to send power and wisdom. As he prays, the wind rises, and after he preaches the new faith, rain begins. His sermon makes it clear that the rain is a means of self-purification of the past, and entrance into the new self and world. The leaflet-hymns of Quetzalcoatl have this renewal as their burden.

As Kate's friendship with Ramón and his lieutenant the soldier Cipriano develops, she learns of the political situation in which they work. The president of the republic, says Cipriano, has the "cravings" of a dictator. His opposition to the Quetzalcoatl movement is based on materialism. He wishes to save his country from hunger and ignorance, while Ramón believes that if a man has no soul it does not matter whether he is hungry or ignorant. Despite this disagreement, the president has given his word that Ramón will not be interfered with. Like Somers in *Kangaroo*, Ramón rejects political power. When he is angered by the opposition of Kate and his wife, he is tempted toward nihilism, but he fears and rejects its anarchic extreme. His intention to avoid politics is challenged by the dangerous opposition of the Church, the Knights of Cortes, and a certain "black" faction. But with Cipriano and his army behind him, he has not much to fear, and he feels it would be better to abandon everything than to be pushed in the direction of any party. When Cipriano tempts him with the idea of a holy war, his answer combines Lawrence's earlier thinking about leadership with vitalistic pluralism of religion. Ramón would like to be one of the "Initiates and Initiators of the Earth." To achieve unity, the "First Men" of every people would form a "Natural Aristocracy of the World," for the reason that only such people can be international, cosmopolitan, or cosmic. The mass of people, incapable of this larger view, think in terms of their various ancient religions—Quetzalcoatl in Mexico; Thor and Wotan in the Teutonic world; the Tuatha De Dannan in the Druidic world. The leader's function is that of linking this lesser, more relative religious view with the larger view, achieving unity in multiplicity. The implication is that force would not be necessary because nothing would be destroyed.

Ramón has his own moments of loss of confidence and revulsion, chiefly caused by aspects of Kate's opposition that he partly shares—for example, her dislike of masses of people and joining movements. He insists that one can successfully turn beyond people to "the greater life," but as he encounters the limited, social aspect of mankind, he becomes "sad with a sense of inadequacy." Someone burlesques his ideas by replacing the sacred images of a church with the papier-maché Judas figures used at Easter; Cipriano slips back into personal ambition; Kate's opposition is "sheer repudiation." Ramón's anger is reflected in a leaflet that attacks foreigners and the machines they introduce.

The Church begins to move against him, though cautiously since it is already under governmental restriction. Ramón and Cipriano seek an interview with Bishop Jiminez, and Ramón asks for peace, his argument being that there is room for more than one religion. But he admits that he intends to remove the images from the church at Sayula and replace them with those of Quetzalcoatl, and the Bishop accuses him of the madness of pride. Cipriano regards this as the response of an old Jesuit who wants to keep his job and his power. Ramón is angry and weary.

The "revival" of the Quetzalcoatl religion is, then, quite local and minimal in its direct opposition to Christianity. Ramón enters the church at Sayula with a young priest who officiates at a solemn, respectful ceremony of repudiation and carries the crucifix and the images to a boat that transports them to an island for burning. Lawrence's chapter title, "Auto da Fé," suggesting a reversal of the Inquisition's methods, indicates the extent to which he was aware of the historical implications. As a last rite, the priest removes his vestments, casts them into the flames, and stands revealed in the garment of a man of Quetzalcoatl. There is even a touch of Biblical portent in the vitalistic thunder, wind, and rain that follow this symbolic action.

The attempt on Ramón's life by the Knights of Cortes that follows, raises again the issue of religious justification of even defensive violence. Ramón's acceptance of the necessity of having killed is placed far back on the evolutionary scale—he has what Lawrence calls the "primitive, pure look of virginity and beauty that goes with pristine rudimentariness." It is Kate who expresses the civilized revulsion. As she looks at the bodies of the attackers, she wishes the natives were not so beautiful, even though their dark beauty is that of "half-created, half-evolved things." She wishes that people were "souls," and their bodies "gestures from the soul," rather than manifestations of perverse materialism or "distorted animalism." Violence seems to her, as it did to Lawrence during the war, to have "snapped the threads that bind her to humanity," and she is plunged into a "wan, deathly indifference."

This vitalistic "dryness" of spirit is overcome through her relationship with Cipriano, in whom she feels the power of an "ancient phallic mystery" that brings her a feeling of "supreme passivity." Her journey with him to the end of the lake, in a scene full of timeless life and movement, is imaginative preparation for the vitalistic transcendence of their sexual consummation. In intercourse, she "fuses" into unconsciousness, her will and self gone. In the marriage ceremony conducted by Ramón that follows, the man is the "rain from heaven," the woman the "earth that is strength to him throughout the long twilight of the Morning Star"; that is, the retirement of Quetzalcoatl, and the period of modern vital decadence. Ramón's words express the eternal Lawrencean problem of the connection of human with higher relationships and, perhaps, Lawrence's attitude toward his recent separation from Frieda. The star imagery differentiates the two relationships. Whoever betrays another man, betrays a "fragment," like himself. But whoever betrays the star, the divinely vital connection that is between him and another man, or a man and a wife, betrays all.

This higher relationship for Kate and Cipriano is consecrated when Ramón, for the first time, opens the church for the rites of Quetzalcoatl. This one scene imaginatively resolves all the tensions of Lawrence's

experience and thought since *The Rainbow,* including his anger at opposition and betrayal. By putting the women in the center, between
two rows of men, he gives them a central sustaining position, and they
crouch on the floor as the men, masters of the activity beyond the love
relationship, salute Quetzalcoatl. Again the Morning Star is the equili-
brator, greater than the worshippers, and symbol of "the new dawn"
they must not betray. The "wine of the spirit" and the "blood of the
heart" must be mingled and dedicated to the star. At this moment of
expression of the vitalistic sacrament, Ramón's wife, Carlota, enters,
calls upon Mary and Jesus to take his life and thereby save his soul,
and, when he is unaffected, collapses, a dying woman. Cipriano is the
vitalistic accuser— charitable but fundamentally compassionless, she has
extinguished her own life. Only Kate is sympathetic, and doubtful of
the rightness of this view.

Cipriano now wants to advance the new faith as a state religion. But
Ramón insists that it spread of itself, and writes open letters—to the
clergy calling for a greater catholicism, and to the socialists urging them
to forget their grudges. He redirects Cipriano toward the higher aim by
urging him to assume the "living Huitzilopochtli," and engaging him
in a ritual that echoes distantly the love between men of the bathing
scene in Lawrence's first novel, *The White Peacock,* the attempt at
brotherhood of the wrestling scene in *Women in Love,* and the recognition through touch of "The Blind Man." This is followed by Cipriano's and Kate's assumption of places in the Quetzalcoatl pantheon.

Now, as the warrior god Huitzilopochtli, Cipriano must officiate at
the execution of the surviving attackers of Ramón, who, rather inconsis-
tently with the realistic substructure of the fable, and with Ramón's
rejection of political involvement, have been held as prisoners when
they might have been turned over to the civil authority. It is as if Lawrence here could not avoid the civil and moral implications of his theocratic position. Ramón's servants, guilty of personal betrayal, are gar-
rotted. The four attackers from outside are permitted to draw twigs,
one of which bears the green leaf of Kate's incarnation of Malintzi, who
pardons once. The losers are executed and their bodies placed at the
feet of the statue of Huitzilopochtli, while the souls are given to Quetzalcoatl, who tells them to make their peace now with "sun, wind, and

waters," and to go with courage. Kate's revulsion against Cipriano because of his participation in the executions is overcome when she sees in him a quality that is not *will* but the higher *wish* to which the will was only instrumental, and she again consents to be Malintzi.

At this point Lawrence had taken the theocratic implications of his theme to their furthest extension, in the right not only to punish, but to take life. He had imaginatively resolved his long-standing debate with Frieda, with the world, and with himself. Why, then, did he go on with it for three more chapters? And more hesitantly?

He provides Ramón with an appropriate wife in the gentle, loyal Teresa, who has the power to make him "great in the flesh while she herself remains inconspicuous, indeed almost invisible." But Kate hates what seems to her Teresa's subjection. Her own "handsome, ruthless" female power, she realizes, is second-rate compared to Teresa's; but this does not keep her from making plans to leave Mexico. When Cipriano reacts to her decision with stoic emotionlessness and tolerance, she fears losing contact with him. Without him to submerge her will, she would become one of those "horrible elderly females, charmless but avid, who look for scarcer and scarcer prey." Her going to Ramón and Cipriano to make a submission continues the ambiguity of her position. When she says she wishes to stay, Ramón's gentleness makes her feel she is a fraud. Ramón's advice, representing that side of Lawrence that believes in ultimate self-reliance, is that she should follow her own best desire. But Cipriano's intervention is an assertion of the side of Lawrence that believed in male mastery.

This more personal, less "philosophical," and rather tentative victory over Kate's scruples and will constitutes a second, more characteristically open ending. Lawrence does go on to a final triumph of the Quetzalcoatl movement (which violates the letter if not the spirit of Ramón's resolve to avoid politics). The Church and the Knights of Cortes fight a "kind of war" against the men of Quetzalcoatl. After Cipriano's army wins a battle, President Montes outlaws the Church, and establishes the new religion as the state religion. But the dominant, humanly realistic ending is the struggle, apparently endless, to keep Kate within the orbit of Lawrence's reformation.

The small colony of kindred spirits that had for so long been Lawrence's devoutest desire takes the form of a successful national, and potentially international organization. This result, which seems from the biographical-critical vantage point to have been inevitable because of the action-reaction patterns of his life and work to this point, is an intellectual tour de force that can arouse only partisan reactions. What gives the novel esthetic, emotional, and ethical validity is not the perfection of a new religious, social political system but the qualitative struggle towards it, and against it. Lawrence himself soon felt that leadership of a nature compatible with his religious vision was no longer possible.

Criticism tends to rank the novel low. Those who rank it high emphasize its skillful employment of myth, and feel that it is imaginative and prophetic rather than dogmatic and didactic. It is surely a faulty mixture of these qualities. There are passages of imaginative evocation of the dangers, disturbances, and harmony and peace of Lawrence's vitalistic experience as good as anything he ever wrote. But the formal religious development is often embarrassingly pseudo-poetic, preachy, and posturing. And the involvement, despite disavowals of desire for political power, with punishment, execution, war, and state sanction, suggests a theocratic intolerance potentially as anti-life as the status quo Lawrence opposed.

4. Mediterranean & English Salvations

T HE DANGER in discussing the few years of life remaining to Lawrence after his return to Europe in 1925, is the temptation to see an absolute climax (or anticlimax) for his career where further development was not fatally impossible. He was only forty-four at the time of his death, March 2, 1930, and there is no ultimately certain indication that his creative powers were failing. His imagination had been perennially renewed and extended by change of place, and during these last years in Europe, mainly in Italy, he was very productive, especially in the short forms.

Just as he had finished *The Plumed Serpent* in February 1925, he had come down with a critical illness that had been diagnosed, apparently for the first time in his medical history, as a tubercular breakdown. Another in the lifelong series of difficult, alienating experiences with government authority had followed when, at the United States border, he had been prevented from entering and had had to appeal to higher authority against the letter of the law concerning foreigners who might have contagious diseases. Back at the New Mexico ranch, where he had regained the strength needed for a move to Europe, he dealt once more with his brotherhood-betrayal theme in the play based on the Biblical story of the friendship of David and Jonathan. In September, the month of his birthday, and ironically the advent of a personally hazardous season among the cycles of natural vitality, he had gone first to England for a month of visiting, on to Baden-Baden for a briefer visit with Frieda's relatives, and then in mid-November had reached Spotorno on the Italian Riviera.

His residence in Spotorno and, for a much longer time, at the Villa Mirenda near Florence was, of course, largely for reasons of health. But his continuing alienation from the civilizations of the north, particularly England, was a strong intellectual and emotional factor. He began to re-experience both the modern decadent Mediterranean he had fled, and its clues to natural and religious sources of the vital way of life. This experience is often developed in his stories through a sun symbolism that, though it had origins as far back as *The Trespasser,* had been profoundly affected by his American experience. In the essay titled "New Mexico" he said of this influence:

> I think New Mexico was the greatest experience from the outside world that I have ever had. It certainly changed me forever. Curious as it may sound, it was New Mexico that liberated me from the present era of material and mechanical development. Months spent in holy Kandy, in Ceylon, the holy of holies of southern Buddhism, had not touched the great psyche of materialism and idealism which dominated me. And years, even in the exquisite beauty of Sicily, right among the old Greek paganism that still lives there, had not shattered the essential Christianity on which my character was established. Australia was a sort of dream, or trance, like being under a spell, the self remaining unchanged, so long as the trance did not last too long. Tahiti, in mere glimpse, repelled me: and so did California, after a stay of a few weeks. There seemed a strange brutality in the spirit of the western coast, and I felt: O, let me get away!
>
> But the moment I saw the brilliant, proud morning shine high up over the deserts of Santa Fe, something stood still in my soul, and I started to attend. . . . In the magnificent fierce morning of New Mexico one sprang awake, a new part of the soul woke up suddenly, and the old world gave way to a new. . . . it is curious that the land which has produced modern political democracy at its highest pitch should give one the greatest sense of over-weening, terrible proudness and mercilessness: but so beautiful, God! so beautiful! . . . Just day itself is so tremendous there. It is so easy to understand that the Aztecs gave hearts of men to the sun. For the sun . . . is of a brilliant and unchallengeable purity and haughty serenity which would make one sacrifice the heart to it. Ah, yes, in New Mexico the heart is sacrificed to the sun and the human being is left stark, heartless, but undauntedly religious.

This feeling, which seems to have been reflected in *The Plumed Serpent,* is expressed now as a softer, strongly sexual Mediterranean sun pride and power. At the same time the leadership idea is replaced by a renewed emphasis on, and hope in, a more humanly limited quality of vitalistic relationship. In 1928 Lawrence wrote to Witter Bynner, with whom at Chapala he had argued the necessity of leadership:

> On the whole, I think you're right. The hero is obsolete, and the leader of men is a back number. After all, at the back of the hero is the militant ideal: and the militant ideal, or the ideal militant seems to me also a cold egg. We're sort of sick of all forms of militarism and militantism. . . . On the whole I agree with you, the leader-cum-follower relationship is a bore. And the new relationship will be some sort of tenderness, sensitive, between men and men and men and women. . . .

Then he added, as if Bynner might mistake this for capitulation, a statement that reveals the reformist side of his new emphasis: "But still, *in a way*, one has to fight, but not in the O Glory! sort of way. I feel one still has to fight for the phallic reality, as against the non-phallic cerebration unrealities. . . ."

This new fight was carried on against odds that would have broken many men. Lawrence was now in middle age. His letters speak calmly, almost deprecatingly of bronchial hemorrhages worse than those he had suffered in America. He was confined to bed for days at a time. Ironically, in the Italy of his sun-symbol of vital renewal, the season was often rainy. Once, out of its denial of his need, he dreamed of a flood back in New Mexico in which his horse was drowned and he was able to find only a "bunch of weird, rather horrible pintos." He had never known a spring so impotent as that of 1926, when, after five days of sun, the weather reverted to gray and wet. February was the bad month for him to get through, to the resurrection of spring. For a man who had lived intimately with disintegration and death from childhood, and had felt at times a desire to lapse into them, what was now going on was a newly crucial contest for life.

In his fiction his perception of nature, always acute, is revivified, diversified and softened by the more civilized landscape. At the same time, his satire is enriched by his encounter with the milieu of health, pleasure, and culture seekers. The strong sexuality of the peasant contrasts boldly with the dilettantism in life of the sophisticated and the bourgeois. For myth he returns to what is more traditional in his education and experience, Pan and Dionysus, and Isis and Osiris superseding Quetzalcoatl. Whatever his mistrust of an anthropocentric view of life, the world of his fiction becomes more humanized. Ultimately his imagination turns again to England, the original and deepest cause of his *saevo indignatio,* in an attempt to establish new roots in native ground.

This attempt was in part a response to the political activity in Europe that was to culminate in World War II. In 1924, as an older writer who had a following, sometimes evangelical, among the young, he had begun a correspondence with Rolfe Gardiner about the youth movement springing up in Germany, and Gardiner's hopes for one in England. From the first, Lawrence criticized the regimentation inherent in nationalistic efforts by affirming his belief in the "pagan many gods" and the animistic vision. Chaos, he said, did not bother him as much as "abstract, or mechanical," order. There was life in the crumbling of the "white ideas," the "oneness," into many pieces, with "all sorts of wonder coming through." He continually advised Gardiner to "fight free of stunts and regimentation." Yet there is no doubt that Gardiner's plans appealed to his old hope for a colony of kindred souls, if not to the evangelistic spirit that had reached a climax in *The Plumed Serpent,* and he seems to have thought of joining him in such a venture on an English farm. His exile was now troubled by the weary feeling that it was "time to go home," the phrase he used in a letter to Aldous Huxley in late 1927. To Gardiner he wrote with characteristic stubborn humor in 1928: "Perhaps I'm due to go back to the Old England: and perhaps you are the whale that will spit forth my Jonahship on to the destined coast. . . . Max Mohr says we must all have roots. But at a certain point the business of the thistle is to roll and roll on the wind. Pazienza!" The anti-heroic nature of such humor, and his reawakened sense of the existential human being to whom sexual fulfillment would be a "tenderness," a humanly profound salvation no matter what the involvement in the meanness of the world, were safeguards against his latent ambition to be the prophet-leader.

In the spring of 1926 he wrote of his long standing alienation in very simple terms: "Frieda says we must live more with other people: which I think is true. It's no use trying to be exclusive. . . . If we are to live, we must . . . not cut ourselves off." To Gardiner he had written: " . . . I shall be very glad to abandon my rather meaningless isolation, and join with some few other men, if I can." But it was in his correspondence with Dr. Trigant Burrow, whose social psychology deeply interested him during his last years, that he engaged in the most self-searching analysis.

> What ails me is the absolute frustration of my primeval societal instinct. The hero illusion starts with the individualist illusion, and all resistances ensue. I think societal instinct much deeper than sex instinct—and societal repression much more devastating. There is no repression of the sexual individual comparable to the repression of the societal man in me, by the individual ego, my own and everybody else's. I am weary even of my own individuality, and simply nauseated by other people's. I should very much like to meet somebody who has been through your laboratory, and come societally unrepressed. Is there anybody? If it weren't for money, the peasants here wouldn't be bad. But money is the stake through the bowels of the societal suicide.

While, of course, such a confession contains no solution to his problem, it indicates a considerable mellowing of Lawrence's attitude toward the world around him. And one cannot help wondering if this would not have resulted in increasingly poised and witty creativity and counsel if the official world had not turned on him again in censorship of *Lady Chatterley's Lover*, his paintings, and the poems *Pansies*, and if he had lived on.

I

The short stories of Lawrence's last years seem to reflect the recession of his insistence on leadership and an elaborate religious program, and the emergence of a new awareness of simpler human needs. In them he is acutely sensitive to the evil of, the arrest or destruction of the vitality and hope of the young. Frequently he takes up the shallow popular genres of the naturalistic shocker, the story of the supernatural, the ghost story, and the murder story, and transforms them into vitalistic parables, as if to say: Here is the real meaning of those frightening events towards whose shallow or false explanations we are so credulous.

The chronology of some of the stories is in doubt. Most of them cluster during the period from late 1925 into 1928, the year of completion and publication of *Lady Chatterley's Lover*, and contain the themes and the quality of imagination of that last major effort. A few, like "Smile" and "The Overtone," may be of earlier vintage. The former seems to reflect the conflict of the friendship with John Middleton Murry in 1923, and the latter may date from 1924.[1]

"Smile" cruelly expresses Lawrence's insight into the existential confusion that contradicts both the ideal concept of right relationship, and the vitalistic, resembling somewhat the first part of Camus' *The Stranger*. The English husband journeying to his wife's deathbed in France, knows what he ought to feel because of his training in the proper feelings. He has always taken life seriously, and now, during his journey, seriousness overwhelms him. "His dark, handsome, clean-shaven face would have done for Christ on the Cross, with the thick black eyebrows tilted in the dazed agony." When he thinks of a bit of sentimental memorial verse, his "monk's face" shows no sign of the contempt, "even self-contempt," with which he regards its bathos. Actually he is no longer capable of much feeling at all.

At the convent to which his wife had retreated from the world, this seriousness yet incapacity to feel is involved in a subtle vitalistic comedy of manners. When the Mother Superior leans toward him, he is frightened by even such a slight, innocent female advance. Lawrence does a subtly beautiful and unexpected thing with the hands of the nuns, which, as they gesture and fold and disappear in the sleeves of the habit, are "like sleeping birds, momentarily rousing." To the husband they are "nice hands" he would like to touch. The ultimate contradiction of his monkish seriousness occurs when he sees the beautiful composure of his wife's face. Something "leaps like laughter" in him, he gives a "little grunt," and an "extraordinary smile" comes over his face.

---

1. See Harry T. Moore's discussion in *The Life and Works of D. H. Lawrence*, pp. 250, 276.

Answering smiles appear involuntarily on the faces of the nuns, that of the young having "a touch of mischievous ecstasy," that of the mature one, "the pagan Etruscan smile with its archaic humor, subtle, unabashed, and unanswerable."

Fearing that his wife has seen him, he replaces his smile with a look of super-martyrdom. In life she had been willful and obstinate and, though she loved him, had left and returned a dozen times; now even in death she is provoking. He forces himself to dwell on his own imperfections, and surprises the nuns with a snarled *"Mea culpa!"* But his smile involuntarily returns, and the nuns and he see an answering mocking smile on the face of the dead woman. He can only flee, the "voluminous figures of the nuns with framed faces and lost hands" following and seeming to bear down on him. The seriousness of the situation has become archetypal modern and ancient sexual comedy.

"The Overtone" is quite unconventional and uncharacteristic in technique, its title coming from the psalmlike interior monologue that expresses the meaning of the failure of love for an older couple as it is felt by a young woman. Lawrence's characteristic opening exposition of the vitalistic irony of the situation he will explore, is absent. A young-looking but middle-aged husband pretends to read while his wife talks to two other women. Outdoors, the night is lustrous from a white moon that "goes like an unashamed and naked woman across the sky," an image of vitalistic promise of fulfillment that reaches back through Lawrence's work to his struggle between loyalty to his dying mother and the young women who were in their way constraining, and his restless effort to break through to fulfillment. The wife talks of state-endowment of mothers (realized in Mussolini's Italy), which she and another older woman approve because for them vital relationship has failed. The girl is attentive not to the overt meaning of the words but to the overtone of the wife's blighted heart. The husband, bored by such abstract talk of sex, lives again the crisis that six months after his marriage left him unfulfilled and immature. The scene is created in terms and images that closely resemble those of Lawrence's immediately pre-war and wartime fiction. The night's great circle is the pupil of an eye, full of the "mystery of the fire of life that burns unquenchably." High on a hill under the moon, a situation of exposure in vitalistic communion that in *The*

Rainbow was Ursula's test of Skrebensky, he asks his wife to give herself in intercourse.

> . . . he wanted to unglove himself. Quite clear, quite, quite bare to the moon, the touch of everything, he wanted to be. And after all, his wife was everything—moon, vapour of trees, trickling water and drift of perfume— it was all his wife. . . . And now, he would come perfectly clear out of all his embarrassments of shame and darkness, clean as the moon who walked naked across the night, so that the whole night was an effluence from her, the whole of it was hers, held in her effluence of moonlight, which was her perfect nakedness, uniting her to everything.

But she, needing "a shadow between them," commits the vitalistic sin of thinking his man's body ugly, hates his love-making and is "ravaged" by his consequent hate, so that forever after there is a distance between them, and no children.

The psalm-like overtone of the young woman's response, in which she grieves over the wife's despair, and wonders whether she herself can avoid such a mistake, culminates in a credo that harmonizes Lawrence's Pan-Christ conflict in a way that may be unparalleled in clarity and apparent serenity anywhere else in his work. Christ is the day-god of the human, responsible, social world; Pan, the night-god of the nonhuman, unconscious, vital force.

> But I am a nymph and a woman, and Pan is for me, and Christ is for me.
> For Christ I cover myself in my robe, and weep, and vow my vow of honesty.
> For Pan I throw my coverings down and run headlong through the leaves, because of the joy of running.
> And Pan will give me my children and joy, and Christ will give me my pride.
> And Pan will give me my man, and Christ my husband.
> To Pan I am nymph, to Christ I am woman.
> And Pan is in the darkness, and Christ in the pale light.
> And night shall never be day, and day shall never be night.
> But side by side they shall go, day and night, night and day, for ever apart, for ever together.
> Pan and Christ, Christ and Pan.

> Both moving over me, so when in the sunshine I go in robes among
> my neighbours, I am a Christian. But when I run robeless through the
> dark-scented woods alone, I am Pan's nymph. . . .

The husband and wife cannot hear this overtone. For them it is too late, and the young woman is simply glad to get away from them.

Most of the stories published during these last years, with perhaps the exception of "In Love," seem to be clearly the work of the first three years of the return to Europe, from 1925 into 1928. In "None of That" Lawrence recalled the potentially violent psychic antagonisms of the international cultural mixture to be found in Mexico, a situation that has also challenged the imagination of Katherine Anne Porter. The Mexican who tells the story of the brutal victory of a bullfighter over the will of an American woman, wanders about Europe, his painting only a sedative for the pain of his own victimization by the woman, and the horror of her ultimate fate.

The bullfighter's animal power is revealed in his eyes, "more marvellous than those of a lion or tiger because they are not afraid to look into people where their courage lives, and melt it." Various women have taken him as lover and lived because they did not oppose him, but he speaks obscenely of all save two humble Mexican Indian women. The American woman is characterized by a "false exterior innocence, enthusiasms that pall," and a desire to know any man who seems to have a "dramatic sort of power." In her relationships she is "dauntless and unscrupulous," making others "dance like marionettes in a tragi-comedy." European and American men have nearly always given in to her; but the Mexican men soon understand her nature and shun her. Her way of saying "I'm having none of that" when they expect her to become their mistress expresses her hate of their active maleness, and consequent cruelty to their bodies. She insists that what she wants is to live the life of the imagination, and through it to change history, but she only makes "human messes." When she talks of such an atrocity as the "famous case of the raped nuns," she says it is nonsense that a woman can be broken by such an experience, since the imagination can rise above anything.

Though she is warned by the narrator that the bullfighter is a sort of beast, and a deadly one, she responds to his challenge of her courage by trying to touch his imagination. Her failure produces in her a torturing tension between body and imagination, her mind saying that he is nothing, her body that he is the marvelous possessor of something she does not have. In the hysteria of this tension she vows that if her body proves stronger than her imagination, she will kill herself.

The narrator pleads with the bullfighter to leave her alone, but he is ruthlessly intent on defeating her and getting her money. Hating her too much to make love to her personally, he turns her over to a half-dozen of his bull-ring gang with orders not to bruise her. In three days she dies of nervous collapse. The authorities soon drop her case because of lack of evidence, and the distraction of a revolution. Here, Lawrence's insight into the conflict between vital power and anti-vital will and detachment is a means of understanding a sensational crime, and of heightening its essential horror.

In "Sun" the "stark, heartless" religious experience of the sun in New Mexico is softened, the sun god here being the Apollonian healer and lover, humanized by his insouciant maleness. The rather commonplace situation of an American woman seeking health on the Mediterranean, develops into a vitalistic marriage with the sun through the intricate interplay of realistic detail with a central symbol that marks Lawrence's best short fiction. Setting, character, and action suggest a parable of emergence from darkness, coldness, and deathliness. Even the wife's departure from New York is at midnight of a black night with the sea heaving like the "serpent of chaos." Everything human suggests her husband's vitalistic limitations and her essential need and direction. It is "all ashore" for him and "out to sea" for her. The harbor is domesticated sea, its ferry boats "like great dishes piled with rows of lights." Her nervous, willful behavior in her modern woman's freedom (as opposed to the poise and peace later found in the vitalistic relationship) is suggested by the phrase "Liberty flung up her torch in a tantrum." The symbolic play of colors begins at once, especially on grey for the dead world she leaves behind. Even in Italy, where she must conceal her golden nakedness when people appear, her robe is dove-grey, a device to make her invisible to the world. And grey suddenly proliferates when the husband appears toward the end: dark-grey suit, pale-grey hat, grey, monastic face of a business man, grey city face, "gold-grey eyes of an animal that has been caught young and reared completely in captivity." The color of sunlight and naked, tanned flesh is, of course, the countering corollary of inward goldness and warmth of feeling. In this Mediterranean place even the shadows are not grey or black.

The five parts of the story are beautifully proportioned to the stages of vitalistic resurrection. Part I ends when the wife, having achieved her own wholeness, turns to the transformation of her child into the "true male" who has the "power of the sun" and is vitally the sun's child. Through her mating with the sun, she loses the torment of her anxiety for the child and even laughs at the "fear and civilized tension" in him. At the end of this part, as his skin turns from white to gold-duskiness, he almost gives her the "challenging, warm look of the true male." Part III ends with the climax of his lack of fear of a snake, and her ability to face such danger for him without hysteria. The snake, she realizes, is a part of the place with her and her child, to be accepted, and treated with caution.

The vitalistic cycle of the sun from winter to spring also times the movement of the parts. By Part IV the month is March and the sun is growing very powerful. As it gains power, so do mother and child, and Lawrence is ready to engage the tame, grey husband in an ironic re-encounter. He arrives to the pagan, sardonic laughter of Marinina, an Italian woman who possesses the "shrewdness and humor that underlie all long experience, racial and individual." Her attitude, contained in an epigram, expresses Lawrence's mature view of the tragic response to life that was his first heritage: "Tragedy is lack of experience." Before the golden power of his wife and child, the grey man is abashed and admiring. Not completely the straw man of allegory, he too has the potentiality of vital power and does not want to return to their old relationship.

At the end of Part IV this divided modern family is confronted with the family of an Italian peasant dining in simple unity outdoors near the green wheat that produces the bread of their vitalistic communion. Part V seems something of an afterthought, as if Lawrence, following his practice of not pre-plotting, is drawn into exploring the possibilities of a relationship between the American wife and the peasant. The peasant is in the tradition of the simpler, lower-class Lawrencean hero, extending from George in the first novel, *The White Peacock*, to Mellors, the gamekeeper in *Lady Chatterley's Lover*. He has the "air of quiet superiority" that belongs to individuals, and though stout in the peasant fashion, belongs to Lawrence's physical tradition through his sunburnt face, his brown moustache, and thick brown eyebrows. He has a "violent generosity of blood," and the "wild animal faculty" of being able to work unseen. When he and the vitalistically resurrected woman unexpectedly meet, a "flame goes over his eyes," and a "flame over her body, melting her." She has even considered the possibility of conceiving his child from the "meeting of an hour" rather than from the "long civilized identification of her life with a man's life." Now as the two families dine in sight of each other, she realizes that she will have to bear her husband's child because he has his own "desperate kind of courage in desire," and will try to join her in the sun. She rebels against his "smelling of the world, its fetters, and its mongrel cowering." "Her conviction that the sun *knew* her, in the cosmic carnal sense of the word" has brought her a feeling of detachment, and a certain contempt for human beings altogether. Intercourse with the peasant would at least resemble the "procreative sunbath" she truly wants. But she yields to her husband, a yielding that, Lawrence says at the end, is a "link in the fatal chain of continuity."

"Glad Ghosts" is a wonderfully skillful and poignant transformation of the ghost story into a parable of vitalistic salvation that resembles, in situation and development, "The Ladybird." The narrator-protagonist is concerned with his vision of "the quick body" within the living dead rather than with the traditional ghost story teller's haunting spirits. His anti-life antagonist is the spiritualistic, aristocratic old woman who dominates her family through fear. His ally in his "secret mission in an enemy country" is the daughter-in-law; their mutual vitalistic understanding transcends class barriers.

> She and I were "friends" in a bare, stark, but real sense. I was poor, but didn't really care. She didn't really care either. Whereas I did care about some passionate vision which, I could feel, lay embedded in the half-dead body of this life. The quick body within the dead. I could *feel* it. And I wanted to get at it, if only for myself.

She didn't know what I was after. Yet she could feel that I was It, and, being an aristocrat of the Kingdom of It, as well as the realm of Great Britain, she was loyal—loyal to me because of It, the quick body which I imagined within the dead. . . . She and I had a curious understanding in common: an inkling, perhaps, of the unborn body of life hidden within the body of the half-death which we call life; and hence a tacit hostility to the commonplace world, its inert laws. We were rather like two soldiers on a secret mission in an enemy country. Life, the people, was an enemy country to us both. But she would never declare herself.

She had married Lord Lathkill, who even before the war was afraid because, though he was "sure of circumstances," he was by no means sure of the "man in the middle of the circumstances." Now, years later, his voice husky from a wound in the throat, he is "possessed by a monomaniac fear." The tradition of bad luck in the family has been confirmed by the death of their children. His wife's struggle against his emptiness and fear is destroying her beauty. Her summary judgment of the situation, when the narrator makes his latter-day visit to the Lathkill house, is: "To be the living dead, that's awful." Also guests are an aging Colonel who believes that he is haunted by the troubled spirit of his unfulfilled first wife and that his "manhood is killed," and his young wife to whom, in his spiritualistic fear, he has "denied his body."

The narrator's reaction to the situation is that a man should take the young Lady Lathkill in his arms and by "cherishing her body, start her life flame" again. He forces liveliness in this haunted house by making the murmuring servants speak loudly and decisively, by insisting on and praising common burgundy at dinner, and by calling the Obelisk Memorial Service for the war dead a "thing of wet mob-emotions." What the house needs is "a spring cleaning," with "Bacchus and Eros to freshen it." The Colonel, whose notion of commands from his dead wife has been encouraged by the cold, spiritualistic elder Lady Lathkill, should be a "fat, healthy, jolly old boy." His vitalistic effort reaches a climax when the younger people, Lord Lathkill and the Colonel's wife, and the narrator and Lady Lathkill, in dancing together oppose the life force of their rapport to the death force in the old woman. The Colonel realizes that his sin against the dead wife who haunts him was his not being kind to her body. As his vitalistic revelation develops, Lawrence utters a characteristic outraged cry against what he regards as Christianity's part in this unkindness: "Oh, Jesus, didn't you know that you couldn't be crucified alone?—that the two thieves crucified along with you were the two women, your wife and your mother!"

The narrator's function as exorciser of ghosts and savior of the living dead is then extended to sexual relationship with young Lady Lathkill, whom he visits as a very real ghost in the haunted bedroom. Both she and the Colonel's wife conceive children during this night of vitalistic resurrection, the one the "blonde, springlike" son of the narrator, the other the "dark" child of the less alive man, Lord Lathkill. Lawrence's vitalistic savior characteristically wanders in "uneasy and distant parts of the earth." Those to whom he has brought peace cannot understand this, and want him to return. They are, in a sense, the ghosts of pain and deathliness Lawrence had fled from after the war become no more than the hopeful creatures of a story, and, through it, the recipients of a long distance message.

"The Virgin and the Gipsy," dedicated to Frieda and written near a time of reconciliation with her daughter Barbara, now a young woman, is a beautifully organized exploration of, and attack on, the anti-life forces ranged against such young women. The two whose mother had left their father when they were little girls, live in a stone house in a stony, bleak countryside. Compared with the valley in which the house is situated, by a river that eventually rages, the upland is at least high, open, and "naked," and it is there that Yvette seeks the vitalistic man, the gipsy, and experiences the revelation of life in the gipsy camp's bright, warm, transient shelter, so unlike the vitalistically claustrophobic home.

Season, weather, and flowers become metaphorical of her need and search. Late winter rain and mud in the valley hamper the young people's activity. In this anti-life ambient the only flower is the snowdrop, whose characteristics and name are connected with the father's idealism and spirituality, which permit him to dismiss the vital side of his errant wife.

> . . . in the pure loftiness of the rector's heart still bloomed the pure white
> snowflower of his young bride. This white snowflower did not wither. That

other creature, who had gone off with that despicable young man, was none of his affair.

Outside the stone house and the pure heart, the real snowdrops resemble Yvette, palely alive in treacherous moral weather. When she is with the gipsy on the upland, "the waking sleep of her full-opened virginity" is like a snowdrop in the sunshine.

Yvette and her sister are ranged against an old maid aunt and, as in so many of these late stories, a dominant, life-devouring old woman, their grandmother. The latter is one of the "morally clever" whose power is gained by catering to righteous feeling.

> The rector still "loved" his delinquent wife, and would "love her" till he died. Therefore hush! The rector's feeling was sacred. . . . Astutely she gave a sigh of homage to the rector's fidelity to the pure white snowflower, while she pretended to disapprove. In sly reverence for her son's great love, she spoke no word against that nettle which flourished in the evil world.

The stone house, then, is ruled by a substitute matriarchy based on denial of vital human reality. In his camp the gipsy is the master and the center of life. Even his way of moving, loose and supple, suggests his freedom and aliveness. As always in Lawrence, but more plainly now, these qualities have survived because he is a cultural outlaw in a conscious way that extends the traditional gipsy position. Society has trapped him only once, when he served in the war. Now he is harder, less trusting, as is the gamekeeper in *Lady Chatterley's Lover*. Response to Yvette's need and appeal would expose him to the grave danger of the vindictive power of society.

Yvette is exposed to this power in many ways. When it is discovered that she has used for her own purposes, intending to replace it, money she helped gather for a memorial to the war dead (a bête noire to Lawrence, representing an anti-life preoccupation with violent death) both her father and her aunt insanely exaggerate her moral failure. When she makes friends with a Jewess who, during the interim of getting a divorce, is living openly with the man she loves and intends to marry, her father expresses the ultimate fear and judgment implicit in his moral position: she must stop before she ends in a criminal-lunacy asylum. She experiences the ultimate self-doubt of the vitalistic rebel when she actually wonders if she is "one of the semi-criminal abnormals."

In the Jewess, as in the gipsy, Lawrence chose a member of a persecuted group to function as vitalistic antagonist to decadence. Ironically, it is her strong Hebraic moral sense that has precipitated her immediate unacceptability, since she is divorcing her husband on principle. Lawrence allies her "dark," outcast heritage with the northern indomitable fighter of such postwar stories as "The Border Line." Her lover is the "remnant surely of some old uncanny Danish stock." His "tenderness" for the Jewess is based on his sense of outraged justice, "the abstract morality of the north blowing him, like a strange wind, into isolation," and his defense of the gipsy, who had looked after the horses in his regiment during the war, is grounded in vitalistic values—the gipsy is a man who had as one good trait a gift with horses, and as the other, the strength to escape from death. He himself has survived, with the gipsy's help, the deathly experience of being buried for twenty hours under snow (a supporting detail of the freezing of the sensibility, vital struggle theme).

Yvette's danger of succumbing to the anti-life reaches a climax, and is temporarily resolved, through the spring flooding of the river—a bursting of bounds by a natural force that sweeps away the prison house, so apparently substantial, and drowns her major moral enemy. It is irresistibly analogous to a violent bursting out of repressed vitality, and a concomitant nihilism. Her bedroom, the one area of hope of life in the house, is left intact, but her deathly chill must be relieved by the naked contact of the gipsy's body, which is the saving grace of the vitalistic hero, rather than the sinful degradation feared by her family.

Yvette emerges from this experience as what Lawrence calls a "fighter within the pale." After a policeman, who feels the "unmarried man's terror" of a young woman in bed, has brought her down to her family clothed and in her right mind, she grieves for the vanished gipsy, but knows it is wise to say nothing. She receives a letter from him saying that he "lives in hope of saying the goodbye" that was interrupted by the flood. Lawrence's final antisocial, vitalistic irony is that only through the signature does Yvette realize he has a name.

In these stories the search for a total solution of cultural decadence through a prophet-leader—extending from *Aaron's Rod* through *The Plumed Serpent*—is absent, and along with it the argument, the heroics, and at times the dehumanization through Lawrence's own kind of religious abstraction and zeal. The manner is frequently more engaging because of the comic spirit, the greater relaxation and warmth, as in Joyce the dedicated but precious Stephen Dedalus is followed by the common but more lovable Leopold Bloom. At the same time there is a sharp emphasis on the inevitability of the "social cage," a bitter form of defeat for a man who had so strongly believed in the possibility of escape and a new life. The fight continues, but the emphasis is on minimal, partial victories "within the pale." The prophet-leader now is a skirmisher, moving on to fight another day.

"The Rocking-Horse Winner," probably the most frequently anthologized of Lawrence's stories, is a wonderfully sustained, shocking exploration of the vital, human cost of the abstract value of getting on in the world. It is rare among Lawrence's mature stories in its revelation of his great warmth for children, so clear in his early work. In the opening exposition, the reflexive play of the value terms is like a seed from which the story must develop a life or death struggle. The tone, that of the fairy tale, at once turns the social-psychological aspect of the situation towards the archetypical.

> There was a woman who was beautiful, who started with all the advantages, yet she had no luck. She married for love, and the love turned to dust. She had bonny children, yet she felt they had been thrust upon her, and she could not love them. They looked at her coldly, as if they were finding fault with her. And hurriedly she felt she must cover up some fault in herself. Yet what it was that she must cover up she never knew. Nevertheless, when her children were present, she always felt the centre of her heart go hard.

As Paul pursues his mother's love through luck on his rocking horse, that simple simulacrum of the natural that is so real to a child's imagination turns into a frantically galloping perversity. The boy's eyes become increasingly hard and cold, like those of the imitation horse, until near the end they are "like blue stones." And when his mother, her burst of terrible anxiety confirmed, feels that her heart has turned into a stone, the rhythmic terror of Lawrence's apprehension of the dehumanization of life comes to rest like the last stroke of a hammer.

On the realistic, psychological side, he creates in detail the ambiguous social passion of the parents that has replaced love, the child's sensitiveness to adult anxiety, and his picking up of a false clue to action from the mother's vague identification of lack of luck and money with her empty life. The muddle of values is revealed in such verbal confusions as the boy's identification of his uncle's "filthy lucre" with "filthy lucker." Characteristically, though all of the adults are involved in Lawrence's indictment, it is pronounced by the least respectable, the gambler uncle.

"Two Blue Birds" sardonically explores the relations of a writer with his wife and his secretary—the eternal triangle with a modern, Lawrencean twist. Though the wife and husband have no vital intimacy, they remain married in a modus vivendi of the freest sort. The secretary adores the intellectual husband platonically and serves him unquestioningly. The wife has unsatisfactory affairs. The husband-secretary relationship, which in its fundamental emotional unreality resembles the sentimentality of the popular song of the period, "The Blue Bird of Happiness," is attacked by the wife, just as the real bluebird on the lawn "draws a feather from the breast of her opponent."

She is antagonized by the service and adoration of not only the secretary but her family, and by her husband's "air of easy aplomb and good humour which is so becoming to a man, and which he only acquires when he is cock of his own little walk, made much of by his own hens." He dictates away "like the voice of God to Samuel" though the secretary must work hard for a small salary and gets "nothing from him as a man." The wife's attack on this spurious happiness coincides with his dictating an article based on the abstract esthetic notion that "what the modern novel lacks is architecture," while the bluebird fluttering around the feet of the secretary as if it were the bluebird of happiness is attacked by another. She suggests that there should be something lively in the life of a novelist. When the secretary, not understanding the point, the life-art connection, disclaims being involved in anything "cheap," the wife makes the vitalistic, reverse value judgment: "You don't call that being cheap? Why, I should say you got nothing out of him at all, you only give! And if you don't call that making yourself cheap—my God!"

"The Lovely Lady" develops a sons and lovers situation into a savage exposé of a mother's life-arresting parasitism. By feeding on sensation and the lives of the young, she preserves her looks even at the age of seventy-two. Characteristically Lawrence begins by mocking the appreciative language of sophisticated dilettantism, in both art and life.

> She really was a wonderfully preserved woman, of perfect *chic*. Of course, it helps a great deal to have the right frame. She would be an exquisite skeleton, and her skull would be an exquisite skull, like that of some Etruscan woman, with feminine charm still in the swerve of the bone and the pretty naive teeth.

Her secret is the "invisible wire" that connects her "fine, little eye-wrinkles" with her will. The movement of the story is toward the breaking of that wire, with a fatal ping. Her vitalistic antagonist is a niece, a plain woman of thirty, who is in love with her son. He, at thirty-two an unsuccessful barrister dependent on his mother's money, which she has made by collecting the preserved loveliness of antiques, is prevented from responding because his secret physical passion is paralyzed by the fascination of his mother.

One of the mother's beauty secrets is sunbathing. The place she uses for this expresses her nature—on the side of loveliness, pretty furnishings; on the side of deathliness, a little, yew-walled square. Here she serenely soaks up the sun's power for her own uses, while the niece bathes uncomfortably on top of the stable, thinking bitterly that if she has no other lover, she will have the sun. Through the rain-pipe extending from the stable roof to the enclosure below, she hears the mother reveal her secret.

> "Too much sun is as bad as too little. Enough sun, enough love thrill, enough proper food, and not too much of any of them, and a woman might live for ever. If she absorbs as much vitality as she expends! Or perhaps a trifle more!"

At the climax of these musings on the means of vital self-preservation, the niece learns that the son's father had been an Italian Jesuit who was the most perfect, poignant lover in the world because he gave himself to a woman "as he gave himself to God," and that the mother is responsible for the death, from her vital vampirism, of another son. Impersonating this son, the niece accuses her through the rain-pipe; the old woman's nerve, the wire of will, snaps; all the signs of her age, and her concealed malice, assert themselves; and she shortly dies. The result for the young couple is, of course, not a triumphant change of natures and situation. The niece is aghast at the outcome of her action. The son bitterly protests that while he has a heart, it is almost "sucked dry" by his experience of people who want power over others. The lovely lady's will leaves only a small sum to them; all the rest, with her valuable antiques, goes to found a museum bearing her name.

"In Love," which may be a rewriting of a much earlier story,[2] begins with the familiar situation of two sisters—here an older girl threatened with spinsterhood and now about to marry quite unromantically, and a younger still free of such jeopardy of peace of mind. The engaged sister is worried about spending a weekend with her fiancé in the intimacy of the little farm he has started for them, as at least an escape from suburbia. They have known each other for years, and she likes the feeling of comradeship when they work together at the farm; but she loathes his having fallen "in love" with her, and his cuddling and petting her. She feels that she is "at least as complicated as the motor-cars" he is so competent with, and needs "just as careful handling in starting off on the matrimonial road."

In the evening of their day at the farm, she endures his arm around her waist, but his attempt to be "lovey-dovey" seems idiotic, and she escapes by getting him to play some Tchaikovsky to "stir her up a bit." The music only makes immediate, human contact more impossible, and she slips outside into the cool October night, where she feels "like Mazeppa's horse, about to dash away into the infinite." Avoiding some real horses she comes across, she hides in an old willow. His search for her lacks "all male magic," and she thinks of him in Stephen Fosterish terms as "Poor Old Joe." They respond to each other vitally only after they express their real feelings. He has been playing a false movie-lover, Valentino role that he thinks will please her and get himself over the

---

2. See Harry T. Moore, *The Life and Works of D. H. Lawrence*, p. 255.

interval before they are married. Actually she loathes Valentino. Now, because she sees her fiancé's "honest, patient love" and "queer, quiet, central desire," a "hot flush goes over her heart," and she experiences real, vitally based love for him.

"Rawdon's Roof" directs Lawrence's vitalistic humor at a sophisticate who has vowed: "No woman shall sleep again under my roof!" Proprietary and humorously gallant toward his wife, from whom he is separated, he is having an affair with an unhappily married woman who is in love with him. His freedom from responsible involvement is threatened when she decides she can no longer stand her husband's making love to her to get his troubles off his mind, and seeks the sanctuary of Rawdon's roof. Her appearance disturbs the whole household— Rawdon, the narrator of the story, who is a visitor, and Rawdon's butler. The latter is slow in appearing because he has been in bed with his girl under this inviolable roof. Rawdon gets the wife back to her husband by means of the butler, flashlights, and an umbrella, while the narrator happens onto the butler's girl hiding in the spare bedroom, her rosy posterior projecting from the bedclothes. When Rawdon says pathetically, on his return, "Why aren't women content to be what a man wants them to be?" the narrator's answer is, "You start at the wrong end." The vitalistic low comedy of this is in direct line with the spirit of parts of *Lady Chatterley's Lover,* and many of the paintings and *Pansies* poems. The narrator is in sympathy with the butler and his girl and finds that Rawdon's roof looks just the same for her having "slept" under it. While by this stage in the reading of Lawrence's fiction, one is aware of anti-life and vitalistic "types," the variation, the sense of fresh observation, the easy colloquialism, and even, occasionally, the old aggressive attitude of carelessness about form, prevents an empty formalism.

"The Man Who Loved Islands" is a Kafkaesque fable of the existential ambiguities of man's effort to order life in a utopian way. Its three parts range through failure to be a master of productive enterprise and other people, and failure to realize a reasonable, happy personal detachment in less ambitious circumstances, to antipathy to anything remotely suggestive of the human.

On the first island, the anonymous man of fable begins his attempt to "regain Paradise" by spending money. He restores, builds, improves the land, and creates a little society of workers—farmhands and bailiff, a skipper for his yacht, an old carpenter and his wife, and a mason whose children help with the work—of which he is to be the "ideal Master." Lawrence's commentary on this takes the ironic and, one cannot help thinking, wistful form of arguing the good reasons for success.

> Well, it was ideal. The Master was no tyrant. Ah, no! He was a delicate, sensitive, handsome Master, who wanted everything perfect and everybody happy. Himself, of course, to be the fount of this happiness and perfection.
> But in his way, he was a poet. He treated his guests royally, his servants liberally. Yet he was shrewd, and very wise. He never came the boss over his people. Yet he kept his eye on everything, like a shrewd, blue-eyed young Hermes.

After five years even such a man, who suggests the vitalistic hero of "The Ladybird" by his wearing a ring with the Egyptian scarab of re-birth on it, must give up. The people defer to him, and in his presence are full of adulation, but they express a "subtle mockery." Only the old carpenter, absorbed in his work, is sometimes sincerely rude to him. The bailiff's wife sentimentalizes his role as Master into his being "so wonderful with the children" that he makes her think of "our Saviour Himself." The families begin to quarrel, and some of them leave. Ideal relationship deteriorates completely into the human frailty of the mainland.

Materially, too, things go wrong. The bills pile up. A bumper crop is followed at once by a series of misfortunes. Drastic attempts to cut expenses do not work. The place itself is characterized by the ambivalence Lawrence always found in life.

> The island itself seemed malicious. It would go on being hurtful and evil for weeks at a time. Then suddenly again one morning it would be fair, lovely as a morning in Paradise, everything beautiful and flowing. And everybody would begin to feel a great relief, and a hope for happiness.
> Then as soon as the Master was opened out in spirit like an open flower, some ugly blow would fall.

The island even has a human history that manifests itself in the present by the "upsurge of violent lusts and imaginations of cruelty" (the kind of thing Lawrence frequently felt in Druidic Cornwall and Aztec Mexico). And the isolation, with its dislocation of the sense of time, contributes to this.

> But once isolate yourself on a little island in the sea of space, and the moment begins to heave and expand in great circles, the solid earth is gone, and your slippery, naked dark soul finds herself out in the timeless world, where the chariots of the so-called dead dash down the old streets of centuries.

The defeated searcher for the earthly paradise sells his island at a loss to a hotel enterprise that makes of it a "handy honeymoon-and-golf island."

In Part II, he moves to a smaller island nearby, taking only the unadulatory old carpenter, and a widow and her daughter. Here, with so few people, in a place that has no human past, there is no longer a world, but a refuge. For a while, no longer a master, he finds a peace that resembles the naturally situated, nonhuman peace that was sometimes the Nirvana of Lawrence's reaction. All desire gone, his spirit is "like a dim-lit cave under water, where strange sea-foliage expands upon the watery atmosphere, and scarcely sways, and a mute fish shadowily slips in and slips away again." His writing "spins softly from him as if it were drowsy gossamer." He lives in "the mist of eternity."

His fall from this otherworldly Paradise is through sex. Despite his nervous dislike, he becomes the lover of the housekeeper, caught by her will and the "automatism of sex." He conceives of another kind of sexual relationship, "a new fresh delicacy of desire," yet he laments that by falling into desire at all he has lost "his place in the rare, desireless levels of Time to which he had at last arrived." He returns to the mainland world, to find that he does not fit in any more. Finally, after marrying the housekeeper and providing for her and their child, he buys at an auction his third and last island, very remote, buildingless and peopleless.

Here he lives alone, visiting ships with his boat his only tie to the world. But sometimes even the sheep, trees, and bushes are too like people.

He wanted only to hear the whispering sound of the sea, and the sharp cries of the gulls, cries that came out of another world to him. And best of all, the great silence.

When winter approaches, snow and eternal night wall him in. He takes a "cruel satisfaction" from the thought that soon nothing will be alive. But a dream of the heads of men swimming in the bay horrifies him with the possibility of unexpected human approach. He destroys all remaining signs of the human, even tearing the brass label from his stove and obliterating all other lettering in his cabin because, like human speech, it has become depraved and obscene, and at last he stands on an unrecognizable island. At the end, the first signs of spring appear, but he feels only the breath of new snow upon him, and death by freezing is near.

If the story shows, as Lawrence said it would, "how tiny an island must be before one can presume to fill it with his own personality," that presumption, of course, ends in denial of humanity and death. In view of Lawrence's own tendency toward utopian leadership, disillusion, nihilistic anger and revulsion, and isolation, it is impossible not to see the story as in part a rather terrible self-examination. As at the end of *Women in Love,* where hope for the freezing soul had lain in a non-instrumental relationship and the warm, more human direction of Italy, so now, after heroic leadership had failed, the real if much more vulnerable and minimal hope lay for Lawrence in the individual fight against the anti-life, and in the very warm quality he called "tenderness."

If one thinks back over the long history of Lawrence's association of cruel denial of life with the crucified Christ, dating from one of his first stories, "A Fragment of Stained Glass," it seems inevitable that he would one day transform the story of the crucifixion and resurrection into a vitalistic myth. The immediate stimulus of "The Man Who Died" was his discovery of a symbol when, at Eastertime of 1927, he saw in a shop window a toy rooster escaping from an egg. The story he evolved is, especially in the first part, a beautifully and somewhat classically modulated legend of the vitality of a man struggling to recover from a great defeat and trauma.

The season is, of course, spring, the time of natural and Christian resurrection. A peasant, one of those for whom Christ died, is proud of his young rooster, exceptional in his vital way—"a dandy rooster, in that dirty little yard with three patchy hens," as Lawrence puts it ironically and colloquially. When the rooster listens "to the challenge of far-off unseen cocks, in the unknown world," the peasant, afraid that he will fly away, ties him with a cord. His breaking of the cord coincides with Christ's awaking, numb and cold in the tomb, from the "long sleep" of his spiritual mission, which has also been an enslavement. He is reluctant to return from the nullity of death, and his only strength is that which comes from revulsion. He leaves the tomb with the caution of the "bitterly wounded," and begins his lifeward journey in the "sickness of unspeakable disillusion."

The direction of this journey is the Lawrencean vitalistic way from the city to the natural world of "herbage" and birds which his spiritual mission had denied him. In his first attempt to help the humanity that had crucified him he is an accessory to the peasant's entrapment of the escaped cock, and his reaction to this parallel of his own fate is to exclaim hopelessly: "Humanity! Especially humanity in authority! There was only one thing it could do." The peasant's offer of a refuge originates in his fear of, and dejection under, authority, rather than in courage and nobility, so that the vitalistic resurrection begins under unfavorable socio-human conditions. Lying in the yard under the morning sun, Christ feels no desire, and the rooster cowers in a corner. Yet through its diminished crowing, he understands the challenge from life to death—

> . . . a vast resoluteness everywhere flinging itself up in stormy or subtle wave-crests, foam-tips emerging out of the blue invisible, a black and orange cock or the green flametongues out of the extremes of the fig tree. They came forth, these things and creatures of spring, glowing with desire and with assertion.

As he observes the peasant, he feels that he has been wrong to "seek to lift up what belongs to the earth." And when he meets "Madeleine," he says to her: "The teacher and the saviour are dead in me; now I can go about my business, into my own single life." He views his relationship with Madeleine as the problem of a mean between excesses: her first excess having consisted of her catching men as the "old, willful

Eve," and her second, of wanting, in her repentant Christian role, to give more than she takes. He has risen for "the woman or women, who knew the greater life of the body, not greedy to give, not greedy to take."

As summer and his healing advance, he seeks an "uncaring, unstriving self" that is beyond words. "The word is but the midge that bites at evening. Man is tormented with words like midges, and they follow him right into the tomb. But beyond the tomb they cannot go. Now I have passed the place where words can bite no more. . . ." He feels that nothing is so marvelous as to be "alone in the phenomenal world." He will be a physician, a healer of bodies rather than souls, and when he takes leave of the peasant, he liberates that emblem of his maimed vitality, the cock. Their mutual release is into the "free variousness" of the phenomenal world. He renounces sermons for psalms or songs. Yet he cannot escape the world of men, and Part I closes on the Lawrencean, vitalistic contention with it.

> So he went his way, and was alone. But the way of the world was past belief, as he saw the strange entanglement of passions and circumstance and compulsion everywhere, but always the dread insomnia of compulsion. . . . There was nothing he could touch, for all, in a mad assertion of the ego, wanted to put a compulsion on him, and violate his intrinsic solitude. It was the mania of cities and societies and hosts. . . . The nausea of the old wound broke out afresh, and he looked again on the world with repulsion, dreading its mean contacts.

In Part II, written a year later near the time of publication of *Lady Chatterley's Lover*, Lawrence went on to create the risen Christ's attainment of vital wholeness through sexual union, using as a means of religious continuity the resurrection myth of Isis and Osiris. The woman is a priestess of the goddess who "yearns eternally to make whole the broken body of a man." Her virginity is a means of withholding of herself for this higher, vitalistic purpose. But she too is in contention with a world in which the evils of property, slavery, and compulsion are dominant. When the man who died appears, he is spied on in a way that suggests Lawrence's experience in Cornwall during the war. The priestess's mother and her overseer suggest the landed aristocracy and the gamekeepers of his earliest encounters with class-based authority. And the enslaved peasants parallel the trespassing, poaching miners and their families. Even in the Mediterranean world of sun and color, the temple is hidden among pines on a peninsula, and the shelter of the man who died is a remote cave.

Lawrence's Isis is "Isis Bereaved, and in Search," linked by the lotus to Lawrence's earlier image of the profoundly sensual, at the extreme of reaction in decadence, in *Women in Love.* " . . . she was Isis of the subtle lotus, the womb which waits submerged and in bud, waits for the touch of that other inward sun that streams its rays from the loins of the male Osiris." As a woman in an era of history, she, unlike Cleopatra, has rejected those great men of the lesser, social world, the "eagle-like, rapacious" Caesar, and the "golden, worldly Anthony." She waits for the reborn man, whose sun, once killed, can "rise subtly in the same dark, inward depths" as the lotus.

In achieving relationship with her, the man who died must endure suspicions and accusations that resemble the hazards of his former mission. But though he bears the stigma of a malefactor, she sees in his "worn, hollow, and rather ugly" face the "beauty of the deeper life," and for the first time responds to a man passionally. He, like Mellors in *Lady Chatterley's Lover,* is troubled over giving himself into touch, since he has been tortured to death by mankind. In keeping with the inward sun and moon imagery, and the need for secrecy, and in line of descent from very early scenes in Lawrence's fiction, the ritual of fulfillment and healing takes place at night. As always, there is, afterward, the outer, lesser, social world to be reckoned with. The man who died makes the vitalistic aristocrat's wish for the slaves that the "all-tolerant Pan should watch over" their limitations. The opposition of the mother and her overseer causes him, though he has forsworn preaching, to break into vitalistic warning: "Unless we encompass it in the greater day, and set the little life in the circle of the greater life, all is disaster." The mother will thwart the daughter, who should have retained power in the "little life." Nevertheless he founds his church in a modification of the Christian meaning that is a poignantly retrospective reaffirmation for Lawrence.

"On this rock I built my life." The deep-folded, penetrable rock of the living woman! The woman, hiding her face. Himself bending over, powerful and new like dawn.

At the end there is a return to a mood of acceptance of minimal, transitory achievement in the world and in the vital flux—"The Spring was fulfilled, a contact was established, the man and the woman were fulfilled of one another, and departure was in the air." The priestess of Isis has conceived and needs a place to bear the child, while he has nothing, and the slaves are dangerous. " . . . he must go. For here, on the bay the little life of jealousy and property was resuming sway again, as the suns of passionate fecundity relaxed their sway." Though she asks him to stay, she now wants her singleness of being and the release from anxiety that his going will bring. He promises her that he will come again "as sure as Spring returns," a second coming implicit in the cycle of nature. His final act is a small triumph over the social world when he frightens from his boat the slave who earlier had participated in furtive, mean sexual intercourse.

Only a few of the short stories seem to have been written after the completion and publication of *Lady Chatterley's Lover* in 1928. They do not indicate a significant change of imaginative temper and direction, although the rather savage emphasis on the inevitability of the "social cage" in "Things" may reflect Lawrence's reaction to the attacks on, and censorship of, his work, and his failing health, that now severely limited his movements.

"The Blue Moccasins" is a Lawrencean comedy of outmoded woman's independence and the vitalistic consequences. The central character, a woman who, some forty years ago, was "painfully modern" in her belief that independence meant having no nonsense from men, finds herself manless in the late Twenties, when independence means devoting one's attentions to a variety of men.

Her blue moccasins constitute a rather slight central suggestion of Indian women's more vital attitude toward their men. She has purchased these empty souvenirs in need of repossession, from an Indian woman in New Mexico whom she made use of, as she does all people. The implication is that they will be forfeited if she ever loses her dominance. In England, they hang unused on the bedroom wall of the much younger, unawakened man whom she has married because he is devoted to her. This relationship is interrupted by the war, and after his return he is startled by her age, shuts his eyes to it, and remains "silently and passively obedient." But he gets on her nerves, and she feels that "the highest blessing is to be quite alone."

The vitalistic "resolution" of this situation begins when the rector's daughter (Lawrence has a penchant for taking his revolutionaries from the ranks of the clergy) decides to awaken him. Loss of her own husband in the war was a grief, but she has the unromantically stoic attitude of the young—"You've got to live, so you may as well do it!" The occasion of the contest for him, performance of a play in the church schoolroom on Christmas Eve, contains all of the sardonically contrasting elements of Lawrence's vitalistic comedy. The wife finds the moccasins gone from his room, and discovers that he has given them to the younger woman to wear in the play, "The Shoes of Shagput." She indignantly enters the audience, with its mixture of propriety, interest in the melodrama, and potentially sympathetic response to the human truth of the situation, and as she rages over the loss of "her moccasins! her blue moccasins! of the sacred blue colour, the turquoise of heaven," the love scenes on stage become more shameful. At last in a wonderful social contretemps, she interrupts the play by asking her husband to hand her the moccasins. He does so, but when, between acts, she asks him to abandon the play and drive her home, he makes a Lawrencean, vitalistic choice, though his way of stating it is amusingly common and human, in spirit very unlike such choices during the American phase.

> "Why, she's never once touched me to be fond of me—never once—though she pretends sometimes. But a man knows—. . . . He knows when a woman's just stroking him, good doggie!—That woman's never been real fond of anybody or anything, all her life. . . . She's limited to herself, that woman is; and I've looked up to her as if she was God. More fool me! If God's not good-natured and good-hearted, then what is He—?"

"Things," with its characteristically ironic, continuous development of the meanings of such a modern value term, is a demonstration of the impossibility of escaping the "social cage" to which things lead an idealistic New England couple with an independent income. Some of the judgments these idealists make of people, places and ideas that once made them happy sound like Lawrence's restless reactions in his letters. Paris was, eventually, too materialistic in spirit. Italy, more beautiful and poignant, escaped the cynicism of the French, and they could enter more fully into the vogue for Buddhism, striving to "eliminate from their souls greed, pain, and sorrow." But America entered the war, they felt obliged to help with hospital work, and the result was that they came to think that greed, pain and sorrow would never be eliminated, though they were "too western" to think of abandoning the world to damnation and saving themselves. For New England idealists it had to be "all or nothing." Now they still had Italy, freedom, and beauty, and "beauty" was the watchword of their furnishing a home with things. But, Lawrence says, while their idealism had been "climbing, vinelike, the vertical poles" of their religious, intellectual and artistic interests, their lives had been "running horizontally," so that

> . . . the halo died from around the furniture, and the things became things, lumps of matter that just stood there or hung there, *ad infinitum,* and said nothing. . . . The glow of beauty, like every other glow, dies down unless it is fed. The idealists still dearly loved their things. But they had got them. And the sad fact is, things that glow vividly while you're getting them, go almost cold after a year or two.

Deciding to return to America for the sake of their child's future, they dream of a pleasant apartment, but in actuality their income only permits two small rooms and a kitchenette, and the "things" must remain unpacked in a warehouse, draining their income. They try the West, but become the "slaves of the hideous things" involved in doing their own household chores. In California, in a cabin offered by a millionaire friend, the latest gadgets leave them free to "hear the brutality of the Pacific pounding the coast." They make another try at life in Europe, find it a complete failure, and finally, at the "critical age" of forty, the husband, forced to face a decision to accept a teaching post in a university, becomes a "ratlike creature of baffled fury." After accepting, he is quieter, and even comes to regard the "inhuman furnaces" of

Cleveland as the "biggest thing the modern world has to show." When they have installed their things in an "up-to-date little house," and have had them admired by people to whom they condescend because they are "travelled, Europe-wise, yet democratic," he is able to say: "Europe's the mayonnaise all right, America supplies the good old lobster—what?" He retains "a queer, evil, scholastic look, of pure skepticism," but finds life safe inside the cage.

In "Mother and Daughter," in which Lawrence the vitalist pretends to imitate Balzac by carefully giving facts, the daughter is his person of unfulfilled vitality, still single at thirty despite having lived with a young man for four years, and the mother the anti-life force, somewhat resembling the old woman of "The Lovely Lady" through her power of mockery which "reduces men to nothing" and ultimately drives them away. Her power is "a spell that must be broken," and the magician who accomplishes this is wonderfully unheroic, and wonderfully deflating of moral stereotypes—an Armenian merchant, sixty, grey-haired, and fat, a once ruined millionaire now regaining his fortune. Though his manner is humble, there is in his bearing a certain "dogged conceit." The mother is disgusted by being forced into contact with such scum. But she cannot annihilate him, as she has her daughter's other men, because, says Lawrence, in scum there is nothing to squash. Vitalistically he exhibits a real, if ludicrous potency in his "fat immobile sitting, as if his posterior is connected with the very center of the earth." His thick, fine white hair is "curiously virile," and even his fat, soft hands have a "masculine breeding of their own." His dull eye can "glint with the subtlety of serpents," expressing the cunning of a defeated race which accepts defeat, but gets its own back. Also, in a touch that suggests the patriarchal side of Lawrence's tendency toward theocracy, he is the tribal father, and his love is the feeling of such a man for the fatherless waif. His power brings her "a sense of destiny which is a relief" after the strain of a "free" life. Like the young man in "The Fox," his passion is intensified by the fact that love also brings him valuable property, in the furnishings of the apartment.

The mother, the modern woman of "energy, will, and contempt," feels old and haggard when the daughter turns from her, and she resorts to moral contempt: her daughter has turned out to be "the harem type." The daughter's reply is that since all the harem was left out of her mother, it had to be put back into her child.

2

During these last years Lawrence seems to have been reluctant to commit himself to writing novels because of the cost to his vitality. His short stories and lively essays on what ailed the world were in increasing demand, and now brought him plenty of money for his frugal way of living. Yet during 1926 and 1927 he carried through the enormous task of writing three longhand versions of *Lady Chatterley's Lover*, supervising and correcting a typescript, and seeing the book through the orthographical difficulties of private printing in an Italian shop after he had given up hope of being able to expurgate it either to his English publisher's satisfaction or his own. It seems clear that a new personal imperative drove him to work out full scale his latest vision of a way to life, centered again, as in *The Rainbow*, in the sexual relationship, and characterized by a new quality he called "tenderness."

The need of such a relationship had been strongly implicit in his early short stories—for example, "Odour of Chrysanthemums," "Love Among the Haystacks," and "The Horse Dealer's Daughter." After *The Rainbow* it had been subordinated to the drive toward a religious and quasi-political solution of the problems of modern life. Now, after the failure of the heroics of *The Plumed Serpent*, Lawrence turned to a new, bolder emphasis on sexual fulfillment, as if only this could now counteract the modern world's tendency to manipulate and violate man's basic nature. The enemy here was not puritanical repression, but the sophistication, sophistry and cynicism—the perverseness, compromises, and defeatism—of the intellectual, who should know better.

The novel marks also the possibility of a reconciliation with life at home after the years of intense revulsion, exile, fight and search. Lawrence's living again in Europe was not altogether necessitous and unhappy, and he was corresponding with young men like Rolfe Gardiner about new developments in England and the possibilities of life there.

In the novel his imagination returns to the Midlands as if to see what minimal vital basis of life might now be possible. Middle age, his rapidly failing health, and his conflict with Frieda challenged his original commitment to sexual fulfillment and marriage based on it. The novel is, in a sense, his transcendence of personal bitterness and defeat, and a reaffirmation. It ought to be remembered that Clifford Chatterley's paralysis and impotence, and Mellor's hurt withdrawal from contact, were inevitably aspects of himself.

The controversy over the morality of the novel has tended to center in Lawrence's use of the "vulgar" four-letter words for the sexual organs and intercourse. He had been labeled a "sexual" writer since at least the prosecution and suppression of *The Rainbow* in 1915. Yet by naturalistic standards there had been relatively little sexual detail in his work, and very little "bad language," with which he had only recently begun to experiment in "Sun." Intercourse had been ritualized into "higher," vitalistically religious meaning through rhythmic, metaphorical language and symbolic setting and action, as in the scenes between Ursula and Skrebensky in *The Rainbow*. Now, in *Lady Chatterley's Lover*, it became more nearly a subject in itself, and its value more nearly what his admirers frequently take it to be everywhere in his work. Failures in intercourse are bitterly enumerated and described in blunt, profane confession. The achievement of success is created by direct and metaphorical descriptions of the struggle for mutual orgasm, and sexual play, endearment, and humor involving an unabashed use of the four-letter words which, natural to the speech of the miners of Lawrence's youth, have become not only vulgar but obscene to proper English, and are used to render the act itself obscene. The movement of the language is back, through the vulgate of the dialect with its idiosyncratically personal words like "lass" and "lad," to the vitalistically "democratic" denominators of sexual rapport and praise.

The novel begins with Lawrence's usual sardonic sketch of the previous lives of his characters, exemplifying the instrumental, uncommitted modern view of sexual relationship. His ubiquitous two sisters have a rather more explicit and unattractive sexual history than heretofore. Their upper class, Continental education had insisted on freedom and cultivation of art and social ideals. This emphasis on lack of relationship, and on mind, had resulted in their learning, during the usual affairs, to withhold their inner selves, and the orgasm, and then to use the man in a "spasm of self-assertion that is like the last word" in the arguments they much prefer. Hilda has become a modern Amazon, antagonistic toward men, and reactionary when they are of the lower class. Constance, as was Ursula in *Women in Love,* is more essentially feminine and capable of being vitally moved.

Her situation with Clifford Chatterley in marriage is a more cruel and difficult vital *cul de sac* than heretofore. All ideally based sympathy is on the side of a man whose war-incurred paralysis has made him impotent, and who seems courageously to make the best of it by managing his estate and the colliery from a motorized wheelchair, by cultivating the mind as a writer and as frequent host to intellectuals, and even by encouraging Constance to have a child, through a casual affair, while remaining committed to him. Lawrence's vitalistic sympathy develops toward her profound need of physically tender, fulfilling relationship, and toward the deeper commitment this would cause her to feel.

The lack of vital sexual relationship is accompanied, as always in Lawrence, by a breakdown in all other relationships. There is no courtesy or communication between Wragby Hall and Tevershall village, mine-owner and miner. Superficial order is substituted for "organic human connection." The Hall, clean and orderly without warmth of feeling, reflects the paradox of "methodical and conservative anarchy" that characterizes Clifford's writing and his development of the mines.

Constance's only contact is with the intellectuals gathered around Clifford. Characteristically vitalistic in response is her sympathy for the cultural and racial outsider, the Irishman Michaelis, who worships the "modern bitch goddess of success" without illusion. She responds to "the appeal of timeless, outcast endurance." Though he is a grateful and good lover, his essential hopelessness prevents her achieving the fulfillment of simultaneous orgasm. All of the others but one regard sexual desire as merely "functional appetite," useful but subordinate to their success. The only view to which Constance is sympathetic comes from one of Lawrence's wounded fighters, the soldier Tommy Dukes, whose words poignantly express the Lawrencean dilemma of the critical thinker.

"My God, the world needs criticising today. . . . Therefore let's live the mental life, and glory in our spite, and strip the rotten old show. . . . But once you start the mental life you pluck the apple. You've severed . . . the organic connection. And if you've got nothing in your life *but* the mental life, you are yourself a plucked apple. . . . And then it's a logical necessity to be spiteful, just as it's a natural necessity for a plucked apple to go bad."

In the fifth chapter Lawrence begins to counterpoint to the anti-life of Constance's situation, the natural world of the countryside that holds the clue to the means of salvation. It was, as he said in a letter of this time in which he mapped the Eastwood region, the country of his heart. Even the wood is not untouched by the anti-life. During the war its trees were cut for use as timber, and the game, unprotected, has disappeared. Now there is again a gamekeeper, Mellors, whose task it is to repair the damage to natural habitat and life. He is the life force after the death force, the vitalistic hero on a very realistic, human level, far from romantically idyllic or naively primitivistic. One of the moderns, he carries his full load of problems. His primary mark is not the savage robustness of the gamekeeper in *The White Peacock,* but the inward vitality of a man who has survived the war intact. He combines the vitality of the lower class with enough knowledge through reading, experience, and innate ability (he has risen from the ranks during the war) so that he is neither ignorant nor hopelessly undirected or self-divided.

Like the keeper in *The White Peacock* he has sought sanctuary in the natural, and fears all human intrusion. Constance encounters him while he is caring for the baby pheasants which will restock the wood. In a scene that is wonderfully sensitive to basic sexual responses, their appeal to her denied maternal feeling causes her to weep, and he is drawn from his isolation when he feels both compassion and desire for her. Mellors expects to find in Constance not only an upper-class coolness and impudence but the antagonistic will that characterizes all modern women, including his lower-class wife. Even if he and she should achieve the vitalistic grace of touch and desire, they would encounter the dangerous opposition of society. When he becomes her lover, he refuses to sentimentalize or idealize his role. Constance's move toward him is expressed in socio-political terms as a move from a "democracy of money" to a "democracy of touch." Her title changes from "Lady Constance Chatterley" to "Constance" to "Connie," and finally, most basically, to the anonymity of "Lady Jane" to Mellors' "John Thomas," in which playfully affectionate names for the sexual organs parody the tags of class. This progress relentlessly explores in four-letter words rather than socio-biological nomenclature the failures in intercourse, caused by the woman's withholding of self, that both have experienced. Their intercourse in the wood is part of the symbolic pattern of renewal through the basically natural and vital. Only after their achievement of fulfillment do they move indoors to a more human, social condition, and engage in the humorous play, embarrassment, and banter that give the novel a more relaxed and easy humanity than can, perhaps, be found in any other Lawrence story.

The vitalistically based exchange of allegiance between Wragby Hall and the gamekeeper's hut is expanded through the problem of providing a nurse for Clifford. Constance is freed by the employment of a miner's widow who, having known real touch with her husband, is sympathetic to Constance's need, and can even assume power over Clifford. The resolution of the moral problem of Constance's secrecy, with its deceptions and invitation to nothing more than scandal, though this is dangerous enough, is precipitated by the question of an heir to Wragby Hall. The question involved the whole history of Lawrence's values. He believed in marriage as the ultimate condition of vitalistic commitment and responsibility. He had shown a deep empathy for children, especially for their anguish in loveless families, and had even questioned the rightness of bringing children into a warring world. Though he had seemed, at times, to make sexual fulfillment an end in itself, he had actually labored to place it in just relationship to higher purpose. Now, having brought Constance and Mellors to fulfillment as the basic condition of hope, he gave them issue. The situation he had already created made it possible for Constance to pretend to Clifford that she had done what he encouraged her to do—impersonally and casually found, during her vacation on the Riviera, a suitable father for a Chatterley heir. But the creation of her fulfillment had required loss of her tendency to make the male instrumental. To deny Mellors' paternity would be to revert to this. She tells the truth though this means exposure to the full force of social spite and revenge.

Clifford's reaction is to lose all his tolerance, and, in a perverse combination of spite and morality, to refuse her a divorce. Constance and Mellors have a few allies in the tradition of Lawrence's earlier fiction—her father, who shares the "ancient free-masonry" of male sensuality; her sister with her Amazonish, resentful courage; the miner's widow nurse, for whom a Tevershall baby in a Wragby cradle would be a great revenge for her lost husband. But in the end, Constance can only leave and hope that he will come to his senses. Mellors takes a job as a farm-laborer and waits for his own divorce, filling the first void of separation from Constance with praise of the chastity that follows naturally after their passion. After the six months' waiting period for divorces is over, and another spring has come, they plan to take a small farm and begin life together.

All this suggests that Lawrence was at last able to accept both the sexual and social condition of man without excessive bitterness, and without wishing to transcend it in the nonhuman vitalistic mystery, or to make men into gods with a revolutionary program. His bête noire, vindictive social judgment, was still active in his imagination, but it was now more despicable and ridiculous than nightmarishly frightening.

3

Publication of *Lady Chatterley's Lover*, in 1928, at once involved Lawrence in a fight of much larger proportions than that over *The Rainbow* in 1915. His plans for publication by private subscription were disrupted by extreme attacks in England, for example, in *John Bull*, that resulted in its being banned, and by the activity of such anti-vice crusaders in America as John Sumner, who had once seized copies of *Women in Love*. Made potentially profitable by the notoriety thus created, and unprotected by the usual publishing safeguards, the book was widely pirated. Lawrence made efforts to protect his legal rights, but his main effort went into counter-attacking the charges of immorality, through such a remarkable analysis of pornography and obscenity as the essay of that title, and in the poems of *Pansies* and *Nettles*.

The theme running through *Pansies* is the necessity of a vitalistic revolution. In December of 1928, in a letter to Charles Wilson at home in industrial England, he said of his feeling of urgency, and his intention:

> It's time there was an *enormous* revolution— not to install soviets, but to give life itself a chance. What's the good of an industrial system piling up rubbish, while nobody lives. We want a revolution not in the name of money or work or any of that, but of life—and let money and work be as casual in human life as they are in a bird's life, damn it all. Oh, it's time the whole thing was changed, absolutely. And the men will have to do it—you've got to smash money and this beastly *possessive* spirit. I get more revolutionary every minute, but for *life's* sake. The dead materialism of Marx socialism and soviets seems to me no better than what we've got. What we want is life and *trust.* . . .

To this letter he appended three of the poems he had done for *Pansies*, calling them a "New Year's Greeting to the Willington Men, for 1929." One of them, "It's Either You Fight or You Die" is a good sample of his spirit and the doggerel and diction he adopted in order to reach such men.

> It's either you fight or you die.
> Young Gents, you've got no option.
> No good asking the reason why,
> It's either you fight or you die,
> Die, die, lily-livered die,
> Or fight and make the splinters fly,
> Bust up the holy apple pie.
> You've got no option.
>
> Don't say you can't, start in and try,
> Give nice hypocrisy the lie,
> And tackle the lousy, big blow-fly
> Of money; do it or die.
> You've got no option.

When Lawrence posted the manuscript of *Pansies* in February 1929, to England, and with it the only copy of the introduction to the book of reproductions of his paintings soon to be published, the parcel was seized, and charges of obscenity were made. In June the exhibition of his paintings in London was raided by the police, and forced to close. Lawrence replied to these official proscriptions in the poems of *Nettles* (and others published posthumously in *Last Poems*), continuing the humorous appeal of doggerel and parody, as in "Innocent England":

> Oh what a pity, Oh! don't you agree
> that figs aren't found in the land of the free!
>
> Fig-trees don't grow in my native land;
> there's never a fig-leaf near at hand
>
> when you want one; so I did without;
> and that is what the row's about.
>
> Virginal, pure policemen came
> and hid their faces for very shame,
>
> while they carried the shameless things away
> to gaol, to be hid from the light of day. . . .

And in "Brittania's Baby":

> Oh Brittania's got a baby, a baby, a baby
> Brittania's got a baby, and she got it by and by.
>
> It's called the British Public, the Public, the Public
> It's called the British Public, including you and I.
>
> It's such a bonny baby, a baby, a baby
> It's such a bonny baby, we daren't let it cry.
>
> So we've got a lot of nurses, of nurses, of nurses
> to feed the bonny baby, and keep its tara dry. . . .

The spirit of this counterattack was hardly hysterical or nihilistic. To say that it was unbecoming to Lawrence's maturer side and deeper wisdom is to ignore the liveliness and agility that are identical with his kind of art. To have responded only with seriousness, or to have been above it all, would have been to run the risk of hardening and atrophying. His serious side appeared in poems like "The Triumph of the Machine," and in such late short essays as "Men and Women." And his notebooks contained poems that, often in a remarkably "classical" modulation of tone, rhythm, and diction, expressed his experience of vitalistic wonder, and the recessional of life that became more and more imminent for him as the fall and winter of 1929-30 approached.

The most deeply felt tensions of his experience were accepted in "Kissing and Horrid Strife":

> I have been defeated and dragged down by pain
> and worsted by the evil world-soul of to-day.
>
> But still I know that life is for delight
> and for bliss
> as now when the tiny wavelets of the sea
> tip the morning light on edge, and spill it with delight
> to show how inexhaustible it is.
>
> And life is for delight, and bliss
> like now where the white sun kisses the sea
> and plays with the wavelets like a panther playing
>   with its cubs
> cuffing them with soft paws,
> and blows that are caresses,
> kisses of the soft-balled paws, where the talons are.
>
> And life is for dread,
> for doom that darkens, and the Sunderers
> that sunder us from each other
> that strip us and destroy us and break us down
> as the tall fox-gloves and the mulleins and mallows
> are torn down by dismembering autumn. . . .

His apprehension of his vitalistic god in "The Body of God" is remarkably like that in one of his very early, youthful poems.

> God is the great urge that has not yet found a body
> but urges towards incarnation with great creative urge.

> And becomes at least a clove carnation: lo! that is god!
> and becomes at last Helen, or Ninon: any lovely
>   and generous woman
> at her best and her most beautiful, being god, made
>   manifest,
> any clear and fearless man being god, very god. . . .

One of the very last things he wrote, the unfinished "Prayer," can be glossed by his explanation of vital symbolism in *Apocalypse*.

> Give me the moon at my feet
> Put my feet upon the crescent, like a Lord!
> O let my ankles be bathed in moonlight, that I may go
> sure and moon-shod, cool and bright-footed
> towards my goal
>
> For the sun is hostile, now
> his face is like the red lion. . . .

During the last months of his life, his thoughts and feelings centered again on his religious inspiration and views through his writing an essay on the Apocalypse, to which he had been attracted by the symbolic drawings of Frederick Carter. He recapitulated and re-argued the conceptual results of his vitalistic insight, without recanting anything. The Christian modification of the pagan materials of the Apocalypse, and the uses made of it by the nonconformist religion of his youth, expressed the desire for triumph of the weak, the vitalistically disinherited. He peeled back this overlay to get at the vital integration of man with the cosmos that he felt sure had been the original meaning, and in doing so provided an explanation of the vitalistic "psychology" in all his work, and the imagery and symbolism of his later poems. He also reaffirmed the vitalistically theocratic basis of his political and social views.

Of image, symbol, and myth he said:

> Man thought and still thinks in images. But now our images have hardly any emotional value. We always want a "conclusion," an end, we always want to come, in our mental processes, to a decision, a finality, a full stop . . . . While men still thought of the heart or the liver as the seat of con-

sciousness, they had no idea of this on-and-on process of thought. To them a thought was a completed state of feeling-awareness, a cumulative thing, a deepening thing . . . the oracles were not supposed to say something that fitted plainly in the whole chain of circumstance. They were supposed to deliver a set of images or symbols of the real dynamic value, which should set the emotional consciousness of the enquirer, as he pondered them, re-volving more and more rapidly, till out of a state of intense emotional absorption the resolve at last formed. . . .

The true symbol defies all explanation, so does the true myth. You can give meanings to either—you will never explain them away. Because symbol and myth do not affect us only mentally, they move the deep emotional centres every time. The great quality of the mind is finality. . . . But the emotional consciousness of man has a life and movement quite different from the mental consciousness. . . .

. . . the older a myth, the deeper it goes in the human consciousness, the more varied will be the forms it takes in the upper consciousness. We have to remember that some symbols . . . can carry even our modern conscious-ness back for a thousand years . . . for four thousand years, and even beyond that. The power of suggestion is most mysterious. It may not work at all: or it may carry the unconscious mind back in great cyclic swoops through eras of time: or it may go only part way. . . .

His remarks on man's relation with the sun reveal something of its symbolic, vitalistic meanings for him:

All we see is a scientific little luminary, dwindled to a ball of blazing gas. In the centuries before Ezekiel and John, the sun was still a magnificent reality, men drew forth from him strength and splendour, and gave him back homage and lustre and thanks. . . .

And some of the great images of the Apocalypse move us to strange depths, and to . . . an escape from the tight little cage of our universe . . . into the vital Cosmos, to a sun who has a great wild life, and who looks back at us for strength or withering. . . . Who says the sun cannot speak to me! . . . When I can strip myself of the trash of personal feelings and ideas, and get down to my naked sun-self, then the sun and I can commune by the hour, the blazing interchange, and he gives me life, sun-life, and I send him a little new brightness from the world of the bright blood. The great sun, like an angry dragon, hater of the nervous and personal conscious-ness in us. . . . We have lost the sun. And he only falls on us and destroys us, decomposing something in us: the dragon of destruction instead of the life bringer.

His sense of vitalistic relation with the moon touches on his most pervasive and personal female symbol.

And we have lost the moon, the cool, bright, every-varying moon. It is she who would caress our nerves, smooth them with the silky hand of her glowing, soothe them into serenity again with her cool presence. For the moon is the mistress and mother of our watery bodies, the pale body of our nervous consciousness and our moist flesh. Oh, the moon could soothe us and heal us like a cool great Artemis between her arms. But we have lost her, in our stupidity we ignore her, and angry she stares down on us and whips us with nervous whips.

Relationship with sun and moon is, of course, part of oneness with the entire cosmos.

The cosmos is a vast living body, of which we are still parts. The sun is a great heart whose tremors run through our smallest veins. The moon is a great gleaming nerve-center from which we quiver forever. Who knows the power that Saturn has over us, or Venus? But it is a vital power, rippling exquisitely through us *all the time.*

Lawrence's ubiquitous horse is a basic source of vital connection on earth.

How the horse dominated the mind of the early races, especially of the Mediterranean! You were a lord if you had a horse. Far back far back in our dark soul the horse prances. He is a dominant symbol: he gives us lordship: he links us, the first palpable and throbbing link with the ruddy-glowing Almighty of potence: he is the beginning even of our godhead in the flesh. And as a symbol he roams the dark underworld meadows of the soul. . . .

The symbol of the dragon is representative of a

fluid, rippling potency which can lie quite dormant, sleeping, and yet be ready to leap out unexpectedly. Such are the sudden angers that spring upon us from within ourselves, passionate and terrible in passionate people: and the sudden accesses of violent desire, wild sexual desire, or violent hunger, or a great desire of any sort, even for sleep. The hunger which made Esau sell his birthright would have been called his dragon: later, the Greeks would even have called it a "god" in him. . . . Modern philosophers may call it Libido or *Elan Vital,* but the words are thin, they carry none of the wild suggestion of the dragon.

Toward the end of his essay, Lawrence made a numbered recapitulation of the socio-political applications of his religious views. Their anti-individualistic, anti-Christian spirituality and otherworldliness, and anti-political democracy nature can be indicated through key sentences. 1. "No man is or can be a pure individual." 2. "The State, or what we call Society as a collective whole *cannot* have the psychology of an individual." 3. "The State *cannot* be Christian." 4. "Every *citizen* is a unit of worldly power." 5. "As a citizen, as a collective being, man has his fulfillment in the gratification of his power-sense." 6. "To have an ideal for the individual which regards only his individual self and ignores his collective self is in the long run fatal." These, he thinks, are the things that the Apocalypse shows, by its very negations of them. In his reassertion of vital power and aristocracy he is not far from his position in *The Plumed Serpent.* It is as if, after the human simplicity of *Lady Chatterley's Lover,* the Bible and Carter's drawings had reawakened all his old ardor for leadership and ritual. Toward the very end he works his way free of argument to a statement of human yearning that is more in keeping with his recent temper, and the tender side of his imagination.

> . . . we can see how deeply the apocalyptists are yearning for the sun and the stars and the earth and the waters of the earth, for nobility and lordship and might, and scarlet and gold splendour, for passionate love, and a proper unison with men. . . . What man most passionately wants is his living wholeness and his living unison, not his own isolate salvation of his "soul." Man wants his physical fulfillment first and foremost, since now, once and once only, he is in the flesh and potent. For man, the vast marvel is to be alive. For man, as for flower and beast and bird, the supreme triumph is to be most vividly, most perfectly alive. Whatever the unborn and the dead may know, they cannot know the beauty, the marvel of being alive in the flesh. The dead may look after the afterwards. But the magnificent here and now of life in the flesh is ours, and ours alone, and ours only for a time. We ought to dance with rapture that we should be alive and in the flesh, and part of the living, incarnate cosmos.

This is a remarkable affirmation of life to have come from a man who had good reason to be bad-tempered or defeatist because of his beleaguerment by the censors, and because of truly desperate illness. He died not long after, on March 2, 1930.

At the very beginning, Lawrence had thought his fiction would be didactic. There was much to fight in a world that from childhood was oppressive with ideal, moral, and social anti-life. There was much to discover about the lost or enslaved vital nature of man, and much to teach.

His insight into the psychological, religious, and political crisis of contemporary life became enormous, ranging far into the future. He understood the nature and the danger of the contest between the democracies, fascism, and Marxism for the minds of men, and the decadence of religious and moral values that caused that contest. He knew what frightful actions, in the name of an ideal, the proponents of new forms of social industrial organization were capable of. He felt more intensely than perhaps any other writer the violation of the sensitive flesh of man that was committed in the name of efficiency and intellectual sophistication. And he feared the nihilism that lurked always at the extreme edge of the social upheaval, and of his own reformist passion.

In the scale of the modern artist's degree of balance between negative destructiveness and affirmative creativity, he takes a place comparatively near the center. In maturity a seasoned and cunning fighter, he could indeed shake his contemporaries' confidence in their attitudes and ways of life. And he could carry his temptation to political engagement to the point of an imaginative religious-social revolution in Mexico. But he always returned from these sorties to the simpler, human center of his drive toward triumphant life—insouciance, joy, procreativity, and vital harmony of relationship in marriage and in the community. The force that hurt man lay not only in contemporary social conditions but in the evolutionary flux of the life force. But this he could accept.

Of course, he was not effective politically, and indirectly he may well have had occasional pernicious influence, although the aid his ideas gave to fascism has been greatly exaggerated. Marxists, of course, and

Marxist critics can find little to take or praise, except perhaps his realization of, and insistence on, the new importance of collective man. He seems most likely to have an eventually beneficent effect in the democracies, if they survive the contest with Marxism and come to greater awareness of the problem of the happiness and welfare of the basic vital human being in the increasing tendency of the state to make him instrumental, as populations grow and economic-industrial organization becomes even more complex.

To speak of these things is not to sever the connection between his art and his message. The art is tremendously moving, flexible and virtuosic as it explores the anti-life and the means to vital resurrection. It is least satisfactory when, as in *Apocalypse*, he becomes intoxicated with the symbols of vitalistic power and grandeur. It is at its best when his attention is centered on the human struggle for fulfillment, in the contemporary condition, as in *The Rainbow, Women in Love,* and *Lady Chatterley's Lover.*

Index